ALABAMA NOTES

Volumes 1 and 2

Compiled By

FLORA D. ENGLAND

CLEARFIELD

Reprinted for
Clearfield Company, Inc. by
Genealogical Publishing Co., Inc.
Baltimore, Maryland
1990, 1997, 2001

Library of Congress Catalogue Card Number 76-39656
International Standard Book Number: 0-8063-0750-1

Made in the United States of America

PREFACE

The data presented in *Alabama Notes,* volumes 1 and 2, were collected by me while doing research for persons in the counties of this area. I hope the publication of this data will serve a need.

I do not dare to hope that the data are completely free of error. It is therefore suggested that interested parties obtain photo-copies of critical documents. These can be obtained from most Alabama counties by writing to the Judge of Probate at the county seat of the appropriate county.

I regret that I have been unable to continue this series.

Flora D. England

ALABAMA NOTES

Volume 1

Table of Contents

Mahan Family of Perry County

Will of Mary Mahan "of Cahawba Co., Ala." from Will Book A,
pages 7-8: Mentions son, Archimedes; Children: Edward
James Christian, John Polly and Archimedes. Extr., Archimedes. Dated 4 Aug., 1820. Witnessed by Henry W. Stephens,
Samuel Neighbors, Allen Neighbors. Recorded 26 June, 1823.

From Minutes of Probate Court, Book K:

p. 25. Feb. 11, 1863. Came John W. Melton and Seaborn
Driver, and applied for letters of administration on the
estate of A. M. Mahan, dec'd. Bond for $100,000.00 with
Joseph W. Morton and James Edwards as securities.

p. 26. Same date. The administrators were given leave to
keep up the plantation and employ the slaves on it, for the
year 1863.

p. 54. June 18, 1863. Came John S. Mahan jointly with
John W. Melton and Seaborn H. Edwards, and applied for
letters of administration on the estate of A. M. Mahan,
dec'd. He also gave bond for $100,000.00 with N. J. B.
Suttles and J. W. Watters as his securities.

p. 129. Nov. 9, 1863. J. W. Melton, administrator of A. M.
Mahan, asked that the dower of Mary Mahan, the widow, be set
apart for her. Decedent owned 800 acres of land in Township
19, Range 9, and 1020 acres of land in Township 19, Range 10.
Mary and A. M. Mahan were married in this county. The heirs
of A. M. Mahan, dec'd, are:

Laura and Martha Mahan, minor children of decedent,
  who reside with their mother, the said widow
J. C. Mahan, a minor, now in the Army at Demopolis, Ala.
Mary, wife of S. A. Edwards, who resides in Perry Co.,
  Ala.
Harriett DeShazo, a widow, who resides in Perry Co.
James C. Melton, wife of John W. Melton, Perry Co.
Margaret, wife of Wm. Curry, who resides in Talladega
  County, Ala.

p. 131. Nov. 23, 1863. Came Wm. S. Miree, E. A. Young,
E. W. Garrison, E. Q. Heard, and Jesse M. Heard, and reported that they had alloted to Mary, the widow of A. M.
Mahan, her dower in the lands he owned at the time of his
death. Also, the appraisers, E. Q. Heard, C. A. Cosby, &
E. A. Heard, filed an additional appraise bill of said
estate.

p. 131. Nov. 23, 1863. Came also John W. Melton and J. S. Mahan and filed a report of the sale of Personalty of said estate, made in Noxubee Co., Miss.

From Minutes of of Probate Court, Book N:

p. 249. Sept. 15, 1870. Came J. W. Melton, S. A. Edwards, and J. S. Mahan, administrators of the estate of A. M. Mahan dec'd, and filed their accounts for a final settlement of said estate. Publication to be made in the Southern Republican, a newspaper published in Demopolis, Marengo Co., Ala.

pp. 275-7. Oct. 10, 1870. Final settlement and distribution of estate of A. M. Mahan. Estate divided into 8 equal parts. Each of following heirs received $76.55:

1. Margaret, wife of W. H. Curry, of Talladega Co., Ala.
2. Jane C., wife of J. W. Melton
3. Harriett DeShazo, widow of J. W. DeShazo, dec'd.
4. Mary A., wife of S. A. Edwards
5. John S. Mahan
6. Martha M., wife of R. Q. Pryor
7. Laura T. Mahan
   -- all these of Perry Co., Ala.
8. Elizabeth F., wife of T. C. (?) Monroe, who resides in Union Co., Arkansas

Note: The widow is not mentioned.

Minutes of Probate Court, Book K:

p. 164. Jan. 17, 1864. N. J. B. Suttles applied for letters of guardianship on the estate of James C. Mahan, giving bond for $15,000.00, with S. A. Edwards and J. M. (?) Watters as his securities.

p. 196. Feb. 1864. Estate of Archey Mahan. Came John W. Melton, S. A. Edwards and John S. Mahan, the administrators of the estate of A. M. Mahan, deceased, and filed their accounts and vouchers for a final settlement of said A. M. Mahan's administration of the estate of Archey Mahan, dec'd. Notice of hearing to be published in the Marion Commonwealth.

Note: There should be other papers re: Archey Mahan's Estate.

From Minutes of Probate Court, Book K:

pp. 199-200. March 14, 1864. Distribution of the estate of Archey Mahan, by the executor, A. M. Mahan, deceased. Each heir received $1669.90. Heirs named:

1. Mrs. Sarah Bates
2. Mrs. Rebecca Roper (Rofer?)
3. Henry Mahan
4. Wm. Mahan (?)
5. Emma C. Mahan
6. John R. Mahan

p. 213. March 14, 1864. Mary Mahan made guardian of Eliza S. Driver, Martha M. Mahan and Laura T. Mahan. She gave bond for $48,000.00 with John W. Melton and John S. Mahan as her securities.

p. 395. Dec. 15, 1864. Estate of James C. Mahan, dec'd. John S. Mahan, administrator. Bond for $10,000.00 with John W. Melton as his security.

Minutes of Probate Court, Book H:

p. 727. Jan. 10, 1859. A. M. Mahan, Sr. appointed guardian of Sarah Ann, Rebecca, William, Henry, Emma Coke and John R. Mahan, minor heirs of Archimedes Mahan, Jr., dec'd, bond at $20,000.00 with John W. DeShazo and John W. Melton and Seaborn Edwards as securities.

From Minutes of Probate Court, Book M:

pp. 174-5: April 13, 1868. The estate of James C. Mahan, dec'd was divided among the following:

1. Jane C., wife of John W. Melton
2. Harriett DeShazo
3. Mary, wife of Seaborn A. Edwards
4. Lizzie, wife of S. (?) C. Monroe
5. Martha W., wife of R. Q. Pryor
6. John S. Mahan
7. Laura S. Mahan
8. Margaret, wife of W. H. Curry

Each heir received $39.65.

From Deed Book B, pp. 28-9: 16 May 1829. John Mahan and
his wife Rebecca, of Shelby County, Ala., sold to James
Sample of Perry County, Ala., for $100.00, 80 acres in
Township 19, Range 11, in Perry Co.

John and Rebecca Mahan acknowledged their signatures to the
above deed before Thos. Payne and Green McElroy, justices of
the peace in Shelby Co., Ala.

From Deed Book B, p. 30: John and Rebecca Mahan of Shelby
Co., Ala., sold another 80 A. in same township and range, to
Jacob Denton of Perry Co. 16 May 1829.

From Deed Book B., p. 463: 19 Aug. 1833. Dunklin Sullivan,
Gabriel Benson, Archimedes M. Mahan and William Ford, Commissioners of Roads and Revenue for Perry Co., Ala., sold
some lots in Marion to Willis Nall.

From Deed Book F. p. 528. March 7, 1843. Archimedes Mahan
and Wm. S. Miree, commissioners appointed by the Orphan's
Court of Perry Co., to sell the real estate of Amry Day,
dec'd, sold some of it to Randolph M. Day.

From Deed Book G, p. 686:

   Jan. 24, 1846. Exum B. Melton sold to Archimedes Mahan
and Wm. S. Miree, trustees, of the neighborhood of Perryville
and vicinity, for the purpose of keeping a permanent school-
house at or near Perryville, for $1.00, five acres of land
on the west side of the road leading from Perryville to Selma,
on the line that divides the land of said Melton from the
land of Alfred Fuller, with the privilege of the tanyard
spring, forever. Land in T19, R9.

From Deed Book H, p. 481:

Nov. 10, 1847. Archimedes Mahan bought some land from
James M. Fike and Wm. S. Miree, who had been appointed by
the Orphans' Court to sell the real estate belonging to
the estate of Wm. Edwards, dec'd. T19, R9.

John Saunders Ford Estate

Hale Co., Ala., Probate Court. File No. 16:

Mary, the widow of John Saunders Ford, filed a petition
for homestead exemption on June 27, 1896. "See Probate
Record E, p. 182."

John S. Ford owned land in Sec. 29, Township 22, Range 4,
124 A. in all. He died in 1883; his widow has been living
on this land ever since. The decedent also occupied these
lands in his lifetime, but owned only a half interest in
them. The heirs of John S. Ford are:

1. Simeon Ford, who resides in Perry Co., Ala.
2. A. P. Ford,   "
3. Sarah M. McCauley   "
4. Martha Lester   "
5. Carlos Ford   "
6. Keziah F. Sheverell, who resides in Montague,
   which is in Montague Co., Tex.
7. J. M. Ford, who resides in Hale Co., Ala.

Also from File No. 16:

P. A. Tutwiler, administrator of the estate of John S.
Ford, deceased, filed a petition on Feb. 28, 1888, to sell
the land belonging to said estate to pay the debts of same.
"See Probate Record D, p. 111."

The heirs are named again, in different order:

1. John M. Ford
2. Simeon H. Ford
3. Alexander P. Ford
4. Sarah, wife of Felix McCauley
5. Charles Ford
   -- all of whom reside in Perry Co., Ala.
6. Keziah F. Sheverell, wife of Oswell Sheverell, who
   resides in Montague, Texas
7. Martha, wife of Wm. Lester, Perry Co., Ala.

All the heirs are over 21, except Charles Ford, who is a
minor over 14 years of age, and is the only surviving
descendent of William Ford, who was a son of said John
Saunders Ford, and who died prior to the death of his
father John S. Ford.

The widow, Mary, is also listed as an heir.

Another document in the file states that John S. Ford died
in January, 1883.

Still another document in this file states that John M. Ford was residing in Hale Co. in 1883.

One Presley Ford left a will in Hale Co., dated in 1906. It is recorded in Will Book A, p. 481. It does not give the names of any of his heirs. There may be other documents there, connected with the probate and the settlement of this estate, which do give the names of the heirs.

From Marriage Record A, p. 87, Hale County:

p. 87: John S. Ford married Mary Holbrook on 23rd Dec. 1874.

p. 133. John M. Ford married Bettie Holbrook on 21 April 1879.

For further information about this Ford family, see our "Notes on some families of Perry Co., Ala."

Hale County was formed in part from Perry, about 1867.

McDonald Deeds from Dallas Co., Ala.

From Deed Book A, p. 358. James McDonald sold to Oliver C. Brooks, the SE¼ of Section 19, Township 16, Range 10, E., containing 160 A.; also a fraction east of Cahaba River of Section 24, Township 16, Range 9. 25 Jan., 1822.

From Deed Book F, page 540: 1st October, 1838. James McDonald bought at a sheriff's sale, Lot. No. 70 in the Town of Cahaba, in Dallas Co., Ala., for $76.00. It had belonged to Bartram Robison.

From Deed Book F, pp. 549-50: 2 Oct., 1838. Deed of Mortgage from B. Roberson to James McDonald. "Whereas, James McDonald has become responsible to Matt Gayle for a debt due from me to said Gayle, for $479.62, and whereas I am indebted to said McDonald for articles purchased at a sale of the estate of Joseph C. Huddleston, deceased... to secure said debts to said McDonald ... I assign to him all my real estate, etc. (Signed) B. Roberson." Witnessed by Hanson Raiford and Wm. S. Phillips.

From Deed Book H, p. 61:

28 Feb., 1840. Braddock McDonald and Edy, his wife, sold to Joseph Walker, for $200.00, the E½ of SW¼ of Sec. 36, Township 15, Range 11, containing 82 A. /The name is also spelled McDaniel./

From Deed Book H, p. 214: 23 July, 1840. Braddock McDonald and edy, his wife, sold to Green Underwood, for $570.00, a plantation, the W½ of SE¼ of Sec. 13, Township 15, Range 11; also all that part of E½ of NW¼ of Sec. 20, T15, R11, that lies on the north side of Soapstone Creek.

Edy and Braddock McDonald appeared in person on 23 July, 1840, before Abram Pierce, a Justice of the Peace in Dallas Co., Ala., and acknowledged their signatures to the above deed.

From Deed Book H, p. 216: 27 Aug., 1840. Braddock McDonald gave a mortgage to Green Underwood on the following property:

one yoke of oxen   one sorrel horse   15 head of cattle
one small 2-horse wagon   15 head of hogs

as security for a debt of $200.00, to be paid before Jan. 1st, 1841.

From Deed Book K, pp. 357-8. 7th May, 1838. Isaac N.
Campbell, sheriff of Dallas Co., sold to Henry B. McDonald,
under a writ of execution from the circuit court, for a
debt of $1040, land that had belonged to Morgan Mills,
at public auction, for $50.40: E½ of SW¼ of Sec. 2, and
E½ of SW¼ of Sec. 12, in Township 13, Range 11, 160 A.

From Deed Book N, pages 108-9: Oct. 24, 1848. Henry B.
McDonald and his wife, Elizabeth (Betsy), sold to Nixon
Cox, for $1510.00, 445 acres in Dallas Co., Ala.

On 26 Oct., 1848, Henry B. McDonald and wife acknowledged
their signatures to above deed before a justice of peace
in Wilcox Co., Ala.

I found no reference to Henry B. McDonald in Dallas Co.,
after 1848.

There are other deeds in the name of James McDonald up
through 1875; may be others of still later date.

From Deed Book N, Dallas Co., Ala., pp 487-8:

4th Jan., 1850. Margaret McDonald, of Cumberland Co., N. C.,
for love and affection, deeded to Nancy C. Holston, her
child, nine Negroes now in possession of said Nancy, in
Alabama; and after the death of Nancy, said Negroes are
to go to Nancy's two children, James J. and Margaret Ann
Holston.

Note: The name Holston is also spelled Holsten.
        The name of James J. Holsten is given in one place
        as William J. Holston.

        I do not know whether this last McDonald deed has
        any reference to the other McDonald family.

Anderson Family of Marengo County

Estate of Wm. Anderson, dec'd.

From Will Record A, pp. 38-43: 16 Aug. 1824. The court
appointed Thos. Anderson administrator of the estate of Wm.
Anderson, dec'd, with the assent of the widow, Tellitha
Anderson. Thos. Anderson made bond for $2500.00 with
Jordan Anderson and Thos. Hightower as his securities.

The court appointed Sherod Parker, James Harper, Joel H.
Malory, Thos. Hightower and Joseph Brackenridge to appraise
the estate of Wm. Anderson, dec'd.

Same, p. 39: 3rd Mon. in Sept., 1824. Thos. Ringgold, Judge
presiding. James Goodwin, Neill Thompson, Richard Rut-
ledge, Samuel Nellums, and Wm. Goodwin were appointed to appraise that part of Wm. Anderson's estate which lay in Perry
Co. (Apparently livestock only.) Ransom McElroy, J. P. in
Perry Co., qualified these appraisers by administering to
them the usual oath.

p. 40. 9th Oct., 1824. Samuel H. Nelms, clerk of the County
Court of Perry Co., Ala., certified that Ransom McElroy was
a justice of the peace in Perry Co.

Purchasers at the sale of Wm. Anderson's personal property
in Perry Co., on 8th Oct., were: Lewis Howell, Stewart
George, Wiley Howell, Samuel H. Nelms, J. K. C. Pool, James
Goodwin and Neill Thompson.

p. 40. 20th Oct., 1824. James Harper, Sharod H. Parker, &
Joel H. Mallory returned an inventory of Wm. Anderson's
estate, sworn to before John McFarland, J. P.

pp. 40-41: Purchasers at the sale of Wm. Anderson's property
in Marengo Co., on 20th Oct., 1824, include: Sherod Parker,
Joel H. Malory, Thos. Hightower, Jordan Anderson, Joseph
Brackenridge, Leonard Pearson, & Wm. Burks.

pp. 42-3. Thos. Anderson, adm. of Wm. Anderson, filed acct.
of what he rec'd and paid out for the estate. Balance left,
$5.84, which the adm. is to retain for his services. No
list of heirs or distributees was found.

The administrator listed payments to the following:

1. To Drs. Fluker and Burrows, for medicine & attention
2. To Jordan Anderson, for services
3. To Wm. Mills for land rent
4. To Richard Buckaloo
5. To Joseph Brackenridge
6. To Jacob Lindsey
7. To Silas Morgan
8. To Roderick Easley, administrator of Samuel Easley, dec'd, on a judgment obtained against Thos. Anderson, as security of Wm. Anderson, dec'd, on a note.
9. To the clerk of the Circuit Court of Marengo Co., for costs in a suit of Thos. Anderson, adm. of Wm. Anderson, versus Alfred Yarbrough.

The administrator's receipts show only money he collected from the sales of property, and money collected from J. Nolen on a note due.

Estate of Jonathan Anderson

Will of Johnathan Anderson, from Will Record A, pp. 188-90:

1. Plantation to wife, Mary Anderson
2. A child's share to my grandchildren, the children of Calvin and Phebe Downy, viz.: Reuben, Peyton, John, Samuel and Stephen Downy; Polly Hall, Betsy O'Neal; Ann Downy and Sarah Downy
3. A child's share to Sarah, Martha, Milla, and Elizabeth White -- what their mother would have got.
4. One child's part to the children of my son William Anderson, now dead.
5. To my sons Stephen Reuben John James and Jesse, each a child's part. (No punctuation.)
6. Executor's: Jesse M. Anderson, and my wife, Mary.

Will dated 23rd March, 1837; recorded Jan. 28, 1838.

From Minutes of Probate Court, Book A&B, p. 376:

4th Dec., 1837. Jesse M. Anderson and Mary Anderson, named in the will of Johnathan Anderson as executor and executrix, offered said will for probate. They gave bond for $31,000 with David Curry, Stephen Anderson, and Robert Pritchett as their securities.

The court appointed the following to appraise the estate of Johnathan Anderson, dec'd:

Phillip Agee, Noah Agee, Obadiah Thomason, Jeremiah
     Pritchett and Henry Hare

There are several other documents in MPB Book A&B, Book D,
and Book E, but nothing of genealogical value until the
following:

Minutes of Probate Court, Book E, p. 245: 21 March, 1848.
Court ordered that a citation issue to Jesse M. Anderson,
as adm. of Johnathan Anderson, to appear in next term of
court and file new bond, with other security, in order to
release Robert Pritchett, one of his present securities.

Same, p. 260: 8th May, 1848. Jesse M. Anderson filed new
bond for $1000.00 with R. B. Anderson and Henry W. Hatch
as securities.

Same, p. 474. 12 Nov., 1849. R. B. Anderson, one of the
securities of Jesse M. Anderson as executor of Jonathan
Anderson, dec'd, asked to be discharged from further liability as such. Jesse M. Anderson cited to give new
security.

Same, p. 509. 11 Feb., 1850. Jesse M. Anderson filed new
bond for $1000.00, with H. W. Hatch and Gray B. Jones as
his securities.

From Minutes of Probate Court, Book F:

p. 147. Sept. term, 1851. Came Jesse M. Anderson, executor
and moved that satisfaction of the amounts decreed by the
Court in favor of Stephen Downey and Wm. H. Reed and wife,
Clarissa (formerly Clarissa Anderson), against him, at the
September term of Court, 1839, be entered. Executor has
fully paid off said decree. The receipts of Stephen Downy
and of Wm. H. Reed and wife, Clarissa, showing that they
had received their shares of the estate of Johnathan Anderson, are recorded.

p. 152. Sept. term, 1851. Jesse M. Anderson resigned as
executor of the will of Jonathan Anderson, and moved that
John B. Bruce, sheriff of Marengo Co., be appointed administrator of the estate.

The court appointed the following to appraise the personal
property belonging to the estate of Johnathan Anderson:

Ennis Loftin   Hugh Goodwin   John Baggett
      James W. Hall   John Gildersleeve

p. 161. 18 Oct., 1851. John B. Bruce, adm., petitioned
the court to allow him to sell the real estate belonging
to Johnathan Anderson, dec'd. Court ordered that the heirs
be notified of this petition. --(but there is no list of
heirs recorded here.)

p. 167. Nov. 1851. The administrator was given permission
to sell the 1851 cotton crop; also the slaves and personal
property not specifically bequeathed in the will.

p. 227. March term, 1852. Jesse M. Anderson, late executor
of the will of Johnathan Anderson, filed his accounts for
a final settlement of his executorship. Publication in the
Linden Free Press.

p. 249. June 1852. Jesse M. Anderson turned over to
John B. Bruce the balance in his hands, $96.65.

p. 481. Feb., 1854. John B. Bruce filed his accts. for a
final settlement of the estate of Jonathan Anderson. The
court appointed F. W. Siddons guardian ad litem to represent the minor heirs at the hearing.

p. 503. April, 1854. The final account of John B. Bruce
as adm. of the estate of Jonathan Anderson is allowed, and
ordered recorded. "See Final Record, Book B, p. 157."

Compiler's note: I could not locate any Final Record.

p. 511. May, 1854. Stephen Anderson, one of the heirs of
Jonathan Anderson, is now dead. He had assigned his share
of Jonathan's estate to Reuben B. Anderson. The court
therefore ordered that Stephen's share, $486.33, be paid
to Reuben B. Anderson. N. B. Leseuer was adm. of Stephen
Anderson, dec'd.

p. 522. June, 1854. Jesse M. Anderson filed the receipts
of Phebe Ann Hamilton and of Jackson Pope and his wife,
for their shares of the estate of Jonathan Anderson.

p. 579. Nov. 24, 1854. Joseph Agee filed in Court a power
of attorney from Anderson Pope and Sarah J., his wife,
authorizing him to collect and receipt for their shares
of the estate of Jonathan Anderson, dec'd.

p. 642. April 27, 1855. Jesse M. Anderson filed the receipt of Eliza D. and James C. Etheridge for $149.13, in full of their share of Jonathan Anderson's estate.

Compiler's note: Nothing is indexed in Minutes of Probate Court, Book G, under the name of Jonathan Anderson.

From Miscellaneous Records, Book 4, pp. 97-8: Account of the sale of personal property belonging to the estate of Jonathan Anderson, dec'd, on 6th Dec., 1851. Purchasers include:

Jesse M. Anderson   Andrew Jackson   Jonathan H. Anderson

Reuben Downey   Jesse F. Hall   James C. Anderson

Reuben Anderson   James B. Anderson

A. F. Fountain   Ennis Loftin   Jesse H. Peeples

Estate of Jordan Anderson

Marengo Co., Ala. Will Record A, p. 191: Will of Jordan Anderson, Sr., mentions:

1. Son Thos. Anderson (executor)
2. Wife Mary
3. Grandaughter Catherine Anderson
4. Daughter Sarah Goodwyn
5. Daughter Nancy
6. Daughter Mary
7. Grandaughter, Nancy A. Hill, daughter of Mary Anderson
8. Daughter Martha Anderson
9. Son Jordan, Jr.

This will is dated 17 Aug., 1837, and was recorded on Feb. 9, 1838.

Witnesses: William Adams and Constance Adams.

Land mentioned in the will was in Section 2, Township 15, Range 3, East.

From Minutes of Probate Court, Book A&B:

p. 365. Sept. Term of court, 1837: Thos. Anderson
offered for probate the will of Jordan Anderson, Sr.,
dec'd. Court ordered that citations issue to the heirs,
who are:

1. Thos. Anderson

2. Sarah Goodwyn

3. Nancy Adams

4. Mary Hill

5. Martha Anderson

6. Jordan Anderson

7. Catherine McCoy (McCary?)

p. 369. 19 Oct., 1837. Will Goodwyn contested the will of
Jordan Anderson. A jury summoned to decide the issue on
1st Mon. in Nov.

p. 371. Tues., Nov. 14, 1837. Thos. Anderson, Executor,
and Will Goodwyn, the party contesting the validity of the
will. By consent of both, the issue is withdrawn as to
the personal property of the estate. Then will was proved
on oath of Wm. Adams, one of the witnesses. The executor
filed his bond for $20,000.00 with J. H. Bondurant and
E. B. Adams as securities.

Court appointed the following to appraise the estate:

Wm. King   David Curry   Austin Eskridge   Wm. Hogan

Peter R. Gunn   Daniel McNeill

p. 396. 2 June, 1838. Came Thos. Anderson, adm. of Jordan
Anderson, dec'd. None of the heirs appeared in court to
show cause why the petition to sell the lands for division
among the heirs should not be granted; and same is granted.

Court appointed following commissioners to sell the lands:

William King   Felix G. Adams   Thos. Ringgold

p. 406. Oct., 1838. The above-named commissioners reported the sale of Jordan Anderson's land to Thos. and Jordan Anderson, at $1.00 an acre.

From Deed Book E, p. 381. 11 June, 1838. We, Thomas Anderson and Louisa, his wife, Wm. Goodwyn and Sarah, his wife, Benjamin Adams and Nancy, his wife, James N. Hill and Mary, his wife, and Martha Anderson, convey to Jordan Anderson, our claim to land in Marengo Co., Ala., that descended to us from our father, Jordan Anderson. Land in Section 2, Township 15, Range 3, East.

Estate of Jordan Anderson, Jr.

Marengo County, Alabama

Will of Jordan Anderson, Jr., recorded in Will Record A, page 276.: Mentions his wife, Nancy, and children (their names are not given). "Furniture bought by me for the use and keeping of the Linden Hotel". William King named executor.
Witnessed by James R. Jones, B. Adams, Wm. H. Mounger, & D. H. Smith.
Dated 5 May, 1848.

From Minutes of Probate Court, Book F:

p. 75. Dec., 1850. Came Wm. H. Mounger and resigned as administrator of the estate of Jordan Anderson; and Nancy Anderson is appointed administrator de bonis non with bond for $10,000.00; Benj. Adams and Wm. M. Byrd her sureties.

Compiler's note: There should be other papers dated between 5 May, 1848, and Dec., 1850. These I did not find.

p. 99. Feb. 8, 1851. John B. Bruce, sheriff of Marengo County, returns the writ of dower issued to him to assign to the widow her dower in the lands of Jordan Anderson.

p. 105. March 4, 1851. Nancy Anderson, administratrix of Jordan Anderson, moves the court that John T. Taylor, administrator of the estate of Wm. H. Mounger, be required to make settlement of the administration of said Mounger on the estate of Jordan Anderson.

Estate of Jordan Anderson, Marengo Co., Ala.

From Minutes of Probate Court, Book F:

p. 153. Sept. term, 1851. John T. Taylor, administrator of
Wm. H. Mounger, deceased, late adm. of Jordan Anderson, dec'd
by his attorney, files his acct. for a final settlement of
the administration of Mounger, in his lifetime, on the
estate of Jordan Anderson. Citation to Thos. Anderson, a
minor under 14, to show cause why a guardian should not be
appointed for him.

p. 167. Nov., 1851. Nancy Anderson, adms. of Jordan
Anderson, given leave to sell at public auction a slave belonging to said estate, for the purpose of paying the debts
of the estate.

p. 185. Dec., 1851. Wm. H. Mounger, adms. of Jordan Andersc
having died without making a final settlement of his administration on said estate; and John T. Taylor, adm. of said
Mounger, having filed his accounts for a final settlement of
the administration of said Wm. H. Mounger on the estate of
Jordan Anderson; ... comes also Nancy Anderson, the present
administratrix, and Thos. Anderson, minor heir of Jordan
Anderson, by his guardian ad litem, Nancy Anderson, etc.
... John T. Taylor paid over to Nancy Anderson $1272.13.

Estate of Mary Anderson
Marengo Co., Ala.

From Minutes of Probate Court, Book A & B (One vol.):

p. 373. 8th May, 1837. Thos. Anderson was appointed admini-
trator for the estate of Mary Anderson, dec'd. Bond for
$2400.00 with David Curry and Thos. Ringgold as his sec.

From Minutes of Probate Court, Book F:

p. 150. Sept., 1851. Ordered by the court that citations
issue to Reuben Anderson, Jesse M. Anderson, Joseph Hare &
his wife, Wm. Reed and his wife, and to Johnathan H. Anderso
Andrew J. Anderson, Sarah J. Anderson, Wm. J. Anderson and
Benjamin F. Anderson, to appear in court and show cause why
letters of administration should not be granted to the
sheriff, coroner, or other suitable person, on the estate of
Mary Anderson, dec'd.

p. 181, same volume. Dec., 1851. The next of kin failing to appear in court, John B. Bruce, sheriff, is appointed administrator of the estate of Mary Anderson.

p. 511. May, 1854. Bruce's accounts allowed as filed, and ordered recorded. "See Final Record, Book B, pp. 166-8".

Compiler's note: I am unable to locate, in the probate office of Marengo County, any "Final Record"; and no one of the present staff there knows what became of these volumes.

From Miscellaneous Records, Book 4, p. 101: Account of the sale of property belonging to the estate of Mary Anderson, held on Dec. 6, 1851. Brittain T. Pope bought some of the Negroes.

From Deed Book G, p. 311. 2 Nov., 1838. Stephen Anderson sold to Jesse M. & Mary Anderson, executor and executrix of the estate of Johnathan Anderson, dec'd, land that was to go to the use of the heirs of said Jonathan Anderson. Martha, wife of Stephen Anderson, joined in the deed.

Stephen and Martha Anderson acknowledged their signatures to the above before Phillip Agee, J. P.

Minutes of Probate Court, Book D, page 206: Came Calvin Anderson and applied for letters of guardianship on the estates of Thos. D., Jane B., Claudius B. and Wm. W. Anderson, minor children of Calvin Anderson. Bond for $160.00 with C. C. Bonds and Thos. J. Woolf as his securities. Feb. 26, 1845.

Minutes of Probate Court, Book F, p. 588. Dec., 1854:

Jonathan Anderson appointed guardian of Stephen Anderson, minor son of Stephen Anderson, dec'd, late of Arkansas.

From Will Record B, p. 64: The will of Jesse M. Anderson, dated Nov. 13, 1865, mentions his wife, Eliza, and children, their names and numbers not given. It is witnessed by O. B. Crocker, J. K. P. Jackson, and Shield Jackson. It was proved by J. K. P. Jackson on 10 Dec., 1866.

From Marengo Co., Ala., Marriage Record for 1818-36:

p. 39.   Anderson, Wm. to Elizabeth Yarborough, 8th Aug.,1822
Releigh Hightower, bondsman; Alex'r McLeod, J. P.

p. 56.   Anderson, Bailey W. to Olive Cook, 23 Jan., 1823
by John Jackson, J. P. Alex'r Birdson, Bondsman.

p. 93.   Anderson, Jonathan to Susan Davis, 1st Sept., 1825
by Lewis Anderson, J. P. Calvin Anderson, bdsmn.

p. 119. Anderson, James to Pemellea Davis, 10th Aug., 1826
by M. Porter, J. P. Bondsman: Clement Dunaedmony

p. 129. Anderson, Calvin to Ovilla Silmon, 16 Feb., 1827
by James Bakley, J. P. Bondsman: Jno. E. Anderson

p. 140. Anderson, Mason L. to Tiner (?) Dunn, 9 Sep., 1827
Bondsman: A. Dunn

p. 170. Anderson, Jesse to Dorothea Smith. License dated
11 Sept., 1828. Bondsman Calvin Downey. No
minister's return.

p. 196. Anderson, Alexander to Mary Skinner, 20th July, 1829
by M. Porter, J. P. Bondsman, Ralph Grayson

p. 252. Anderson, Baily W. to Louisa Burton, 22 Mar., 1832
by John Collier, M. G. Bondsman: Geo. Cunningham

p. 255. Anderson, Burbon to Malinda Warren, 5 July, 1832
by Wm. Clark. Bondsman: Geo. W. McDonald

p. 263. Anderson, Thos. to Louisa Hill, 15 Nov., 1832
by Wm. J. Alston, JCC. Bondsman: J. H. Bondurant

p. 2.   Birdsong, Alexander to Marion Anderson. License
dated Feb. 10, 1819. by Ichabod Watkins, J. P.

From Marriage Record for 1836-51:

p. 48.   Anderson, Calvin to Ann White, 27 Nov., 1838
by T. J. Ford, J. P. Bondsman: Thos. J. Woolf.

p. 50.   Anderson, Jordan to Nancy Adams, 2 July, 1839
by Thos. S. Abernethy. Bondsman: David H. Smith

p. 59.   Anderson, Thos. M. to Ann E. Machau, 25 Nov., 1840
         by T. S. Abernethy. Bondsman: James M. Rembert

p. 184. Anderson, Jos. C. to Francis Dumas, 3 July, 1845
         by Woody Jackson, J. P. Bondsman: A. D. Thomason

p. 433. Anderson, Jonathan to Ellender J. Reid, 15 July, 1851
         by John Agee, J. P. Bondsman: Wm. H. Reed

Compiler's note: The next two volumes of marriage records,
up to 1865, have no indices.

Anderson Deeds from Marengo County Records

A:63.   Jan. 9, 1823. James Holley and Sarah, his wife,
         both of Marengo Co., Ala., appoint our friend, Wm.
         Anderson of same state and county, our attorney, to
         sue for and take into his possession...all moneys,
         goods and Negroes coming to us from the estate of
         our grandfather and grandmother, King and Sarah
         Freeman of N. C., acknowledging that it is forever
         beyond our powers to collect any part of said
         estate.
         Witnesses: Bailey W. Anderson, Alexander Birdsong,
         Stephen Davis

A:256:   I, Jacob Calahan, of Clark Co., Ga., appoint Lewis
         Anderson, of Marengo Co., Ala., my attorney, to
         transfer a piece of land in Marengo Co., that was
         transferred to me by Polly Glover. 25 July, 1825.
         Witness: Wm. L. Anderson (in Marengo?)
                   Ethelred Sorrell, J. P. in Clarke Co., Ga.

A:277:   28 Nov., 1825. Eli Davis and Dorcas, his wife, sold
         land in Section 2, Township 15, Range 3, East, to
         Jordan Anderson, land lying next to Wm. Anderson.
         Witness: Isaac Smith, John C. Jones.

A:349.   1st July, 1826. Bowen Bennet to William Anderson.
         Land in Section 11, Township 15, Range 3, East.
         Witnesses: Jacob Mitchell
                     John C. Jones

A:475   21 May, 1828. Deed of Partition: Wm. Browning and
John E. Anderson had bought land jointly from the
U. S. Govt., and are now dividing it between them-
selves. Land in Sec. 15, T15, R4E.
Witness: A. A. McNeil
James Moreland

B:128. 7 May, 1825. Bailey W. Anderson, and Olif, his wife,
sold to B. W. Johnson, for $200.00, land in Sec. 10,
T15, R3E.

B:369   9 April, 1832. Dallas Co., Ala. Reuben Anderson
of Dallas Co., Ala., and Sarah, his wife, sold to
Thòs. B. Creagh, of Wilcox Co., Ala., land in the
State of Ala., Sec. 9, T17, R5E.

B:423. Marengo Co., Ala. 6th Oct., 1832. Wm. Anderson &
Elizabeth, his wife, sold to David Hogan, land in
Sec. 2, T15, R3E, next to Jordan Anderson, Which was
granted to him (Wm. Anderson) by Eli and Dorcas
Davis, by deed bearing date 14 Nov., 1827. 6 A.
Also 160 A. granted to him the said Wm. Anderson,
by the U. S., by two patents bearing date 15 Apr.,
1824.

B:15   1 Mar., 1828. Allen Glover and Geo. S. Gaines, &
Ann, wife of said Geo., sold to Alexander Anderson,
land in Sec. 23, T17, R4E.
Witnesses: M. Porter,J. P.
Wm. Ranken, J. P.

B:252   5 July, 1831. John E. Anderson, and Cynthia D.,
his wife, sold to John D. Catling, land in Sec. 15,
T15, R4E.
Witnesses: David Hogan
Edward Johnson
George Cunningham

B:470. 23 Feb., 1831. Wm. Anderson and Elizabeth, his wife,
of Marengo Co., Ala., sold to Jas. P. Hainsworth,
land in Sec. 11, T15, R3E.

B:39.   Bond of John E. Anderson as sheriff of Marengo Co.
His commission from the governor dated 9 Dec., 1828.
Securities on the bond: Elisha Lacy, John Holland,
Alexander Anderson, Thos. Anderson, Wm. Anderson,
Wm. Browning, John Anderson, Bailey W. Anderson.

C:18   John E. Anderson, of Sumter Co., Ala., sold to
Micajah McGee, of Marengo Co., Ala., for $750, 3
slaves, now in possession of Thos. Ringgold, of
Marengo Co. 24 June, 1833.

C:340. Sumter District, S. C. Marriage Contract between Samuel D. Carter and Margaret Anderson. She had an estate in her own right, apparently in Sumter District, S. C., including land in Green Swamp and Shotpouch (?), in which she owned ¼ part, and some Negroes, which John Anderson, Sr., bequeathed to John Anderson, Jr., for his lifetime, and after his death to his children, of which Margaret is one. She also owned ¼ of 2/3 of a tract in Clarenden Co., S. C., in Santee Swamp, said to be near Scot's Lake, and 32 Negroes, which land & Negroes were part of the estate of John Anderson, Jr. By this marriage contract her property was put in trust, with following as trustees:

> Thos. J. Wilder
> Henry Vaughn

The contract is dated 5 Jan., 1830, and witnesses by:

> John A. Nettles
> Amos A. Nettles
> John Anderson

C:130 1st Jan., 1833. Bourbon Anderson and wife Malinda, of Marengo Co., Ala., sold to Wm. M. Burwell, of Franklin Co., Va., land in Sec. 4, T16, R4E.

C:132. 8th Jan., 1833. Alexander Anderson and Mary, his wife, of Marengo Co., Ala., to Wm. M. Burwell, of Virginia, land in Sec. 4, T16, R4E.

G:406. 24 Dec. 1835. Greene Co., Ala. Wm. Anderson sold to M. B. and M. E. Matthews, land in Sec. 7, T17, R4E. Frances, the wife of this Wm. Anderson, joined him in making the deed.
Witnesses:
> A. M. Dowling
> D. B. Smith

Estate of Elias Read
Wilcox Co., Ala.

Will of Elias Read, dated Sept. 20, 1841, from Will Book
One, p. 411:

All property real and personal to wife, Elizabeth,
during her widowhood, or until she becomes dissatisfied.
Then lands to be equally divided among my sons:

Wm. H. Read

Briant Read

Marion Read
My wish is that my wife shall remain on the plantation.
If she marries again, she can take as much with her as
she brought when we married.
Witnesses:
James Whitted
Benj. D. Carter
Mosed Whitted

From Minutes of Probate Court, Book 4:

p. 366. Feb. 1, 1844. Elizabeth Read, widow of Elias
Read, dec'd, produced will of Elias for probate.

p. 399. April 15, 1844. A jury of 15 summoned to appear
on May 18th next, to inquire into the validity of said
will. (Apparently the witnesses came not when summoned.)

p. 405. May 2, 1844. Names of the jury:

John Watkins	Ausburn Henry
	Abijah Miller
James Smith	Abraham Hillier
John E. Brantley	Solomon W. Portis
Geo. M. Hamner	Eaton Lee
Wm. Boyd	Wm. Bonner, Sr.
Wm. Bonner, Jr.	Hiram Holt
__?__ J. Grigsby	Harmon Bussey

p. 412.   May 18, 1844. Will established by the jury,
          and ordered recorded.

p. 421.   21 June, 1844. Elizabeth Read given letters
          testamentary as executrix of the will of Elias
          Read. She gave bond with Isaac Mixon and Wm. G.
          Chambers as her securities.

From Minutes of Probate Court, Book 5:

p. 221.   May 26, 1859. Marion Read, a legatee mentioned
          in the will of Elias Read, made application that
          his legacy under said will be distributed to him.
          Citation to Elizabeth Read, executor of said will,
          notifying her of the hearing of said petition.

Compiler's note: Nothing more is indexed about this matter in the General Index to Probate Minutes. There is
always the possibility that the other documents may be
there, but not in the index.

From Memorial Record of Alabama, Vol. 2, p. 740:

     A biography of Amderson M. Sellers says that he was
born in Lowndes Co., Ala., in 1829, son of William Calvin
and Levina Anderson Sellers.

          Anderson Deeds from Dallas Co., Ala.

E:445.   6th Dec., 1832. Power of attorney from Alexander
          Anderson to Major Wm. C. Hogan, to sell the NW¼ of
          Sec. 19, T17, R11, the same land granted by the
          U. S. to Joseph Anderson, assignee of Wm. Anderson,
          and by said Joseph sold to Alexander Anderson.
          This document mentions Joseph Hamilton, clerk of
          the Court of Please and Quarter Sessions, in
          Jefferson Co., Tenn.

E:325.   Deed of Partition. Dallas Co., Ala. 24 Dec.,
          1849. James Anderson of Greene Co., Ala., and
          Virginia E., his wife, one of the daughters of
          John Spaight, deceased, late of Wilcox Co., Ala.;
          Robert J. English, of Dallas Co., Ala., another
          of the daughters and heirs of said John Spaight
          (sic); Ashley W. Spaight, son and heir of said
          John Spaight and

Matilda M. George, wife of James George, widow and heir of said John Spaight, dec'd, by Ashley W. Spaight, her trustee, legally appointed to receive the title to her distributive share of the estate of her former husband, said John Spaight, dec'd...

These are all the heirs of John Spaight. By this deed, they divided among themselves the slaves that had been the property of John Spaight.

The signatures of James and Virginia E. Anderson, and of Robert J. and Georgia A. English, were acknowledged before A. C. Jackson, J. P. in Dallas Co., Ala., on Dec. 24, 1849.

A. W. Spaight acknowledged his signature to this deed before Thos. G. Rainer, clerk of the County Court of Dallas Co., Ala., on 2 Feb., 1850.

Correction to item near bottom of page 23: Robt. J. English of Dallas Co., Ala., and his wife, Georgia, another of the daughters and heirs of said John Spaight, dec'd.

0:1 6th Nov., 1845. Alexander Anderson, and Eliza R., his wife, of Knox Co., Tenn., gave deed to Ezekiel Pickens of Dallas Co., Ala., to land in NW¼ of Sec. 19, T17, R11, in Dallas Co., Ala., the same tract bought by the late Joseph Anderson (then Comptroller of the U. S. Treasury) from the Govt. of the U. S., and by him conveyed to the said Alexander Anderson.
Witnesses:
>   James M. Witeker (?)
>   Samuel W. Bell

Alexander and Eliza R. Anderson acknowledged their signature to this deed before Arthur R. Grozier, notary public in Knox Co., Tenn., on 6 Nov., 1845.

P:362-3. 10th Oct., 1853. John W. Craig mortgaged some slaves to Aly W. John, Jesse B. Anderson, Samuel H. Gilmer, James Gilmer, Jr., of Perry and Dallas Counties (in Ala.), they being endorsers of a promissory note he made, payable to John J. Craig, as administrator of James W. Craig, dec'd.

Philen Family of Wilcox Co.

From Minutes of Probate Court, Book 5:

p. 159.   June 14, 1845.   Wm. F. Fountain, Joshua Philen &
Sidney Philen, heirs of Peter Philen, dec'd, vs.
Manassah Philen, administrator of Wm. Philen, dec'd.

"In this case, on application, it is ordered that
notice issue to Manassah Philen, adm. of estate
of Wm. Philen, dec'd, to appear at next term of
court, and file his accounts with said minors for
a final settlement of the guardianship of said
Wm. Philen, dec'd, in his lifetime, with said
minors." (?)

p. 175.   Aug. 18, 1845.   Wm. Fountain and wife, and others,
versus Manassah Philen, adm. of Wm. Philen, dec'd.
Settlement of the guardianship of Wm. Philen, in
his lifetime, with Wm. Fountain and wife, and others
is continued till 3rd Mon. Sept. next.

Compiler's note: I did not find the settlement of this
guardianship, but did not make an exhaustive search, as I
was not certain my client needed this.

From Minutes of Probate Court, Book 3:

p. 435.   Aug., 1840.   Estate of Peter Philen, dec'd.   Came
Wm. Philen, the adm., and made his final settlement
and distribution of the estate.   Named heirs:

Fereby, the widow, and the following children:

1. Dau., Mary, wife of Edward F. Farrington

2. Dau., Fereby, wife of Joel Mixon

3. Dau., Jane, wife of Isham J. Clarke

4. Son, Wm. Philen

5. Son, Manassah Philen

And the following grandchildren, being children of the
deceased children who had died previous to the death of
said Peter Philen, the intestate:

6. Catherine Kelley, wife of Wm. L. Morse, and dau. of Elizabeth Philen Kelley, wife of James Kelley.

7. Elizabeth Philen Walker, wife of Andrew Walker, and dau. of Peter Philen, Jr., dec'd, who was a son of Peter Philen, the intestate,   and

   Harrison, Chapman R., Catherine, Joshua, and Jackson Philen, minors, and children of Peter Philen, Jr., dec'd, who was a son of Peter Philen, the intestate.

8. Eliza Ann and Martha Philen, children of Riley Philen, dec'd, who was son of Peter Philen, Sr.

9. Wesley Philen and Susan (Philen) Walker, wife of John M. Walker, who are the children of John Philen, dec'd, who was a son of Peter Philen, the intestate.

10. Wm. Chaney and Sarah Chaney Kelley, wife of Asa Kelley, children of Sarah Philen, daughter of Peter Philen, Sr., the intestate, who married Charles Chaney, now dec'd.

Ferebe, the widow is entitled to 1/5 of the personal est.

Mary and Edward F. Farrington are entitled to 1/10 of 4/5..

Compiler's note: There are 29 more documents connected with this estate. I did not summarize them all.

From Minutes of Probate Court, Book 5:

p. 36.   Dec. 16, 1844. Wm. F. Fountain was appointed guardian of the minor heirs of Peter Philen, viz.:

             Harrison Philen
             Chapman Philen
             Isham Philen
             Jackson Philen

p. 183.   Aug. 18, 1845. The minor heirs of Peter Philen are named again: Catherine Philen who married Wm. F. Fountain; Joshua Philen; Jackson Philen; and Chapman Philen. Wm. Philen, dec'd, had been their guardian.
           Note discrepancies in lists of minor heirs.

Estate of Brittain Belk, Wilcox Co.

From Minutes of Probate Court, Book One:

p. 111. Nov. 13, 1826. Sarah, widow of Brittain Belk, dec'd, applied to be made administratrix of his estate, and asked that Stephen Day, a citizen of Wilcox Co., be jointly concerned in said administration. Bond for $1200.00 with Wm. Fisher and Blakely Higginbotham as their securities. Appointed to appraise the estate:

Ezekiel Glover

Samuel Williamson

Daniel McLean

Compiler's note: There are 7 documents relating to this estate in MPC Book 2. I read them all, but found no list of heirs. Stephen Day was still adm. in 1830.

From Minutes of Probate Court, Book 3, p. 157:

17 July, 1837. Sarah Belk, guardian of Darling, Mary and William Belk, heirs of Brittain Belk, dec'd, asked to have her appointment as guardian amended so as to include Augy Myram Belk, minor heir of Brittain Belk, who is over 14 years of age; also to show that said Brittain Belk was the son of heir of Darling Belk, dec'd, late of Mecklinburg Co., N. C. She gave bond for $300.00 with Green A. Fisher and Geo. D. Fisher as her securities.

From Minutes of Probate Court, Book 5:

p. 196. Aug. 18, 1845. Came Sarah Belk, guardian of the minors heirs of Darling Belk, dec'd, and filed the rec'ts of H. J. Belk, M. A. Tolbert, and M. Z. Belk, heirs at law of said decedent's estate.

Compiler's note: Nothing else about these matters is indexed in either Book 3 or Book 5. There may be other papers, not indexed.

From Deed Book E, p. 362. 24 Nov., 1838. Edward T. Farrington of Clarke Co., Ala., sold land in _____County to Anderson D. Etheridge of Monroe Co., Ala. Witnesses: John F. Pate, Barnett R. Mobley

More Anderson Deeds from Dallas Co., Ala

From Deed Book D, p. 14. 5th Nov., 1822. Deed from the
U. S. to Joseph Anderson, Assignee of Wm. Anderson.
165.35 A. NW¼ of Sec. 19, T17, R11.

D:74. 26 Sept., 1834. Reuben B. Anderson, and his wife,
Sarah, sold to John Wisdom, for $80.00, all their
title and claim to the W½ of SE¼ of Sec. 8, T15,
R6E.

D:299. 3 Sept., 1833. Lewis Anderson sold to Isaac
Stephens, for $240.00, the E½ of NW¼ of Sec. 27,
T15, R7. 80.47 A.

Lewis Anderson acknowledged his signature to the
above deed before J. H. Silman and Hugh McPhaill,
Justices of peace in Marengo Co., Ala., Sept. 3,
1833.

Four Mahan marriage records from Perry Co., Ala.:

p. 262. David A. Griffin to Mary Mahan, on 15 Feb., 1827
by Wm. Harris, M. G.

p. 574. Alfred Mahan to Abigail Goggins on 29 Dec., 1831
by James W. Cosby, J. P.

p. 611. A. M. Mahan to Mary Bennett on 21 June, 1832
by Moses Bledsoe, J. P.

p. 687a. David Mahan to Elizabeth Goggins on 6th Oct.,
1833, by Benj. Ford, J. P.

Eubanks marriages from Monroe Co., Ala.

Marriage Record for 1834-1880:

p. 21.   Eubanks, J. J. to Miss Eliza Walker on 3 Dec.,
         1835, by Asa Parker, J. P. Security: S. A. DuBose

p. 53.   Eubanks, Evander to Elizabeth Eubanks on 19 Feb.,
         1839, by Wm. C. Faulk, J. P.

p. 117. Jesse Eubanks to Julia Rauls on 6 Jan, 1848,
         by R. O. Connell, J. P. Bondsman, R. O. Connell

p. 177. Benj. F. Newberry to Josephine Eubanks, "At J.
         J. Eubanks" on 30 Nov., 1855, by John J. Eubanks,
         J. P. Bondsman, B. N. Walker. "Consent"

p. 122. Eubanks, Jesse G. to Catherine Rall on 5th Oct.,
         1848, by J. G. Wallace, J. P. Bndsmn: Malcom
         Graham.

p. 130. Eubanks, John J. to Mrs. Elizabeth Rikard on
         30 Dec., 1849, by R. O. Connell, J. P.
         Bondsman: David W. Kelly   "of age"

p. 206. Eubanks, Thos. J. to Laura Catherine Craps (?)
         on 10th Feb., 1859, by K. O. Connell, J. P.
         "of age"

p. 236. Eubanks, J. B. to Martha A. Newberry at the res.
         of Wm. Newberry, on 30th Sept., 1863, by M.
         McCorvey, Judge of Probate. Sec.: J. J. Eubanks

p. 246. Eubanks, R. H. to M. C. Holman, at res. of Nancy
         Davidson, by M. M. Graham, M. G. on 19th May,
         1865. Sec: G. W. Salter   "of age"

p. 259. Eubanks, Jesse A. to Sarah A. Davison, at res.
         of Mrs. Davison, on 4th Jan., 1866, by M. Mc-
         Corvey, Judge. Sec., J. J. Eubanks. "Consent"

p. 288. Eubanks, Wm. H. to Adelaide V. Craps, at res. of
         Mrs. Bethea, by W. B. Dennis, M. G. on 17 Dec.,
         1867. Security: H. T. Craps

p. 92.   Eubanks, Fannie to Wm. Buck (?) on 20 Oct., 1844,
         by Samuel Kelly, J. P. Security: F. B. Long

p. 56. Robt. O. Connell to Miss Mary Ann Eubanks on
25 July, 1859, by Wm. C. Faulk, J. P.
Security: Wm. A. Graham   "of age"

p. 40. John McCaskill to Caroline Eubanks on 18 Jan.,
1838, by Wm. C. Faulk, J. P. Security: B. N.
Walker.   "of age"

p. 55. Wm. A. Graham to Miss Margaret Eubanks on 25 July,
1839, by Wm. C. Faulk, J. P. Sec.: Robt. O. Connell.

Compiler's note: Earlier records of Monroe Co. were
destroyed by fire about 1833.

Wilkes Data from Greene Co., Ala.

From Deed Book B, pp. 145-6: 29 Sept., 1825:

I, Francis Wilkes, for love and affection, to my two
daughters, Mary T. Wilks and Martha A. Wilks, some Negro
girls; but my wife, Mary Wilks to have the use of them
during her life. Witnessed by:
                        Amos Tims (?)
                        Juliet Tims (?)

From Minutes of Probate Court, Book F:

p. 65. Feb. 12, 1844. Inventory of the personal property
of the estate of Mary Wilks, dec'd, returned by Martha A.
Wilks, administratrix of said estate.

p. 407. Feb. 5, 1849. Robt. F. and Martha A. Stuart,
         admr. and admx. of the estate of Mary Wilks,
         dec'd, gave bond for $7000.00 with Thos. T. Chiles
         and David R. Chiles as their securities. The
         admr. and admx. are permitted to keep the estate
         together for one year.

p. 817. Apr. 13, 1846 (?). Robert F. Stuart, adm. in
         right of his wife, Martha A., permitted to keep
         the estate together for another year. Bond for
         $7000.00 with Benj. Williams and James DeLoach
         as sec.

Compiler's note: I found nothing indexed in Book B about
Wilks. Book C, MPC, has no index at all. Nothing indexed
in Book D. Most of these old indexes are imperfect.

From Minutes of Probate Court, Book G:

p. 32.   Sept. 16, 1846. On application of John W. Wilkes,
         by Wm. F. Pierce, his attorney, citations were
         issued to Robt. F. and Martha Stewart, adm. and
         admx. of Mary Wilks, dec'd, to appear at next term
         of court and file their vouchers for a final
         settlement of the estate. Mary Wilks had been
         administrator of Francis Wilks.

p. 146: James Greer and his wife, Mary T., and Martha A.
         Stewart and her husband, Robert F. Stewart, are
         the only heirs at law of Mary Wilks, dec'd. Jan.
         13, 1847.

p. 211. Apparently a division was made.

p. 162-3. Dec. 14, 1846. Account of John W. Wilkes,
who was admr. of estate of Francis Wilkes,
dec'd. Heirs of said Francis Wilks are:

> John W. Wilkes
> James Greer and wife, Mary T.
> Robt. F. Stuart, and Martha A.,
>   his wife

Advancement had been made to said Mary and Martha in the
lifetime of Francis Wilkes, by deed of gift of one slave
each, valued at $150.00 ea.

Court decreed that John W. Wilkes should get $214.92;
each daughter to get $64.92.

From Minutes of Probate Court, Book H:

pp. 18-19: Nov. 29, 1848. The settlement of the estate
of Francis Wilkes, dec'd, by John W. Wilkes, adm., was
re-opened.

p. 574. Oct. 16, 1850. Robert F. and Martha A. Stuart,
administrators of the estate of Mary Wilkes, asked to be
allowed to sell the lands belonging to the estate, in
sections 11 and 14, Township 22, Range 2, West. The
following are minor heirs of said decedent:

> Aquilla Greer
> Mary Greer
> Roxana (Rosana ?) Greer
> Robert L. Greer

Alexander Falconer was appointed guardian ad litem to
represent the minors.

p. 1054. Feb. 12, 1852. The administrators report the
sale of the land to Robert F. Stuart.

From Bond Book A, p. 9: 2 Jan., 1835. Bond of John W.
Wilkes and Mary Wilkes as adms. of Francis Wilks,
$12,000.00 with Matthew Trussell and Hopkins R. Richard-
son as securities.

From Bond Book A, pp. 24-25: Two bonds of Mary Wilks as
guardian of Martha A. and Mary T. Wilkes, minor heirs of
their deceased father, Francis Wilkes. $7000.00 in each
case, with John W. Wilks and John G. Coleman as her
securities. Dated: 20 April, 1835.

p. 454. 20 July, 1843. Bond of Martha A. Wilks as administrator of Mary Wilks, dec'd. $7500 with James G. George and Samuel C. McNeese and James Greer as her securities.

In passing, I also found two McNeese items:

p. 128. 12 March, 1838. Bond of James G. George as adm. of Wm. McNeese, dec'd. $20,000.00 with Simeon Carpenter and T. M. Hutton as securities.

From Minutes of Probate Court, Book D, p. 384:

March 12, 1838. Delila McNeese, the widow, renounced her right to administer the estate of Wm. McNeese, and James G. George was appointed instead.

Compiler's note: Nothing else is indexed about this estate in Vol. D, and nothing is indexed in Vol. E. There may be other items which are not indexed.

From Minutes of Probate Court, Book F, p. 912:

20 July, 1846. Court received the receipts and release from Delilah McNees to James G. George, as administrator of Wm. McNees, dec'd, which is dated 22 June, 1846; also the receipt of Samuel C. McNees for his share of the estate, dated 8th July, 1846.

Compiler's note: I understand there was a McNees-Wilks connection.

Morisette Family of Perry County

Estate of John Morrisette. From Minutes of Probate Court, Book O:

p. 68. July 17, 1871. Came Edmund P. Morisett, administrator of the estate of John Morrisett, and filed petition asking the court for an order to sell the lands for division. The only heirs are:

Francis Morrisett, who lives near Bell's Landing, in Monroe Co., Ala.

Edmund P. Morrisett, Montgomery, Ala.

-- both brothers of John Morrisett, dec'd, and of full age.

Caroline, a sister of deceased, living at Enterprise, Miss., and married to Dr. A. Baldwin

The minor children of James D. Morrisett, brother of deceased; to wit: Maud, Lalula, and May, who reside at Washington, Ark., in custody of their mother, Mrs. F. B. Morrisett.

The minor son of Geo. G. Morrisett, a brother of dec'd, named Robinson Morrisett, residing at Claiborne, in Monroe Co., Ala., in custody of his mother, Mrs. Cornelia R. Williams.

p. 153. Same volume. Description of the land, which was in Hale and Perry Counties.

p. 220. Nov. 18, 1871. Report of the sale of the lands, on 6th Nov. 1871, in front of the court house, in Perry Co. Land bought by Edmund P. and Francis S. Morrisette, at $12.00 an acre. Total, $11,040.

From Minutes of Probate Court, Book P, p. 171:

Dec. 9, 1873. Final settlement of the estate of John Morrisett. No new family data, except: Caroline M. Baldwin; Robinson Morrisett, a minor, resides with his legal guardian, John McLeod, in Wilcox Co., Ala.; Lalula and May reside with their mother and legal guardian, Fannie B. Morrisette, in Washington, Ark.

The estate was divided into 5 equal shares of $1081.76.

Note: No mention of Maud in this list of heirs.

Morrisette Deeds from Perry Co., Ala.:

Deed Book N, p. 296. 30 Jan., 1857. John Morrisett and
James D. Morrisett sold to Henry Jemison, for $10,000,
480 A. land in T18, R6, in Perry Co., and in T18, R5, in
Marengo Co.

John and James D. Morrisett acknowledged their signatures
to this deed before J. J. Drake, J. P., in Perry Co., Ala.
on 23 March, 1857.

From Deed Book N, p. 624. 8th Feb., 1858. I, Edmund W.
Robards, of Monroe Co., Ala., administrator of the estate
of John Morrisett, dec'd, late of said County, sold to
John Morrisett, for $25,683.10, land in Perry and Marengo
Counties, containing in all 712.43 acres.

From Deed Book G, p. 202. 26 Feb., 1844. Gray Huckabee
and Martha A., his wife, of Greene Co., Ala., sold to
John Morrisette of Monroe Co., Ala., for $700.00, 160 A.
in Marengo and Perry Counties, in T18, R5 and R6.

Correction: From Deed Book G, p. 202. 26 Feb., 1844.
Gray Huckabee and Martha A., his wife, of Marengo Co.,
Ala., sold to John Morrisett of Monroe Co., Ala., for
$500.00, 240 A. in T18, R6, in Perry Co., Ala.

From Deed Book G, p. 526. 10th Sept., 1844. Thos. R.
Borden and Ann M., his wife, of Greene Co., Ala., sold to
John Morrisett, of Monroe Co., Ala., for $700.00, 160 A.
in Marengo and Perry Counties, in T18, R5 and R6.

Deed Book M, p. 164. 3rd March, 1855. Robt. J. Semple,
Mary J. Shields and Edwina Shield, sold to John and James
Morrisett, for $12,888.72, land in T18, R5 and R6, in all
470.36 acres.

From "The Ala. Lawyer", Vol. 6, p. 129: John Morrisett,
of a name long connected with the Claiborne region, lived
at Bell's Landing, not far from the Wilcox-Monroe County
line. He was born in Rogersville, in East Tennessee;
served through the war of 1812, then moved to St. Stephens,
Ala., then the seat of the territorial government of Ala.,
and there formed a partnership with James Lyon. He moved
to Monroe Co., in 1821, after marrying Frances Gaines, a
relative of Gen. Edmund P. Gaines, under whom he had served
in the Army. He then began the practice of law......

Patton Family of Greene Co., Ala.

From Will Record B, p. 121: 12 Aug., 1833. James K.
Patton made guardian of Powhattan E. Patton, 10 years old,
minor heir of James Patton, dec'd. Bond for $12,000.00
with John M. Bates and Wm. L. (or S.) Harrison as sec.

Will of Samuel Patton, from Will Record C, pp. 375-9:
Mentions:

1. Grandchildren, children of my dau., Elizabeth Bates

2. Granddaughters, Margaret L. Willingham and
   Martha E. Fowler

3. Son-in-law, John M. Bates

4. Grandchildren, Children of my deceased daughter,
   Martha, wife of E. V. Levert

5. Debt to John Nelson and B. Vaughn, for slave bt.

6. To son-in-law, John M. Bates, my land on which he
   now resides, with the mill

7. Executors, James D. Webb, Samuel C. Levert, and
   John M. Bates

   Dated 5 June, 1854

   Witnessed by S. R. Williamson
                J. M. Idom
                M. Martin

   Proved 16 Oct., 1854

List of persons in debt to Samuel Patton includes
     John M. Bates, Jr.

From Greene Co., Marriage Record, Book A, p. 21:

License for John M. Bates to marry Elizabeth Patton,
     issued 11 Aug., 1824. There is no minister's
     return showing date on which ceremony was performed.
     "By consent of parent."

Bates notes from Greene Co., Ala.

From Deed Book I (eye), p. 341. 5th April, 1838:

John M. Bates and Elizabeth, his wife, and Eugene V. Levert and Martha, his wife, sold to Robert Dickens, Andrew Walker and Frederick Peck and Thos. M. Johnston and John Erwin, land for Greensboro Cemetery.

From Deed Book A, pp. 76-7: James A. Bates sold to John M. Bates, slaves, in 1823.

From Deed Book A, p. 227. 1st April, 1823. Robert A. Bates sold a slave to John Carson. Deed witnessed by James A. Bates and Henry Wideman.

From Deed Book A, p. 240. 1st December, 1823:

John M. Bates, as sheriff of Greene County, sold a slave to Solomon McAlpin. Slave had belonged to Pleasant Daniel.

From Deed Book A, p. 255. Margaret Bates, of Greene Co., for love and affection, to my grandchildren, Oscar and Margaret B. Watkins, son and daughter of Needham and Elizabeth Watkins, of Greene Co., a Negro man, Charles, aged 25. Delivered to Needham Watkins, natural guardian of said children, in the presence of Thos. F. Moody. 12 Feb., 1825.

Book and page number not recorded. 3rd April, 1857:

John M. and Robert F. Bates gave a mortgage to Thos. M. Johnston, conveying to him their undivided interests in the lands and slaves bequeathed by their grandfather, the late Samuel Patton, in his will, to Elizabeth Bates, to be allotted to the children of said Elizabeth as they reach the age of 21; said lands being the same occupied by John M. Bates, dec'd, in his life-time, and where he resided at the time of his death, including the mill known as Bates' Mill, about 4½ miles north of Greensboro.

From Marriage Record of Greene Co.:

John W. Bates married to Miss Elizabeth Constantine on 30 Nov., 1853, by C. C. Calaway.

Estate of William Bates, Greene Co., Ala.

From Minutes of Orphans' Court, Col. A (?), p. 135:

17 Sept., 1823. Letters of administration granted to Sophia Bates on the estate of Wm. Bates, dec'd. Bond for $5000.00 with Pleasant White and John Coats as her securities.

The following were appointed to appraise the estate of Wm. Bates, dec'd:

Robert Bell   Walter Chiles   Thomas Seales
Joseph Middlebrooks   Doctor Christopher

From Marriage Record A, p. 37: Wyatt Harper married to Sophia Bates on 21 Dec., 1825.

From Probate Court Record, Vol. C, pp. 46-7. Oct., 1829. Wyatt Harper, guardian of William Bates, one of the minor heirs of Wm. Bates, dec'd. Harper is also administrator of the estate of Wm. Bates, dec'd.

In same volume, a document dated April 13, 1829, mentions cash received for this estate from John Thomas, James Adams, and Andrew Elliott.

Lands belonging to said estate were sold about 1829 by virtue of an Act of the Legislature of Alabama, passed for that purpose. Land in Township 20, Range 5.

From Probate Court Record, Vol. B., pp. 233ff. These documents are dated 1825-6-7. John Coats and Sophia Bates were then administrators of the estate of Wm. Bates, dec'd.

From Probate Record D, p. 799. March 30, 1835. Inventory of Negroes belonging to the estate of the minor heirs of William Bates, dec'd, by Joseph B. Chambers, their guardian.

Same Volume, p. 800. March 31, 1835. Joseph B. Chambers, guardian, in account with the minor heirs of Wm. Bates, dec'd: viz.:

Mary Ann Bates   Martha Bates   Betty Bates
Joseph C. Bates

Same Volume, p. 802. 31st March, 1835. Mary Jane Bates has married Henry Field prior to this date.

Probate Record D, p. 804. Martha Ann Bates has married
Willis B. Harvey. Apparently Elizabeth Bates is still
single.

Same Volume, p. 809: Joseph B. Chambers, who was appointed
in 1828, guardian of Martha Ann, Mary Jane, Elizabeth, and
Joseph C. Bates, resigned March 31, 1835.

Same Volume, p. 958: 28 Sept., 1835: Receipt of John
Morrisette, guardian of JosephC. Bates, for certain notes
deposited in the clerk's office by Joseph B. Chambers,
former guardian. Also the receipt of David Packer, gdn.
of Elizabeth Bates, by his agent, John Morrisette.

Nothing is indexed in Books E, F, G, or H about these
minors.

Bates Data from Wilcox Co., Ala.

From Minutes of Orphans Court, Book C, p. 511: (Date ?)

Came Henry Field, in right of his wife, Mary Jane,
formerly Mary Jane Bates, one of the heirs of Wm. Bates,
dec'd, and filed his petition to sell certain real estate
belonging to said estate, for the prupose of making a more
equitable distribution among the heirs.

It is ordered by the court that notice of the filing
of said petition be issued to:

Joseph B. Chambers, in right of his wife Ann, who
was the widow and relict of Wm. Bates, dec'd.

Willis B. Harvie, in right of his wife, Martha Ann,
formerly Martha Ann Bates

John Morrisett, guardian of Joseph C. Bates, a minor

David Packer, gdn. of Elizabeth Bates, a minor

-- all children and heirs of Wm. Bates, dec'd.

From Minutes of Orphans Court, Vol. 3, p. 58:
17 Oct., 1836. This case having been continued from
time to time, and no one appearing to oppose the petition,
same is granted. Commissioners appointed to make the sale:
Bryant Marsh, Alexander Perryman, James Gamble, John H.
Gamble, Thos. E. Ellis.
Same Vol., p. 65: 21 Nov., 1836. Petitioner comes by his
attorney, and dismisses petition.

Bates Data from Wilcox Co., Ala.

From Deed Book G, p. 162: 23 Jan. 1841. I, Joseph Bates, of Monroe Co., Ala., but at present a citizen of Holmes Co., Miss., sell all my right, title and undivided interest, at law or in equity, as one of the heirs of William Bates, dec'd, to fraction section 6 & 5, Township 13, Range 7, West of Ala. River, for $200.00, to Henry S. Atwood; some of the land being lots in the Town of Dale, alias Prairie Bluff. Witnessed by C. M. Hobbs, and J. H. Smith. Signed: Joseph C. Bates.

From Deed Book G, p. 398: 1st Jan. 1837. Deed recorded in Wilcox Co., Ala., but drawn and witnessed in Perry Co., Ala. Willis B. Harvey and Martha A., his wife, Henry Field and Mary, his wife, and Joseph C. Bates, all of Perry Co., sold to Bryan Marsh, of Wilcox Co., for $5730, 480 A. in Sec. 26 and Sec. 23, Township 14, Range 6. Witnessed by Jack F. Cocke and Woodson Cocke.

Same Volume, p. 399. Elizabeth, wife of Joseph C. Bates, joined her husband in making this deed. "Land belonging to the estate of the late Wm. Bates."

Bates Marriages from Monroe Co., Ala.

Earliest Marriage Record: p. 17. Seymour Bates to Martha A. Sharp, on 25 July, 1835. Security: Joseph D. Boney.

p. 57. Seymour Bates to Elizabeth M. Sullivan, on 9th Oct., 1839, by James P. Wilson, J. P. Security: Henry Sullivan.

p. 105. Richard Clark to Elizabeth Bates, 28 April 1846, by Edmund C. Murdaugh --

Monroe Co., Ala., Deed Book A, p. 574-5. 4th April 1846:

Deed of trust between Adam Carson and Joseph C. Bates. Carson is indebted to Ann Chambers for $12,000.00. He made over his slave-property, in trust, to Joseph C. Bates, to secure the debt. Witness: John Morrisette.

Wilcox Co., Ala. Deed Book K, p. 533. 11 Jan. 1840:

Uriah M. Bates, and his wife, Eliza, sold to Ezekiel Watson, 80 acres on Pine Barren Creek.

Bates Family of Dallas and Perry Counties

From 1850 Census of Dallas Co., Ala., Athens Beat,
House No. 460:

G. W. Bates	age 37	born in S. C.
S. E. Bates	25	born in Ga.
N. A. "	3	born in Ala. (female)
Martha E. "	5	"
G. M. "	1	" (male)

From Minutes of Probate Court of Dallas Co., Ala.
Book W, p. 63ff:

Oct. 16, 1875. Came Alexander W. Brown, and represents
that George W. Bates departed this life about 24 Sept., 1875,
leaving no will, and possessed of property including about
1300 acres of land, worth about $8000.00. He left no
widow, and his heirs are his children, viz.:

1. Nannie A. Morgan

2. Ida J., wife of Samuel Bates

3. C. E., wife of A. W. Brown

4. Sallie, wife of Clark Lyles

    -- all over 21, and residing in this State

5. John Murphy Bates

6. Lucy M. Bates

7. W. W. Bates

    -- the last three are minors and reside in
       this County
    -- and since the death of her father, Lucy
       has married John Lyles

There are 22 documents connected with the settlement of
this estate. Land in Township 15, Range 7, which is SW
of Selma, near the present town of Safford. The documents
mention the Mobley Place (also called the Home Place),
the Sugar Bottom Place, and the Goldsby Place.

From Book W, Minutes of Probate Court, Dallas Co., Ala., pp. 576 ff. Sept. 27, 1876. The following list of heirs gives additional information about them:

1. Mrs. Nannie Morgan, residing in Perry Co., Ala.

2. Ida J. Bates

3. Ella, wife of Alexander W. Brown, residing in Dallas Co., Ala.

4. Sallie, wife of Clark Lyles, residing in Wilcox Co., Ala.

5. Lucy, wife of John Lyles, residing in Wilcox Co.

6. Murphy Bates, a minor over 14 years, residing with Clark Lyles in Wilcox Co., Ala.

7. W. W. Bates, a minor under 14, residing with Clark Lyles in Wilcox Co., Ala.

From Minutes of Probate Court, Book X, p. 53:

Dec. 16, 1876. John S. Lyles and J. E. Wilkerson bought some of the land of the estate.

Alexander W. Brown eventually resigned as administrator of this estate, and the administration was committed to Joseph F. John, who was at the time general administrator for Dallas Co. This was on April 13, 1877. I did not find a final settlement of the estate; nor any account of property being distributed among the heirs.

From Marriage Record of Dallas Co., Ala., for the years 1818-45:

p. 276. George W. Bates was married to Sarah E. Mobley on the night of 14 July, 1844, by Wm. McElroy, J. p.

From 1860 Census of Dallas Co., Ala.:
Athens Beat, Post Office, Liberty Hill.

Geo. W. Bates, age 47, farmer, born in Ga.
          value of real estate $700
          personal property $31,600
S. E.   "   age 35, born in Ga. female
Nancy A. "   13; G. M. Bates, 11, male;
I. J. Bates, age 8, female; Eoline Bates, age 7;
Sarah Bates, age 5; J. M. Bates, age 3, male;
Lucy Bates, age 2 -- all born in Ala.
Also living in this family were: M. E. Raines, female,
school teacher, born in N. C.; Wright Scurlock, age 40,
farm laborer, b. in Ga.; and Susan Scurlock, age 22,
born in Ga.

Inscriptions from Marion Cemetery:

        William Walter Bates (My husband)
        Dec. 16, 1865 June 24, 1901

        Thos. J. Morgan
        Mar. 4, 1832 Feb. 23, 1875

        My beloved son: G. W. Morgan
        Nov. 13, 1869   Nov. 24, 1891

        Lula T., wife of James D. Smith
        June 12, 1871   Dec. 7, 1907

From cemetery between Miller's Ferry and Camden, in
Wilcox Co., Ala. (Canton Bend ?):

Sallie, wife of Clark Lyles, born April ___, 1857, and
        died Jan. 22, 1887.

Children of Sarah Bates Lyles still living include:
Mr. Malcolm Lyles of Kimbrough, Ala., and a Mrs. Lawler
of Camden, Ala.

Mrs. Eva Lyles Wilkerson, daughter of John and Lucy Bates
Lyles, is still living, in Montgomery, Ala. She states
that she was born at the old Bates homestead near Safford.

Compiler's note: Thos. J. Morgan, buried in Marion
Cemetery, was husband of Nannie A. Morgan. George W.
Morgan and Lula T. Smith were two of the children of
Nannie and Thos. J. Morgan. Another of their children
married Marshall Levis. I believe this was Minnie;

Mr. M. M. Frost, of 3617 Caruth Blvd., Dallas 25, Texas,
a grandson of Nannie Bates Morgan, states that she was born
in Athens, Ala., Jan. 23, 1847, and died at the home of her
daughter (Clara, Mrs. A. D. Frost) on Oct. 29, 1934. Mrs.
Clara Morgan Frost is still living (1959) at Venus, Texas.

Minnie Morgan, another daughter of Nannie Bates Morgan,
married Walter P. Levis. One of her sons, M. M. Levis,
resides at 55 Oakdale, Berkeley, California.

Members of the family still living state that John Bates
of Perry Co., and Robt. Bates, also of Perry Co., were
brothers of Geo. W. Bates, of Dallas Co.

So far, I have not found who were the parents of George W.,
John and Robert Bates.

From Marion Cemetery, Marion, Ala.:

>   John Bates, born Dec. 1, 1808, died Aug. 2, 1868
>   Martha Jane Dorroh, wife of John Bates,
>   born June 10, 1829   died Sept. 5, 1899
>   Joel M. Bates   Aug. 20, 1859   Nov. 15, 1900
>   W. D. Bates   Aug. 22 - Oct. 22, 1847
>   Lettie Bates, wife of H. G. Smith,
>   Nov. 17, 1860   May 23, 1927
>
>   in another square:
>
>   John Murphy Bates   Nov. 18, 1856   July 1, 1921
>   Mamie England Bates   July 7, 1855   Oct. 22, 1938
>
>   Robert Bates   March 26, 1807   Feb. 5, 1870
>   Mary D., wife of Robert Bates, and Daughter of Thomas
>   and Sarah Montague, born in Cumberland Co.,
>   Va., Sept. 30, 1823, and died at Marion,
>   Ala., June 10, 1881
>   Prentice R., son of Robert and Mary D. Bates, born
>   in Perry Co., Ala., Dec. 17, 1857, died in
>   Selma, Ala., Sept. 25, 1880
>
>   Annie Underwood, dau. of S. H. and A. B. Underwood,
>   Dec. 29, 1897   June 18, 1904
>   Inf. son of S. J. and Ida Bates, born Nov. 30 and
>   died Dec. 8, 1882

Note: Members of the family still living say that Ida
Bates, dau. of Geo. W. Bates, married Sam'l Bates, son of
John Bates of Perry Co.; and that their daughter, Annie
Bates, married Sam Underwood.

From 1860 Census of Perry Co., Ala., Woodville Beat:

```
John Bates    Age 51    born in S. C.
M. J.    "     30       born in Ala., female
Sam'l    "     11         "
A. F.    "      8         "              "
John     "      6         "
Martha   "      4         "
Julia    "      2         "
Joel     "    11/12        "
```
John Barge, age 18, **farm** manager, born in Ga.
Frances Sherlock (?)**female**, aged 15, born in Ala.

Note: a client states that John Bates had a sister Susan
who married John Barge, and that after her death, some of
her children went to live with their uncle, John Bates, in
Perry Co.

From the 1860 Census of Perry Co., Ala., Hamburg Beat:

```
Robert Bates    age 35    born in S. C.
M. D.     "         36    born in Va.
Prentice Bates      2     born in Ala.
```

William Walter Bates married Nannie Adele Ezelle in Perry
Co., Ala., on June 15, 1898.

From the Minutes of the Probate Court, Perry Co., Ala.,
Vol. P, pp. 368 ff: Dec. 14, 1875. Came Martha J. Bates,
executor of the will of John Bates, dec'd, asking the court
for leave to sell the real estate to pay the debts of the
estate. The devises of the deceased, John Bates, are:

1. Samuel Bates,   over 21
2. John D. Bates
3. Mattie J. Bates, a minor over 14
4. Julia Bates, a minor
5. Lettie L. Bates, a minor
6. Joel Bates, a minor

-- all of whom reside in Perry Co., except John D. Bates,
whose place of residence is unknown.

Living members of this family say that Mattie J. Bates,
dau. of John and Martha J. Bates, married a Craig, and
had:

1. Joe Bates Craig
2. Martha Craig

Martha Craig married a Barclay from near Faunsdale, Ala.,
and had a son, Joe Bates Barclay, and a dau., Martha Craig
Barclay.

Lyle Notes from Wilcox Co., Ala.

From Minutes of Probate Court, Vol. 26, pp. 519-20:

May 16, 1892. Came Wm. Thos. Lyles, and produced for
probate the will of Mrs. Martha E. Lyles, who died on
13 May, 1892.

Decedent left three children:

      1. John S. Lyles,   age 42

      2. Clark Lyles,   age 40

      3. Wm. Thomas Lyles, the petitioner, age 36

-- all residing in Wilcox Co.

From Minutes of Probate Court, Vol. 38, pp. 490-91:

21 June, 1938. Petition of Mrs. Eva Lyles Wilkinson to
probate the will of Mrs. Lucy Bates Lyles, who died
June 5, 1938.

Mobley notes from Dallas Co., Ala.

The will of Abner C. Mobley is recorded in Will Book B, pp. 281-4. It is dated 24 Feb., 1857, and names the following children:

1. Wm. W. Mobley
2. Susan Mobley
3. C. Reuben Mobley
4. Martha Mobley
5. Samuel Mobley

The will also mentions his wife, Lucy M. Mobley.

C. R. Mobley and Wm. W. Mobley were named executors.

The will is witnessed by:

A. W. Ellerbee
John D. Adams
Ansel Tolbert

A codicil, dated Oct., 1862, is witnessed by:

A. W. Ellerbee
H. J. Winn
Simeon Sheppard

The will and codicil were proved Dec. 31, 1863.

From Minutes of Probate Coust, Book N, pp. 323 ff:

A document dated April 3, 1867, names the heirs and distributees under the will of Abner C. Mobley as follows:

1. Wm. W. Mobley, who is executor
2. John S. and Margaret Mayes, his wife
3. Hardaway P. Heath, and Mary A., his wife
4. Geo. W. Bates, and Sarah E., his wife
5. Henry Morgan and Martha C., his wife
6. Elijah L. Coleman as administrator of the estate of C. R. Mobley, dec'd
7. Lucy M. Mobley, the widow

From Minutes of Probate Court, Book N, pp. 326 ff.
Another list of the heirs of Abner C. Mobley, slightly
different:

1. W. W. Mobley

2. Heirs of Mrs. Mary A. Heath, who are minors
    (names and numbers not given here)

3. Mrs. Sarah E., wife of Geo. W. Bates

4. Mrs. Martha C., wife of Henry Morgan

5. Mrs. Margaret A., wife of John S. Mayes

6. Heirs of C. R. Mobley, to wit:

            Mary J. Mobley
            A. C. Mobley

            -- both under 14 years of age

All the heirs reside in Dallas Co., Ala.

Note: Lucy is not mentioned; nor Susan.

Another document relating to the estate of Abner C. Mobley
and recorded in Minutes of Probate Court, Book P, p. 460,
under date Sept. 24, 1869, mentions E. R. Coleman as custodian of the minors, Mary J. and A. C. Mobley. "The Court
does not know the names of the infant heirs of Mary A.
Heath; their father is their custodian."

From Dallas Co., Ala., Marriage Record, 1845-65:

p. 199.   Henry Morgan to Miss Martha C. Mobley, on
          17 Sept., 1857, by Thos. G. Rainer, Probate Judge

p. 219.   Cullen R. Mobley to Miss Laura J. Coleman, on
          2 Sept., 1858, by Thos. G. Rainer, Judge Probate

p. 66.   Hardaway P. Heath to Mary A. Mobley, on 12 Dec.,
          1848, by J. Reeves, M. G.

From 1860 Census of Dallas Co., Ala., Athens Beat,
          Post Office, Liberty Hill:

            A. C. Mobley   age 63   born in Ga.
            Lucy A.   "   50   "
            Samuel   "   19   born in Ala.

From Dallas Co., Ala., Marriage Record 1845-65:

p. 178:　Abner C. Mobley to Mrs. Lucy M. Whiting, on
　　　　 18 Oct., 1855, by Elijah Bell, M. G.

p. 25:　 Abner C. Mobley to Miss Elizabeth E. Pledger,
　　　　 on 9th Sept., 1846, by W. H. McDaniel, M. G.

It is obvious from the above dates that neither of these
wives of Abner C. Mobler was the mother of Sarah E. Bates.

The mother of Sarah E. (Mobley) Bates must have been Ann,
the first wife of Abner C. Mobley. I have not found a
record of their marriage, nor of her surname. She signed
a deed as wife of A. C. Mobley in 1832, and another in
1845, both in Dallas Co. See Deed Book C, p. 124, and
Deed Book L, p. 315.

From the 1850 Census of Dallas Co., Ala., Athens Beat:

House No. 450:	A. C. Mobley	age 53	male	b. Ga.
	Elizabeth E.	50		b. S. C.
	J. M. Mobley	21		b. Ala.
	Wm. M.　"	18		"
	C. R.　　"	14	male	"
	S. G.　　"	15	female	"

From 1840 Census of Dallas Co., Ala.

House No. 1175:　A. C. Mobley:　1 male under 5
　　　　　　　　　　　　　　　　 1 male 5 - 10
　　　　　　　　　　　　　　　　 1 male 10 - 15
　　　　　　　　　　　　　　　　 1 male 20 - 30
　　　　　　　　　　　　　　　　 1 male 40 - 50

　　　　　　　　　　　　　　　　 1 female under 5
　　　　　　　　　　　　　　　　 2 females 5 - 10
　　　　　　　　　　　　　　　　 1 female 10 - 15
　　　　　　　　　　　　　　　　 1 female 15 - 20
　　　　　　　　　　　　　　　　 1 female 30 - 40

From File No. 34, package No. 99, Probate Court of Dallas
Co., Ala.:

Estate of John M. Mobley, dec'd. Aug., 1858. A. C. Mobley,
the administrator, filed a list of heirs, as follows:

1. Margaret A., wife of John S. Mayes
2. Sarah E., wife of G. W. Bates
3. Mary A., wife of H. P. Heath
4. Wm. W. Mobley
5. Susan G. Mobley
6. Martha G., wife of Henry Morgan
7. C. R. Mobley
   -- all of legal age, and residing in Dallas Co.
8. Samuel A. Mobley, son of A. C. Mobley, the
   administrator, who is upwards of 17 years old.

Another document in this file, dated Nov. 11, 1857, gives
the same list of heirs, and says they were brothers and
sisters of the deceased, John M. Mobley.

From same file and package:

"Received of A. C. Mobley, my guardian, $482.89, in
full of my hsare of the estates of John M. Mobley and of
Susan G. Mobley, dec'd. (Signed) S. A. Mobley."

Will of Lucy M. Mobley, Hale Co., Ala.

From Will Record A, Hale Co., Ala., pages 186-7. Dated
18 March, 1882. Persons mentioned:

1. Martha C., wife of Henry Morgan
2. Louisa, wife of Sam M. Willingham
3. Fanny Langham
4. Martha Willingham and her brother, Lee Willingham
5. Lucy M. Willingham, dau. of Louisa and Sam
   Willingham
6. Willy Willingham
7. Jesse W. Coleman of Lowndes Co., Ala.
8. Mitchel M. M. Langham
9. Children of my brothers and sisters that are dead
10. Patsy Burge's children

Executor, Mitchel M. M. Langham
Witnessed by C. Derrick and Thos. Seay.
Codicil dated 20 Mar., 1882.
Proved 17 Feb., 1883, by Clarence Derrick

Estate of Mrs. Lucy M. Mobley. Hale Co., Ala., Probate Coust, File No. 23.

Names of distributees:

1. Jesse W. Coleman, residing in Louisiana

2. Heirs of Martha W. Burge, dec'd:
   Mrs. Julia A. Owens (Ala.)
   E. C. Johnson
   B. S. Evans
   A. P. Evans

3. Heirs of G. W. Coleman:
   Mary C. Boggan
   T. B. Coleman
   John F. Coleman (Texas)
   Margaret B. Brown
   L. E. Coleman
   The children of Noah Lewis (Butler Co., Ala.):
       N. R., Jr.; F. M.; Mary A.; G. W.; E. H.;
       C. H.; S. J.; and Sidney Lewis

4. Heirs of A. W. Coleman:
   J. W. Coleman
   Martha F. Camp
   Theodore Coleman
   N. E. Adams
   E. A. Arant
   T. E. Coleman
   E. J. Adams

5. Heirs of D. W. Coleman:
   B. A. Coleman (Texas)
   Louisa A. Covington (North Carolina)
   Mrs. Cornelia Reed (Ala.)

Fannie Langham is now Mrs. Massey. She is named, along with the above and the other heirs named in the will on the preceding page.

From these documents I infer that Lucy M. (Whiting) Mobley must have been a Coleman.

A client states that Lucy Whiting Mobley was a Coleman, (or was married to a Coleman).

Will of Catherine Bates, Edgefield District, S. C.
Recorded in Will Book C, pp. 176-8.

In the name of God, Amen. I, Catherine Bates, of the
District of Edgefield in the State of South Carolina, being
of sound and disposing mind, memory and understanding,
praised be to God for the same, do make this my last Will and
Testament in manner and form following ---

1. It is my will that all of my estate of every kind whatever that I may be possessed of at my death shall be sold
publicly by my executors hereafter to be named in such lots
as they may think best upon a credit of one year and this
money arising from said sales and what may be otherwise due
me when collected, shall just as much thereof as is necessary
be appropriated to pay all my just debts and when the next
amount of my estate shall be fully apportained my executors
are to apportain what the amount or worth of the children
of a certain Negro wench named Stacey, that I gave to my
daughter Nancy Bowers is which said amount is to be added
to the next amount of my estate and then to be equally
divided into six shares or equal parts.

2. I give and bequeath to my son Jacob Bates the amount or
one of the six shears of my estate as above mentioned.

3. I give and bequeath to my son Andrew Bates the amount
or one of the six sheares of my estate as above mentioned.

4. I give and bequeath to my son John Bates the amount
of one of the six sheares of my estate as above mentioned.

5. I give to my daughter, Elizabeth Long, and the seven
children she had by her first husband, Reason Wootley, the
amount or one of the six sheares of my estate, as above
mentioned, to be divided among them as follows: One-third
part of the said one-sixth of my estate to my said daughter,
Elizabeth Long, and the other two-thirds of the said one-
sixth of my estate to the said seven children my daughter
Elizabeth had by her first husband, Reason Wootley.

6. I give and bequeath to my deceased son, David Bates'
two children, viz., Wilson M. and Ann Catherine Bates, the
amount or one of the six shears of my estate as above
mentioned.

7. I give and bequeath to my daughter, Nancy Bowers, as
much as when added to whatever the increase of a certain

Negroe wench named Stacey shall be valued at, will make
a sum equal to the amount of the one-sixth part of my
estate as before mentioned for it is my intention and will
that my said daughter Nancy shall not receive anything
more in advance or above the rest of my children except
the Negroe wench Stacey which is the reason which I have to
take in the value of the increase of the said Negroe Stacey
into view thereby she will not receive anything more than
said wench along over and above the rest of my children.

8. It is my express will and desire that whatever I have
herein given to my grandchildren, the seven sons and daughters of Reason Wootley shall remain in the hands of my executors until they respectively arrive of age or marry at
which time they are each to have their shares and whatever
interest may be received or due thereon -- and in case of
the death of any of said seven children before marriage,
or they become of age, then what is due them of my estate
shall be equally divided between those that are living.

9. it is further my express will and desire that what I
have herein given to my two grandchildren, the son and
daughter of my deceased son, David Bates shall remain in
the hands of my executors and by them put out to interest
until they shall respectively arrive of age or marry, at
which times my executors are to pay to them what I have
herein given them, but should either of them die before
they marry or come of age, my executors are then to pay
the survivor of them when married or of age, the whole that
I have herein given to them and should they both die before either of them come of age or marry, then my executors
are to divide what I have herein given them among my children in such proportions as they are herein directed to
divide the remainder of my estate.

And lastly, I do hereby constitute erdain and appoint my
sons Andrew Bates and John Bates executors of this my last
will and testament, hereby revoking all former wills at
any time heretofore by me made.

In witness whereof I have hereunto set my hand and seal
this the twelfth day of July in the year of our Lord one
thousand eight hundred and nineteen.

Signed, sealed and acknowledged by the testator as and for
her last will and testament in the presence of us, who
at her request and in her presence have subscribed our
names as witnesses thereto.

                              Catherine Bates, her mark

(continuing the will of Catherine Bates, from the preceding page):

Witnessed by Andrew Taylor, his mark
            John Tillory, his mark
            Tho. Anderson

Recorded Oct. 20, 1825.

Compiler's note: This copy taken from a photostatic copy obtained from the State Archives, Columbia, S. C.

Will of Sarah Mobley of Edgefield Dist., S. C.

In the name of God, Amen.

I, Sarah Mobley, of the State of South Carolina and District of Edgefield, being weak in body but of sound mind and memory, do make and ordain this to be my last will and testament.

In the first place, all my just debts and funeral expenses are to be paid out of my estate.

Secondly, my will and desire is that my beds bedding and household and kitchen furniture be equally divided between my son Wm. Mobley and my daughters Catherine Harriett Mary Ann and Margarette; and my daughter Mariah is to have five dollars in money to satisfy her in place of her not getting any part of the property above named.

Thirdly, my will and desire is that all the balance of my estate consisting of money and notes be equally divided between all my children, viz., Mariah Permenter, Eliza Bland, Margaret Hazle, Wm. Mobley, Jeremiah Mobley, Catherine Gamble, Harriett Herrin, Mary Paul, Ann Cockroft, and John T. Mobley, to each share and share alike.

Fourthly, I do hereby nominate and appoint my son, William Mobley executor of this my last will and testament.

In witness whereof, I do hereunto set my hand and seal this 26th of August 1848.

            Sarah Mobley, her Mark.

Signed, Sealed and acknowledged in the presence of us:

W. Daniel
Sarah McGraw

Recorded in Will Book D, p. 349. Oct. 11, 1848.

Compiler's note: This copy taken from a photostatic copy obtained from the South Carolina Archives.

Cranford Notes from Clarke County

From Deeb Book A, p. 238:

James Monroe, President of the Unites States. Know ye that
in pursuance of Acts of Congress granting land to the last
Army of the United States, passed on and since the 6th day
of May, 182 (?), Josiah Cranford having deposited in his
favor a warrant No. 648 (?), there is granted unto said
Josiah Cranford, late a corporal in Cook's detachment of
the 8th Regiment of Infantry, a certain tract of land,
containing 320 A., the S½ of Sec. 17, Township 14 North,
Range 5 West, in the tract appropriated by the Acts aforesaid for military bounties in the Territory of Illinois ...
This deed dated 5th April, 1818, and signed by Josiah Migs,
Comr. of the General Land Office. Recorded in Vol. 23 in
the General Land Office, p. 521.

Note in Deed Book A in Clarke Co.: "The above came to this
office 25 Oct. and was recorded 5th Nov., 1822."

From Minutes of Orphan's Court, Book B (1829-40):

p. 182. Nov., 1835. Dickson Boutwell appointed guardian
of Louisa, John J., Jesse J., Josiah W. and Wm. W. Cranford,
minor heirs of John Painter, dec'd.

p. 210. July 4, 1836. Hearing of the petition of Samuel
Loftin for a sale of the land belonging to the estate of
the late John Painter. Citation has been served on all the
heirs; all of whom reside within this state; and Dixon
Boutwell, guardian of the minor heirs of Elizabeth Cranford,
deceased, and Sam'l Loftin having produced written evidence
of Ennis Loftin and Josiah Cranford, that the land cannot
be equitably divided without a sale; it is ordered that
Ennis Loftin, Thos. B. Hawkins, and Stephen Gilmore be commissioners to sell said land, and to report 1st Monday in
Sept. next. Notice to be given in the Clarke Co. Post,
published at Sugsville.

p. 265. 7th Aug., 1838. Ordered that citation issue to
Dickson Boutwell to appear on 1st Mon. in Sept. next, to
make final settlement of his guardianship of the minor heirs
of Joseph Cranford.

This day came Jesse Cranford in person, and Josiah,
Wesley, and James Cranford by certificate from justices of
the peace, all minor heirs of John Painter, dec'd --- and
all over 14, and chose Samuel Loftin as their guardian,
Loftin made bond for $1500.00 withChristopher Pritchett
and Wm. W. Alston as his securities.

p. 270. 1st. Oct., 1838. Came Dickson Boutwell, guardian, and made a final settlement of his guardianship of Josiah, Jesse, James and Wesley Cranford, minor heirs of John Painter, dec'd. Josiah and Jesse drew $133.60 each; James and Wesley drew $122.35 each.

p. 279. 7th Jan., 1839. Report of Samuel Loftin, as gdn., for the year 1838.

Estate of John Painter, Clarke Co., Ala.

From Minutes of Orphans' Coust, Book B, p. 167:

6th April, 1835. Charlotte Painter, widow of John Painter, cited to appear in Court and show cause why letters of adm. should not be granted on said estate.

p. 169. 4th May, 1835. Samuel Loftin appointed adm. of estate of John Painter.

p. 171. 1st June, 1835. Sam'l Loftin filed an inventory and appraisement of this estate. Comrs. appointed by the court to divide the estate of John Painter, dec'd.

p. 173. 6th July, 1835. Report of these comrs.

p. 203. 2 May, 1836. Above report set aside as informal & illegal. Five new commissioners appointed to divide John Painter's estate between the widow and the following heirs: Thos. Harris, John H. Martin, Samuel Loftin, Richard J. Painter, and the children of Elizabeth Cranford, dec'd.

p. 226. Jan., 1837. Final settlement by Sam'l Loftin, of the estate of John Painter.

Note: Book C, Minutes of Orphans Court, contains several reports by Sam'l Loftin, as gdn. of Wesley and James Cranford, up through the year 1844.

From Clarke Co. Marriage Record A (1814-34):

p. 216. Josiah Cranford to Elizabeth Johnston. License dated 20th Nov., 1826; ceremony same day by Joel Bell, J. P.

p. 98. Samuel Loftin to Nancy Panther. License issued on 29 Sept., 1818; executed by J. B. Chambers, J. P. (or J.Q.) on 30th Sept., 1818.

The marriage of John Painter is not recorded in this Vol.

From Clarke Co. Marriage Record B (1834-65):

p. 83.   Robert J. Cranford to Martha Lide
              Sept. 28, 1843

From Deed Book H, p. 242:

James A. Cranford and Martha, his wife, deed to Chas. L.
Sisson (?), dated Jan. 24, 1857.

Also from Deed Book H, p. 105:

Robert J. Cranford, and Martha, his wife, of Ouachita Co.,
Arkansas, appoint James H. Cranford, of Clarke Co., Ala.,
to take possession of and bring to me, 3 Negroes; also to
receive any legacy that may be coming to us from the
estate of Cynthia Lide. Dated 25 May, 1857.

The above is not an exhaustive study of the Cranford records.

Abercrombie Notes, Perry Co., Ala.

Will of Isaac Abercrombie from Will Book A, Perry Co., Ala.:

Pages 20-23:   This will names wife, Mary.

> To Thos. Billingsley and Isaac Abercrombie,
> certain Negroes, in trust for the use of my
> daughter, Mary Burroughs
>
> My children: Archibald, James, Isaac,
>   Alexander, and Thos. Abercrombie
>
> Heirs of my deceased daughter, Elizabeth
>   Billingsley
>
> Executors: Thos. Billingsley
>   Isaac Abercrombie
>
> Dated 10th June, 1824
> Probated Aug. 5,1825
>
> Witnessed by: D. Sullivan
>   Chas. Stevenson
>   Henry Scott

From Minutes of Probate Court of Perry Co., Ala.:

Book C, p. 357. June Term, 1842. Francis M. Abercrombie
and Alexander Graham applied for letters of administration
on the estate of James Abercrombie, dec'd.

Book D, p. 95. Dec. term, 1843. Came Frances Abercrombie
and files her petition alleging that she is the widow of
James Abercrombie, dec'd, and so is entitled to one-half of
the lands as her dower. Description of lands. And it
appearing to the Court that Thos. Abercrombie, Wm. Burris,
Syrous Billingsley, Isaac Billingsley, Daniel Long, and
Chas. H. Moore, the heirs of said James Abercrombie,
all resident in this State, and Edward Jackson, tenant in
possession of said lands, have been severally notified...

Book D, pp. 123-4: Jan. 5, 1844:

In the matter of the petition for dower of Francis M.
Abercrombie, widow of James Abercrombie, dec'd: Report of
the commissioners previously appointed by the court to
allot to her her dower in the lands, which are in Secs.
14, 23, and 24, in Township 19, Range 7, East.

Francis M. Abercrombie is now married to James E. Taylor.
After the death of Francis M. Taylor, the dower land is
to be divided between the heirs of James Abercrombie, who
are as follows, he having no children nor lineal descendants:

1. Thos. Abercrombie

2. Archibald Abercrombie

3. Mary Burroughs, formerly Abercrombie, sister of
          said James Abercrombie, dec'd

4. ___ Billingsley, formerly ___ Abercrombie, sister
   of said James Abercrombie, dec'd, and now dead.
   Her children are: Wm., Cyrus, and Isaac Billingsley;
   Eliza Moore, formerly Eliza Billingsley; and
   Mary Long, formerly Mary Billingsley.

Book D, p. 267. Sept., 1844. Came Alexander Graham &
James E. Taylor, administrators, and Francis M. Taylor,
administratrix, of the estate of James Abercrombie, dec'd,
and filed a petition to sell the balance of the land, for
distribution among the heirs. (Names of some minor
Billingsley heirs. Other papers.)

From Marriage Record of Perry Co., Ala., for 1840-51:

No. 1281. James Abercrombie to Francis Withers .....

No other Male Abercrombie marriage is indexed between 1820 and 1863. There are omissions in the index.

From Minutes of Probate Court, Book E, p. 393:

Aug. 7, 1848. Thos. Abercrombie made guardian of James R. and Thos. J. Abercrombie, minors, and children of his former wife, Mary Abercrombie, formerly Mary Pucket, who was a daughter of Richard Pucket, late of South Carolina.

Payne Family of Perry County, Ala.

From Will Book A, Perry Co., Ala., pp. 166-7: The will of Hiram Payne mentions:

Sons: John B. Payne, Wm. Y. Payne, James M. Payne,
            Daniel W. Payne and Hiram B. Payne
Daughters: Nancy A. Payne, Manerva J. Payne, and

Wife: Mariah W. Payne.

John Boyd appointed to sell the land Hiram Payne owned in
            Sumter Co., Ala.

Will dated 13 August, 1844.

Attested by: Charles Coleman, and J. L. Blackburn

From Deed Record B, Perry County, Ala.:

pp. 309-10: Dec. 16, 1831. Dillard Payne and wife Mary, sold land in Perry Co. to Calvin Crews. Deed witnessed by Madison Tubb. Dillard Payne appeared personally on Sept. 15, 1832, and acknowledged his signature to this deed; and Mary Payne, his wife, relinquished her dower rights in said lands on 29 Sept., 1832.

From Deed Record M, p. 307: Thos. Smith and Elizabeth, his wife, sold to Mariah W. Payne, land in Sec. 5, T21, R7, on August 12, 1854.

Note: Many other Payne deeds in Perry Co.

From Will Book B, Sumter Co., Ala.: Will of Lucy A. Adams

p. 292. All property to my husband, Benj. H. Adams, for
his lifetime; at his death, a family of negroes to my
brother, Hardy C. Fluker. Executor, Benj. H. Adams.
Dated 29 Dec., 1855. (1855).

Witnessed by: James L. Hainsworth   S. A. Hainsworth
               Wm. M. McGrew

Proved by Sallie Estill, formerly Sallie Hainsworth
          on Dec. 22, 1863.

Also from Will Book B., Sumter Co., Ala:

p. 88. Will of Wm. F. Adams. All property to my wife,
Locky H. Adams, and she is named executrix.
Dated 19 March, 1853. Witnessed by:

     James L. Hainsworth   Sallie A. Hainsworth
               Elisha A. Hainsworth

Probated Nov. 12, 1855, by James L. Hainsworth.

Also from Will Book B, Sumter Co., Ala.:

pp. 66-9: Will of Wm. Fluker, names wife, Minerva Eliza;
daughters: Cibell McGrew, wife of John C. McGrew; Elizabeth Chiles, wife of Henry Chiles; Ann, wife of James L.
Mosby; Nancy M., wife of Philip G. Edmunds; Laura, wife
of J. G. Coats; and a son, Wm. L. Fluker. Friend, John F.
Vary to be guardian of children by wife Minerva E.
Dated 1st March, 1853. Witnessed by:

     Henry H. Harris   George Wilson   Augusta A. Coleman

Probated 12 June by all three witnesses.

Will of Susan Ware of Perry Co., Ala., from Will Book 2,
Sumter Co., Ala., pp. 388-9, mentions:
     Sons Thos. T. and Wm. N. Ware
     The children of Thos. T. Ware
     Daughter, Mrs. Sophia Leverett, who is executrix.

Dated 9 Nov., 1868

Witnessed by: John M. Jeffries   James Shearer

Probated 14 June, 1869.

Will of Pleasant White, from Will Book 2, Sumter Co., Ala.:

pp. 342-9. Mentions:

1. Dau., Caroline P., wife of Solomon Williams
2. Son, John W. White
3. Son, James H. White
4. Dau., Elizabeth Ann, wife of Alexander Lawson
5. Dau., America Shurley
6. Son, George Sidney White
7. Wife, Frances Churchwell White
8. Dau., Sophia Frances White

Executor, friend, W. W. Coats

Dated Jan. 6, 1857. Witnessed by:

G. R. Crews
H. M. Gilmore

Probated 19 May, 1866.

From Will Book 2, Sumter Co., Ala., pp. 366-7:

Will of Sophia Harper, widow of Wyatt Harper. "Done at my residence in Bellmont Township."   Heirs named:

1. Sons, L. P. and Z. C. Harper
2. Daughters: M. A. Arrington and Sophia E. Grayson
3. Sons: R. L. Harper, G. G. Harper
        L. P. Harper, Z. C. Harper
4. Daughter, M. A. Hadden
5. Heirs of my son, Wm. Bates
6. Heirs of my son, John E. Harper
7. Heirs of my son, J. W. Harper
8. Son, Robert L. Harper

Dated 27 Jan., 1868. Witnessed by:

John A. Nuffer   Michael Grady
C. B. Nuffer

Proved by John A. Nuffer on May 1st, 1868.

Bates Notes from Sumter Co., Ala.

From Deed Book A, p. 481: Robert A. Bates assigned to
Daniel Green, all of his right and title to a tract of
land purchased on 10th Oct., 1834. Receivers' receipt,
No. 2335. Land in Township 19, Range 2, West.
Dated 5th April, 1836. Witnessed by:
G. W. Harper
James A. Bates

Minutes of Orphans' Court, Book 1, pp. 260-1:
May 12, 1837. James A. Bates appointed administrator of
Robert A. Bates, dec'd. Bond for $4000.00 with James Savage
and John Carson as securities.

Same volume, p. 521: Final settlement of estate of Robt.
A. Bates. Names five heirs:

1. Wm. Brewer in right of his wife, Ann C., formerly
    Ann C. Bates

2. James A. Bates, in right of his wife, Sarah G.,
    formerly Sarah G. Bates

3. James H. Spence, in right of his mother, Catherine
    H. Spence, fromerly Catherine H. Bates

4. John M. Bates

5. Needham Watkins, in right of his wife, Elizabeth F.,
    formerly Elizabeth F. Bates

From Minutes of Orphans' Court, Book 1, p. 25:

11 Oct., 1839. Fleming C. Bates appointed adm. de bonis
non of Robert A. Bates. Bond for $2000.00 with James A.
Bates and Kneedham Watkins as his securities.

From Minutes of Probate Court, Book 3, p. 201:

26 June, 1843. Letters of administration on the estate of
Robert A. Bates, heretofore granted to James A. Bates,
revoked, and the administration of the estate turned over
to James Hair, general administrator for the County.

Same volume, p. 232. Aug. 9th, 1843. Balance of estate
distributed to the heirs. Heirs named again.

From Deed Book D, pp. 75-6: 21 Sept., 1838. James A. Bates
and his wife, Sarah G., ... a mortgage.

From Deed Book D, Sumter Co., Ala.:

pp. 668-9: 15 March, 1840. Henry Bates, of Kemper Co., Miss., deed to Gilford Robertson of Sumter Co., Ala.

From Deed Book E, Sumter Co., Ala., p. 245:
Seymour Bates of Mobile Co., Ala., to _____. Dated April, 1839.

From Minutes of Probate Court, Sumter Co., Ala., Book 8, pp. 66:

Jan. 2, 1854. Came Wyatt Harper and James G. Coats, and offered for probate the will of William Bates. Notice to the widow, Martha Bates, and to Lewis Haddon, as guardian of the minor heirs:

> Wm. Bates
>
> Laura Bates
>
> Colonia Bates
>
> Oregon Bates

Compiler's note: I did not make a complete search for Bates date in Sumter Co., as what I found seemed not to be what my client needed.

Rev. Washington Wilkes

Summary of a biography of Rev. Washington Wilkes, from "Memorial Record of Alabama" Vol. 2, p. 992:

Rev. Washington Wilkes was a pioneer Baptist minister of Alabama. He was born in Marlboro District, S. C., on March 26, 1822, son of Elias and Hannah Usher Wilkes.

Elias Wilkes was born in N. C., son of John and Margaret Wilkes.

John Wilkes was in the War of 1812.

Hanna (Usher) Wilkes was a daughter of Thomas Usher, and a relative of James Usher, Archbishop of Armagh.

When Washington Wilkes was about eleven years old, the family moved to Dale County, Ala., and later to Barbour Co. He attended Howard College, 1848-9. He began his ministerial career in 1846.

In 1854, he married Mary E. LaMar, daughter of John and Mary E. (Dubose) Lamar.

John Lamar was a native of Georgia, who came to Dallas Co., Ala., in 1832.

Mary E. DuBose was a daughter of Peter DuBose of Ga.

Compiler's note: There is other information about this subject in this article, but nothing of genealogical importance.

Auberry Notes from Perry Co., Ala.

From Deed Book B, p. 551. 19 July, 1833. Philip Auberry sold to James M. Massey, W½ of SW¼ of Sec. 14, Township 20, Range 8, for $200.00. Witnessed by Sam'l Doneghey, and Chas. Heard.

From Deed Book B, p. 722. 29 Oct., 1834. Philip Auberry sold to Gabriel Benson, for $600.00, the NW¼ of Section 3, Township 18, Range 8, containing 146.12½ acres.

Philip Auberry, in person acknowledged his signature to the deed on p. 551, on 24 Dec., 1833.

Philip Auberry, in person, acknowledged his signature to the deed on p. 722, on 7th Jan., 1835, before Jesse B. Nave, Clerk of the County Court.

From Deed Book D, p. 762. 9th Jan., 1835. Philip Auberry sold to Rebecca Auberry, for $66.66 3/4, the S½ of SE¼ of Sec. 34, Township 20, Range 8, containing 53.46 1/3 A.

Philip Auberry, in person, acknowledged his signature to the above deed on 6th Feb., 1835.

From Minutes of Probate Court, Book I (eye):

p. 469. Feb. 20, 1861. Sam'l A. Heard vs. Phil Aubry. This being the day appointed at a previous term of Court for hearing the petition of Samuel A. Heard, as a relative of Phil Aubrey, praying an inquisition into the alleged lunacy of said Aubrey, the jury, Wm. N. Wyatt and eleven others, who reside in the neighborhood of said alleged lunatic...declared Aubrey non compos mentis. Samuel A. Heard appointed guardian of Aubrey, and gave bond for $5000.00 with A. J. Heard and W. H. Stewart as his securities.

p. 569. Oct. 14, 1861. Thos. Lester vs. the heirs at law of Elizabeth Aubrey, dec'd. Lester appointed to administer the estate of Elizabeth Aubrey. He gave bond for $11,500.00 with M. W. Oliver and C. J. Crews as his securities. The following were appointed to appraise the estate:

Johnson McCauley
M. W. Oliver
Jacob Kinerd

p. 573. Nov. 4, 1861. Same three gentlemen appointed to divide the slaves that had belonged to Elizabeth Aubrey among the heirs.

From Minutes of Probate Court (Perry Co.) Book K:

p. 213. Mar. 14, 1864. James Mason made adm. of the
estate of Philip Auberry, dec'd. Bond for $9000.00 with
C. Heard, James. A. England, and B. Boroughs as securities.

Minutes of Probate Court, Book L, p. 73: James Mason, adm.
filed his accounts for a final settlement of the estate of
Philip Auberry, dec'd.

Minutes of Probate Court, Book L, p. 142. Dec. 13, 1865.
Final Settlement. No balance for distribution among the
heirs of Aubrey. No list of heirs.

Minutes of Probate Court, Book L, p. 407. Dec. 19, 1866.
James Mason resigned as administrator of the estate of
Philip Aubrey. There are assets still unadministered.
Geo. W. Aubrey appointed adm. de bonis non. He gave bond
for $3000.00 with W. M. Ford and Josiah Whitman as sec.

Minutes of Probate Court, Book M, p. 25. June 10, 1867.
Another "final" settlement of estate of Philip Aubrey.
Balance due the administrator, $299.73. No list of heirs.
There may be other papers, not indexed.

From Deed Book O:

p. 586. 16 Nov., 1859. Harvey S. Gary sold to James
Aubry. Witness: M. A. Moseley.

p. 594. ___ Nov., 1859. Philip Aubrey to James Aubrey,
for $4000.00, land in Township 20, Range 8. Witnesses:

P. W. Stedman   E. H. Donaghey

p. 657. 12 Jan., 1860. James Aubrey sold to A. J. Brazelton, and Rebecca, his wife. Witnesses: T. V. Brazelton,
W. P. Law.

p. 706. 6 Feb., 1860. Harvey S. Gary sold to Wm. N. Wyatt,
land mortgaged to said Gary by James Aubrey.

From Deed Book S, p. 191. Geo. W. Aubrey bought some land
that had belonged to A. J. Brazelton, a bankrupt, from
Mason J. Gibson, assignee. 25 July, 1868. He paid for it
2 and 374/563 cents an acre. Land in Township 20, Range 8.

From Deed Book W, p. 493 (indexed as 393)

15 Nov., 1869. Benjamin T. Auberry and Samuel T. Auberry,
for $1500.00, to Jesse B. Lovelace, 187 A. in Townships
19 and 20, Range 8, East.

On same day, B. T. and S. T. Auberry appeared in person
before B. S. Williams, Judge of Probate, andacknowledged
their signatures to this deed.

Note: Rebecca Auberry and Rebecca Heard are buried side
        by side in Marion Cemetery, with inscriptions as
        follows:

        Rebecca Auberry died March 1, 1843, aged 80 years
        Rebecca Heard, born May 22, 1818,
                        died July 6, 1837

The 1820 (State) Census shows a Candler Auberry in
St. Clair Co., Ala.

Derden Notes from Perry Co., Ala.

Marriage Record for 1820-32: No. 471: John W. Derden
married Penelope Pearson on 17 Sept., 1830. No minister's
return is recorded. (The license is dated 17 Sept., 1830)

From Marriage Record for 1832-39: License No. 1052:

License issued to James Derden to marry Elizabeth Tubb, on
6th Aug., 1838. No minister's return showing date of rites.

The Marriage Record for 1840-63 lists no male Derden.

From "Deeds, Mortgages and Bills of Sale," 1826-31:

p. 255. David Durden sold to Jesse B. Nave, a negro slave
named Lewis, aged 15, on 2 May, 1829. Consideration:
$329.90½ paid by said Nave for me, as follows:

$167.90½ balance due from me to the Bank of State of Ala.
150.00 due from me to James Harrison
 12.00 paid for costs in the case of B. Robertson, ad's,
       of Thos. M. Robertson against me in Perry County
       Circuit Court.

From 1850 Census of Perry Co., Ala., Old Town Beat,
         House No. 78:

James Derden	age 35,	farmer, B. S. C.
Elizabeth "	30	born in Tenn.
Rosannah "	9	born in Ala.
Martha "	7	" "
David "	4	" "
Jessee "	2	" "
William "	9/12	" "

Also from 1850 Census of Perry Co., Ala., (Old Town Beat ?):

John W. Boyles	age 38	born in Tenn.
Mary "	32	"
Nancy M. "	12	b. in Ala.
Louisa J. "	2	"
Nancy Tubb	60	born in S. C.

Note: No Dirden, Durden, or Derden is listed in 1790
       Census of S. C.

From Deed Book F, pp. 285-6: Feb. 10, 1840:
James Derden andElizabeth, his wife, sold to Robt. M.
Wallace, for $1212.00, the W½ of NE¼ of Sec. 23, Town-
ship 21, Range 7. 80 A. Witness: John T. Sinclair.

James and Elizabeth Derden appeared personally on Feb.
10, 1840, and acknowledged their signatures to above
deed before John T. Sinclair, J. P.

From Deed Book G, p. 339: Feb. 12, 1838. James Derden
sold to John W. Boyles, for $1000.00, the NE¼ of Sec. 23,
Township 10, Range 14, E., lying in Kemper Co., Miss., in
the district of Columbus.

James Derden appeared personally before John Cunningham
Clark of the Co. Court, in Perry Co., Ala., and acknowledged his signature to the above deed, on 22 March, 1845.

Compiler's Note: The description of land in above deed
                  sounds incorrect, to me.

From Deed Book G, pp. 578-9: 4th March, 1837. John A.
McKeller and David McCraney, are bound untoJames Derden,
...in the sum of $14,000... the condition of the above is
that McKellar and McCranie make good titles to James
Derden for the NE¼ of Sec. 23, Township 10, Range 14, and
the SW¼ (?) of Sec. 31, T10, R15, containing 319 A., in
Kemper Co., Miss., as soon as patents can be obtained for
same, then the obligation to be void.
Witness: Jesse B. Nave.

From Deed Book L, p. 54: 30 March, 1853. Wiley Tubb and
Pheba, his wife, and James Derden, to Sardis Church, for
$1.00, one acre in NW¼ of NE¼ and NE¼ of NW¼, of Sec. 14,
T21, R7.

James Derden and Wiley and Phebe Tubb appeared personally
on the same day, and acknowledged their signatures to the
above deed, before Sid. W. Blackburn, J. P.

From Deed Book L, pp. 522-3: 27 Jan., 1854:

James Derden, of Perry Co., Ala., sold to John W. Boyles,
also of Perry Co., for $450.00, land in Sections 11, 12,
and 14, in T21, R7, East, lying in Perry Co., Ala., 200 A.

From Perry Co., Ala., Marriage Record for 1832-39:

License No. 1057: Issued 8th Aug., 1837. Wiley Tubb to
Phebe Tubb. Executed 10 Aug., 1837, by Jno. T. Sinclair.

License No. 833: John W. Boyles to Mary Tubb. License
dated 15 April, 1835. No minister's return showing date
of ceremony.

John Derden was Judge of the County Court in Perry Co.
in 1820.

From Greene Co., Ala., Marriage Record:

Richard W. Derden to Nancy A. Spiddle in 1851.

Ann Derden to James Short in 1831.

Clarissa Derden to Abner Evans, Jr., in 1831.

From Record of Probate Court, Greene Co., Ala.
Book D, p. 237:
8th Oct., 1832. I have received of John Derden, my legal
guardian, all my portion of the estate of my deceased
grandfather, Wm. Tailor, of Anson Co., N. C.
Signed: Geo. W. Derden

The will of one James Derden is recorded in Greene Co.,
Ala., in Will Book B, pp. 289-90. Heirs mentioned:

1. Wife, Temperance   2. Daughter, Sarah Meador
3. Son-in-law, M. Meador   4. Son, Richard W. Derden
5. John H. Derden   6. James K. Derden

Executors: Sons Richard W. and James K. Derden, and
friend, Eldred Pippen

Dated 29 March, 1841. Witnessed by:

James B. McDonald
Joab Griffith

Proved 12 July, 1841

Tubb Family of Perry Co., Ala.

From "Deeds, Mortgages, and Bills of Sale, 1826-31":

p. 68: Articles of agreement entered into in the year 1802, between Wm. Tubb, Sr., of Greenville District, S. C., on the one part, and John Tubb, Esqr., of same State and District, of the other part; in consideration of $350.00 for a black woman named Charlotte; said sum to lay in the hands of John Tubb, "only as I should want said money to live on occasionally, and should any part remain at the death of myself and wife, it is to be divided equally among my children." Aug. 18, 1802. Wm. Tubb, his mark. John Tubb. Witness: Stephen C. Wood.

On Feb. 25, 1821, Geo. W. Earle, Clerk of the Court in Greenville District, S. C., testified that he believed the signatures of John Tubb and of Stephen C. Wood, on the above document, to be their own handwriting.

Note on this document: Oct. 10, 1819. Paid by me, John - Jeremiah ? - Tubb, to Jenings (?) Tubb, for the use of Elizabeth, the wife of Wm. Tubb, dec'd. $20.00

Compiler's note: The handwriting of the copy in Perry Co. is not too good. The copy in Greenville might be better.

From Bond Book for 1855: p. 85. 3 Nov., 1851. We, James Tubb, James Durden and Wiley Tubb, are bound to James F. Bailey, Judge of the Probate Court, in the sum of $800.00 ... the condition of the above bond is that, whereas James Tubb has been appointed administrator of Thos. Wherry, dec'd...etc.

Same volume, p. 69. 5 Aug., 1851. James Durden and Sam'l Whitman signed the bond of Obadiah Belcher, adm. of Wm. Cone, dec'd.

Same Volume, p. 52. 18 Jan., 1851. James Durden and Wiley Tubb signed the bond of James Tubb, administrator of the estate of Geo. B. Tubb, dec'd.

From Deed Book B, p. 212: Quit Claim and warranty deed drawn in Lowndes Co., Ala., by Geo. W. Derden and Harriett, his wife, who sold to Vincent Sanders, for $400.00, the NE¼ of Sec. 17, T20, R8. Dated 7 March, 1832. Witnessed by Hugh McCall, J. P.; Robt. Perry, J. P.; and Sherrod Sanders.

From Deed Book B, Perry Co., Ala., p. 214:

23 Feb., 1832. I, Seaborn Aycock, Sheriff of Perry Co., by virtue of executions direction to me by the Clerk of the Circuit Court of said County, in favor of John Lockhart & Co., against Geo. W. Derden, commanding me to expose to sale the NE¼ of Sec. 17, T20, R8, sold on 6th Feb., inst. to John Lockhart, for $200.00... I convey to said Lockhart all the title which Geo. W. Derden had in said lands.

The will of John Tubbs, recorded in Will Book A, pp. 73-6, and dated 17 Sept., 1835, mentions his wife, Feraby, and the following legatees:

1. Polly Sanders

2. The children of Nancy Barton, dec'd, namely:

   Malinda
   Polly
   Cary
   Nancy
   Orleana

3. Betsy Sanders
4. Son, James Tubb
5. Lucinda Oliver
6. Celia West
7. Grandson, Vinson Sanders

Witnessed by: Samuel Jemison
              Humphrey Jemison
              Benj. Sinclair, J. P.

Ordered filed Oct. term of court, 1836.

From Minutes of Probate Court, Book G, pp. 95-99:

Jan. 9th, 1854. Final settlement of estate of John Tubb, dec'd. Green B. Sanders, administrator. Amount for distribution, $3144.22, which was distributed as follows:

1. To daughter, Lucinda Oliver
2. To daughter, Cecia West, wife of Anderson West
3. To James Tubb, a son
4. To John Sanders, son of Polly Sanders, and Grandson of John Tubb, dec'd.
5. to Wm. Sanders, also son of Polly Sanders, dec'd

6. To Murrell Sanders, also a son of Polly Sanders, dec'd
7. To Vincent Sanders, son of Polly Sanders, dec'd
8. To Perry Sanders, son of Polly Sanders, dec'd
9. To Lucinda Ragsdale, dau. of Polly sanders, dec'd
10. To ___ Sanders, in trust for his wife, Polly Sanders, who was a dau. of Polly Sanders, dec'd.
11. To ___ Rice, in trust for Elizabeth Rice, his wife, a granddaughter of John Tubb, dec'd
12. To Celia Sanders, dau. of Polly Sanders, and grand-dau. of John Tubb, dec'd.
13. To the children of Cion Sanders, dec'd, names and no. unknown, grandchildren of John Tubb, dec'd
14. To the children of Jackson Sanders, dec'd, names and no. unknown, grandchildren of John Tubb, dec'd.
15. To S. W. S nders, son of Elizabeth Sanders, and grandson of John Tubb, dec'd
16. To Wm. L. Sanders, son of Elizabeth Sanders, dec'd, and grandson of John Tubb, dec'd
17. To Green B. Sanders, son of Elizabeth Sanders, and grandson of John Tubb, dec'd
18. To Rachel Sanders, dau. of Elizabeth Sanders, and granddaughter of John Tubb, dec'd.
19. To ___ Massey, in trust for his wife, Julia Massey, a granddaughter of John Tubb, dec'd
20. To W. R. Sanders, son of Vincent Sanders, dec'd, & grandson of John Tubb, dec'd
21. To T. G. Sanders, son of Vincent Sanders, dec'd, & grandson of John Tubb, dec'd
22. To R. W. Sanders, son of Vincent Sanders, dec'd, & grandson of John Tubb, dec'd
23. To E. J. Sanders, son of Vincent Sanders, dec'd, & grandson of John Tubb, dec'd
24. To John Hughey and Polly Hughey, his wife, a grand-daughter of John Tubb, dec'd
25. To Orlena Russel, dau. of Nancy Barton, dec'd, and granddaughter of John Tubb, dec'd.
26. To Green W. Thompson, son of Malinda Thomas, dec'd, and grandson of John Tubb, dec'd.
Correction:
26. To Nancy Barton, dau. of Nancy Barton, dec'd, and grand-dau. of John Tubb, dec'd
27. To Green W. Thompson, son of Malinda Thomas, dec'd and grandson of John Tubb, dec'd
28. To Orlena Thompson, dau of Malinda Thompson...
29. To Thos. J. Thompson, son of Malinda Thompson...
30. To James J. Thompson, son of Malinda Thompson...

31. To Jefferson, son of Cary Hughey, grandson of John Tubb, dec'd
32. To Betsy Patton, granddaughter of John Tubb, dec'd
33. To James M. Hughey, son of Cary Hughey, dec'd, & grandson of John Tubb, dec'd
34. To Lucinda M. Hughey, dau. of Cary Hughey, dec'd...
35. To Cassaline Hughey, dau. of Cary Hughey...
36. To Clemons (?) Barton, dau. of Cary Hughey...
37. To Anderson Barton, dau. of Cary Hughey, dec'd...

From Sardis Cemetery in Perry Co.:

Rev. James Tubb	July 10, 1799	April 20, 1856
Mrs. H. H. Tubb	July 5, 1801	Dec. 10, 1872

Sion Tubb   1805-1872
Rebecca Perry, his wife,   1801-1900

The Tract Book for Perry Co. shows that certificates to purchase land from the U. S. Govt., in T20 and T21, R7, were issued to:

Wiley Tubb	1836	Owen Tubb	1853
Richard Tubb, Sr.	1828	James Tubb	1828
Byars Tubb	1835	Elisha Tubb	1832
Geo. Tubb	1828	Carter Tubb	1854
Wiley Tubb	1854	John Tubb	1844
James Derden	1843	Sion Tubb	1854
Sion Tubb	1832	Reuben Tubb	1847
Samuel Tubb	1833	James M. Tubb	1842

Compiler's Note: There may be others:

From Minutes of Probate Court, Book D, p. 598: Final settlement of the estate of Richard Tubb, Sr., dec'd. March 16, 1846. Madison and Owen Tubb, administrators, David Wallace, guardian ad litem of the minor heirs. None of the heirs of full age was in attendance, except David Wallace, in right of his wife. Amount for distribution: $19,775.67, which was distributed to:

1. The widow, Margaret Tubb 2. A son, Madison Tubb
3. A son, Owen Tubb 4. Jonathan D. Wallace in right of his wife, Mary, formerly Mary Tubb, dau. of dec'd.
5. Robt. A. Scott, in right of his wife, Sophrona, a daughter of Richard Tubb, Sr., dec'd.

6. A son, Geo. Tubb   7. A son, Reubin Tubb
8. A dau., Martha Tubb
9. Nancy McLaughlin, in right of her mother, Cyrena
   McLaughlin, dec'd, formerly Cyrena Tubb, who was a
   daughter of intestate
10. A son, Felix G. Tubb
11. Margaret J. and Lavona Tubb, in right of their father,
    Jackson Tubb, dec'd, who was a son of intestate

Note in margin says "Decree No. 11 set aside. See Minutes,
Book E, pp. 168-9."

From Minutes of Probate Court, Book E, pp. 168-9:

April 19, 1847. Court ordered that the money decreed to
Margaret J. and Lavona Tubb be paid to Owen Tubb, who had
been made administrator of the estate of Jackson Tubb, dec'd.
The widow of Jackson Tubb was Permelia J.

From Minute Book E, pp. 124 ff. Jan. 3, 1847. Elisha F.
Tubb, administrator, and Nancy Tubb, administratrix, of
the estate of Richard Tubb, Jr., dec'd, petitioned for a
sale of certain lands belonging to said estate. Heirs of
Richard Rubb, Jr., named:

1. Mary E., wife of Thos. Driver, and over 21
2. Elisha Tubb   3. Martha S. Tubb   4. Richard Tubb
5. Isabella Tubb 6. Lenora J. Tubb
   --- all minors
7. and Nancy Tubb, the widow, who is also one of the
   petitioners

James Underwood appointed guardian ad litem of the minors.

From Minutes of Probate Court, Book G, pp. 247-8:

Sept. 11, 1854. James Tubb administrator of Geo. B. Tubb,
dec'd. John H. Chapman, gdn. ad litem of the minor heirs.
Heirs named: F. A. Tubb, the widow, and two minor children, Thos. B. and Georgiana Tubb.

From Minutes of Probate Court, Book G, p. 436:

July 9, 1855. Came Elisha Tubband Nancy Tubb, administrators of R. E. Tubb, dec'd, and filed their vouchers
for an annual settlement. John Moore, guardian at law
for the minor heirs. Distribution made to following:

1. The widow, Nancy Tubb   2. Susan and David Hogue
3. R. E. Tubb, son of deceased 4. Lenora, dau. of dec'd.
5. Isabella, dau of deceased.

From Minutes of Probate Court, Book G, pp. 45-6:

June 3rd, 1850. Owen Tubb, adm. of estate of Jackson
Tubb, dec'd. Heirs named:

The widow, Permelia J. Tubb, now wife of Reuben Tubb
Margaret Jane Tubb
Nancy L. Tubb

From Minutes of Probate Court, Book F, p. 145:

Dec. 23, 1850: Owen Tubb, administrator of the estate of
Felix Tubb, dec'd. Nothing for distribution among heirs;
no list of heirs.

Derden Notes from Greene Co., Ala.:

From 1840 Census of Greene Co., Ala.:

    James Derden: 1 male 15 - 20
                     1 male 20 - 30
                     1 male 50 - 60
                     1 female 50 - 60

    John H. Derden: 2 males under 5
                     1 male 20 - 30
                     1 female under 5
                     1 female 20 - 30

From 1850 Census of Greene Co., Ala.:

    1087. Elizabeth Derden, age 75, born in N. C.
           Richard W. Derden   41   "

    1353. James K. Derden   31 born in S. C.
           Martha A. Derden   17 born in Ala.

From Will Book A, Greene Co., Ala., p. 50:

John Derden was guardian of Geo. W. Derden, aged 19,
minor heir of Wm. Taylor, dec'd, his grandfather.
16 Nov., 1830. James Derden and Thos. T. May were the
securities on his bond.

From Will Book A, Greene Co., Ala., p. 8:

Dec. 1, 1824. James Derden witnessed the will of John R.
          Duke, dated Dec. 1, 1824.

Derden Notes from Greene Co., Ala.

From Minutes of Probate Court, Book F:

p. 87.   Mar. 11, 1844. Petition of Richard W. Derden
as executor of the will of James Derden, to sell
real estate. Citation issue to:

The widow, Temperance Derden

John H. Derden, heir at law

James K. Derden   "

Wm. Meador, in right of his wife, Sarah

pp. 149-50. May 13, 1844. The land belonging to this
estate is in Sumter Co., Ala. No new list of heirs here.

pp. 208-9: July 8, 1844. The estate of James Derden
having been heretofore reported insolvent, the proceeds
were divided among the creditors, to wit:

Eldred Pippin

Richard W. Derden

Mauldin Montague & Co.

From Minutes of Probate Court, Book H:

p. 689. Jan. 14, 1851. On application of Wiley Coleman,
the court issued citations to Richard W. and James K. Derden, heirs of Temperance Derden, dec'd, to appear at next
term of court, and show cause why administration on her
estate should not be granted to Robert Leachman, general
administrator for Greene Co.

p. 712. Feb. 10, 1851. The demurrer of James K. Derden,
to the citation issued to him...he is made administrator
of the estate of Temperance Derden.

Minutes of Probate Court, Book I (eye), p. 427:

April 11, 1853. Final settlement of estate of Temperance
Derden by James K. Derden, adm. The heirs at law are:
Richard W., James K., and John H. Derden; and Sarah, wife
of Wm. Meador. Each received $227.47.

Derden Deeds from Greene Co., Ala.

Book C, pp. 119-20. 6th May, 1828. James Derden, land in Sec. 26, T21, Range 3, Mortgaged to Robt. Freeman. Witnessed by James Yeats and John W. Childress.

Book C, pp. 217-8: 12 Aug., 1828. Deed of trust from James Derden to Wm. Van DeGraaf.

Book C, p. 256: James Derden, quit claim deed to John Hendrick, to land in Sec. 19, T21, R4.

Book C, p. 303: Power of attorney from John Derden to John Derden. 2 Dec., 1829.

Book C, p. 331: James Derden sold to David Jackson, land in Sec. 21, T21, R3. 5th Feb., 1829.

Book C, p. 332: Temperance, wife of James Derden, relinquished her dower rights in said lands, on same date.

Book C, p. 388: James Derden sold a slave to Robert Freeman on 2 March, 1829.

Book C, p. 412: James and Temperance Derden sold land to Robert Freeman on 5 Feb., 1829.

Book C, p. 419: James Derden and Abner Beck sold land to Wm. P. Brown on 26 May, 1828. Land in Sec. 22, T21, R3.

Compiler's note: This is not all the Derden date from Greene Co.

Random Notes from Sumter Co., Ala.

From Will Book 1, p. 25: Will of Aaron Crowson. Mentions wife, Rhody, and children (not named). Executor: Obed Lovelady. Dated 16 Aug., 1834. Witnessed by:

Cyrus Lovelady
E. Tartt

From Will Book 1, p. 101: James Derden witnessed the will of Mrs. Mary Rushing in Sumter Co., Ala., in 1837.

Will of Robert Craig of Gainesville, in Sumter Co.: Names

Brother, James D. Craig, of Cahaba, Ala., executor

Rev. Chas. A. Stillman, pastor of the Presbyterian Church in Gainesville, for the use of said church.

$500 to put a fence around the graves of my wife and children in Pleasant Ridge grave yard in Greene Co., Ala.

Niece, Sallie (Craig) Hudson

Rest to my brothers and sisters; one share to the children of a deceased brother.

Dated 7 Oct., 1860. Proved Dec. 3, 1860.

From Will Book 2, p. 40: Will of Wm. Bates of Sumter Co., Ala. Executors, Wyatt Harper and James G. Coats, to control my estate for my infant heirs. Dated Dec. 14, 1853. Witnessed by Chas. S. (?) Coats and Louis Hadden. Proved 14 Jan., 1854.

From Will Book 2, p. 319. Will of Wyatt Harper names:

Wife, Sophia Harper
Daughter, Sophia E. Harper
Sons, Lewis P. and Jack (or Zack) C. Harper
Executor, friend Stephen Horton
Dated 6 Nov., 1864. Proved 23 Jan., 1865.

From Sumter Co., Ala., Marriage Record 1, p. 306:

Wm. Bates to Martha Ann Lawson on Dec. 19, 1844, by J. M. Rushing, J. P. Bondsman: John L. Flowers. Her father, Jonas Lawson, gave his consent.

From Sumter Co., Ala., Marriage Record 2, p. 510:

Geo. W. Bates to Sarah S. Yarborough, 16 Oct., 1864.

Rev. Wm. W. Lovelady to Mary Ann Rencher, 15 Jan., 1849.
This one from Book 2, p. 52.

Notes from New Prospect Cemetery in Sumter Co., Ala.:

    Thomas Talbot died 1844, aged 18 years
    Sophia C. Talbot died 1844, aged 18 years
    Edmund Talbot died 1854, aged 26 years

    Frederick Porter, born Nov. 13, 1803, died Oct. 12, 1857
        aged 53 y 10 m 29 d

    Ruth Greer Scarborough, wife of Rev. A. R. Scarborough,
      and dau. of W. H. (?) and O. Talbot,
      born in Nashville, Tenn., Sept. 4, 1821
      died May 28, 1880
      Compiler's note: All doubtful, hard to read.

Notes from Hennegan Cemetery, near Epes, Ala.

Located off Highway 11, leading north from Livingston
    toward Epes.

Mrs. Mary M. R. Lipscomb, wife of A. Lipscomb,
    died June 22, 1858, aged 37 years
(Some Lipscomb children buried nearby)

John D. Godfrey, d. 27 April, 1843, in his 24th year
Dozier Godfrey, died 24 Aug., 1843, in his 32nd year
My child: Dozier Elizabeth Godfrey 1843-45

Margaret Lawrence, dau. of Laurence D. and H. M. M.
    Phillips 1845-45
Mrs. Harriet P. Godfrey, consort of Wm. Godfrey,
    died 30 Sept., 1845, aged 54 y 1 m 22 d
Wm. Godfrey, died 22 Jan. 1854, aged 69 y 6 m 4 d

Prudence H. Lowry 1809 - 1873

Sallie J., wife of T. H. Kennedy 1830-1860

My husband: J. P. Willis 1846 - 1904

Our father: Andrew J. Arrington 1827 - 1909
Helen Amelia, wife of Andrew J. Arrington 1837 - 65

Catherine Lowry, wife of J. T. Kennedy 1837-1915
Vernal Habdy Kennedy 1855-1896

Our friend, Major John Phillips, died March 18, 1846,
    aged 60 years
Our friend and relative, Mrs. Martha G. Phillips,
    died May 7, 1853, aged about 44 years

Our friend: Asbury Myers 1816 - 1843
My friend: James G. Myers 1811 - 1840
    Martha Myers 1780 - 1845

Permelia Collier died 29 April, 1842 (1812 ?)
    aged 13 y 2 m 2 d

Rev. H. R. Autry Oct. 12, 1814 Aug. 14, 1888

Other surnames in Hennegan Cemetery: Ogletree, Smith,
Henagan, Greenlea, Cathey, Sawls, Shaw, May, Love, and
Fitzpatrick.

———————————

Notes from Christian Valley Cemetery, Sumter Co., Ala.:

Wm. Gibson 1801 - 1871
Abbie, his wife 1811 - 1884

Lewis Johnson 1807 - 1875

Julia T., wife of Rev. W. I. Powers, died 1886, aged 54

James M. Lee 1820 - 1881
Catherine Rebecca, his wife 1832 - 1862

Wm. Ransome Boling, born in Wilkes Co., Ga.
    Nov. 27, 1799; died 1860

W. B. Coleman 1810 - 1853

Joseph Patton 1796 - 1876
Martha Ann, wife of Samuel Patton Hand 1889 - 1914
Martha L. Cusack, mother of S. P. Hand 1802 - 1876

John P. Rushing 1808 - 1892

(continued next page)

Notes from Christian Valley Cemetery, in Sumter Co., Ala., continued from preceding page:

Drury McMillan   1796 - 1860
Elizabeth McMillan 1824 - 1875
Daniel McMillan   1798 - 1860
Preston McMillan   1862 - 1869
Anna B. McMillan   1859 - 1867
Isaac N. McMillan   1855 - 1873
A. C. McMillan   1854 - 1911

Other surnames in Christian Valley:

Henson   Matthews   Connelley   Hord   Morris   Lee

Williamson   Turner   Larkin   Scales   Seales   Reed

Walston   Crocker   Guller   Martin   Stone   Torry

Speed   Burnett   Boggs   Edmonds   Brockway   Bolton

Elliott   Blakeney   Grady   Wimberley   Scott   Nixon

Davidson   Pearce   Houston

Two inscriptions from Uniontown Cemetery, Uniontown, in Perry Co., Ala.:

Thomas Bondurant, born in Buckingham Co., Va., in
1792, died 1869
Mary, his wife, also born in Buckingham Co., Va.,
in 1809, died in 1869, aged 59 years.

Dallas Co., Ala., Deed Book A, p. 370:

I, Robt. J. W. Reel, for $3600.00, paid by
Richard Radcliff of Autauga Co., Ala., for certain slaves.
Dated 29 Jan., 1823, and witnessed by

John Radcliff, Clerk of the Circuit Court
of Dallas Co.

Thomas Golaspe

From Greene Co., Ala., Tract Book:

p. 251. Caleb Eubanks patented land in Township 20, Range 4, East, Sec. 6, on May 13, 1834. Patents Nos. 1644 and 1645.

p. 264. John Darden patented land in Township 21, Range 4, Sec. 7, in 1825

James Darden in same township and range in 1824.

From an early book of mixed records in Greene Co. Court House, not bound:

p. 99. 2nd May, 1823. Caleb Hughbanks appointed overseer of the road from McGee's Spring Branch to Greensborough, on the old A. D. Kinard Road

From Greene Co., Ala., Record of the Probate Court, Vol. D., p. 168: Receipt of Mary Hopkins for property of her husband, Hardy Hopkins, which he inherited from the estate of Matthew Strickland, dec'd, of North Carolina. Jubal Carpenter, executor of the estate of Hardy Hopkins, dec'd. Dated 1832.

From Minutes of Probate Court, Greene Co., Ala.:

Book H, p. 401. Estate of John Watts to be administered by Robert Leachman, administrator-general for the County. Dated 1850.

Graves by Highway 22, about 4 miles from Plantersville, Ala. County not known to me.

Caroline P. Welch   Apr. 23, 1824   Aug. 31, 1852
Julia A. A. Welch   Jan. 13, 1838   Feb. 12, 1852
Two other stones, inaccessible; gate locked.

From cemetery in Plantersville:

Mary E., wife of Peter Haley
Feb. 9th, 1830   April 22, 1904

Robert Royston Fuller   1877 - 1950

From Deed Book C, pp. 429-31. Dallas Co., Ala.:

Charleston District, S. C. 26 April, 1832. Whereas a
marriage has been solemnized between Jacob Martin Lee of
Charleston District, S. C., and Rebecca B. Fishburn, of
Barnwell District, S. C., and said Rebecca had slaves in
her own right, and also an undivided interest in two
plantations in Colleton District, S. C. ... said property
should be settled to provide for the issue of said marriage. Therefore, I, Jacob Martin Lee, for $1.00, sell
unto Cornelius K. Ayer of Barnwell District, all these
Negroes and plantations belonging to the estate of my wife's
father, Thos. J. Fishburn, dec'd, lying in Colleton
District, in trust, for his life. Residuary legatee, Mrs.
Eliza M., wife of Dr. C. K. Ayer.

Witnessed by: Pinckney B. Myner (or Minyer)
              Isaac Youngblood

Compiler's note: There is another deed relating to this
property on pp. 430-31, same volume, but no additional
family data.

Notes from Canton Bend Cemetery, on Highway 28 between
Miller's Ferry and Camden, Wilcox County, Ala.:

John L. B. Robins, son of Littleton Robins and Martha,
his wife, was born in Worcester Co., Maryland, June 11,
1802; emigrated to Ala., in 1838; and died Nov. 30, 1850,
age 48 y 5 m 16 d

Henrietta, widow of John L. B. Robins, and daughter of
Lemuel and Hannah Showell, was born in Worcester Co., Md.,
Jan. 28, 1806; emigrated to Ala. in 1838; and died
Feb. 22, 1872, aged 66 y 24 d

Andasia Robins, wife of Wm. T. Purnell,
                April 4, 1846   March 14, 1924
Martha Robins Pharr   1831 - 1902
Geo. Mathews Pharr   1830 - 1903
Wm. Lindsey, son of Geo. Matthews and Ida Lindsey Pharr,
              Dec. 3, 1892 - Apr. 26, 1916
Mary, infant dau. of G. M. and M. W. H. Pharr,
              died 3rd June, 1851, aged 7 m 12 d

Inscriptions from Canton Bend, continued

Samuel W. Robins b. 4th Feb., 1828   d. 3 Dec., 1853
                    ae. 25 y 10 m
Mary S. Johnson, daughter of Littleton Robins and his
                  wife, Martha, born July 23, 1808,
                  died Dec. 7, 1851, ae. 43 y 4 m 15 d

Anna Maria Gibson, wife of Samuel A. Gibson,
                  died Feb. 16, 1851, aged 19 y 11 m 10 d

Charles B. Savage died Oct. 28, 1858, aged 23 y 5 m 3 d
M. Adele Savage died Dec. 20, 1858, aged 1 y 18 d

Mother: Margaret Ellen, wife of J. J. Kimbrough,
          March 26, 1838   March 12, 1908
Father: John J. Kimbrough, May 8, 1839   Jan. 24, 1893

Samuel W., son of J. and S. F. Robins
          died Sept. 20, 1863, aged 4 y 10 m 15 d

Sallie, wife of Clark Lyles, born April ___, 1857
                            died Jan. 22, 1887
Barnett Lyles Dunaway, wife of Hunter L. Dunaway,
                  Jan. 30, 1886   Jan. 20, 1937

Husband: John Thomas Lyles, Oct. 2, 1882 - Dec. 23, 1908

Columbus Marion Jackson, Jan. 26, 1847 - Apr. 11, 1906

Dr. Alexander Reed   born in Winchester, Va., in 1784
                      emigrated to Ohio in 1798
                      married in 1805
                      joined Presbyterian Church in 1808
                      removed to S. C. in 1827
                      removed to Ala. in 1832
                      died 28 Sept., 1834, aged 50 y 6 m 3 d
                      left wife & 2 sons in Ala.
                      and a dau. in Missouri

Columbus F. McMillan Dec. 25, 1825   Dec. 24, 1875

Elizabeth A., wife of C. F. McMillan
            Jan. 11, 1835 - May 3, 1881

John B. Primm, born at Laurens Court House, S. C.,
              Sept. 18, 1825; died Wilcox Co., Ala
              July 29, 1887
Henrietta A., wife of John B. Primm,
              Feb. 28, 1834   Feb. 28, 1868

Our beloved pastor, who served us in this place without
intermission for ten years: Rev. John C. Wear,
    born in Tenn., Oct. 7, 1807
    died in Camden, Ala., June 22, 1874

*
Thos. H. Seaver died Oct. 30, 1852, aged 31 years

Wm. Monroe Bryant   Mar. 15, 1836 Jan. 22, 1915
              "He surrendered with Lee"

Ann, wife of Wm. Monroe Bryant, d. July 10, 1914

Other surnames in Canton Bend Cemetery:

Fuller   Alford   Smith   Graham   Harwood   Miller
    Marsh   Cook   Moore   Tait

From "Acts of Alabama": Dec. 4, 1819. An Act to provide
for the sale of lots in the Town of Cahawba and to build
a bridge over the Cahawba River in the Town of Cahawba.
Commissioners to take charge of the public property in
Cahawba:
              John Taylor, Sr.
              Alexander Pope
              Waller O. Beckley (Walter or Waller)
              John Howard
              John W. Rinaldi
              Thomas Casey

Nov., 1820. The (acting) Governor was authorized to pay
D. & N. Crocheron $4500.00 in addition to the sum hereto-
fore allowed them, for building the State House in Cahawba.

---

* Two more inscriptions from Canton Bend, omitted by
mistake in typing:
Geo. H. Strother Jan. 1, 1820   Sept. 21, 1890
Mother: Selina G. (or C.) Wear, wife of Geo. H. Strother,
        Aug. 19, 1841   Sept. 21, 1895

Acts of Alabama, 1827-9:

Act establishing an academy in Perry Co., named Oak Grove Academy. The trustees, who are to constitute a body corporate:

> John Barron
> Robt. Jemison
> John J. Wolf
> Geo. C. King
> Jabez Curry
> Seabourn Mimms
> Friend O. Love
> Joseph Adair
> Edward Harper
> R. B. Walthal

Inscriptions from Myrtlewood Cemetery in Livingston, Ala.: (Sumter Co.)

Mary Howie, consort of Wm. Howie,
> Dec. 29, 1799   Aug. 19 (?), 1841

Isabella Stephenson, oldest dau of
> Samuel B. and Susan H. Boyd
> April 6, 1831   June 29, 1836

George W. Dainwood   Jan. 23, 1829   May 22, 1905

C. T. Roan   Oct. 9, 1907, aged 69 years (CSA Cross)

From "Southern Argus", a newspaper published in Selma, Ala.:

Issue of April 18, 1873: Fannie Brazelton married to Lee R. McKee, of Selma, at the residence of H. H. Hurt, in Marion, Ala., on April 17, 1873.

Died in Selma, Mon. last, Mrs. Laura Kennard, daughter of Mr. J. W. England of Perry Co.

Issue of June 27, 1873: Rev. J. C. Waddell, a native of Selma, has become editor of the "Central Texan", in Calvert, Texas. His kinsman, Mr. Thos. F. Martin, is one of the proprietors, and is in charge of its mechanical department.

From "Minutes of City Court of Selma" for 1866-9:

p. 1: 5th March, 1866. Organizational meeting of the Court:
Names of Attorneys present, with W. S. Burr, Judge, presiding:

E. W. Pettus	J. R. John
T. B. Wetmore	W. H. Fellows
N. H. R. Dawson	S. N. McGraw
J. T. Morgan	John T. Heflin
James W. Lapsley	Geo. C. Johnson
Jon'n Haralson	R. H. Chapman
J. C. Compton	Sumpter Lea
W. J. Mims	P. G. Wood
John White	Geo. W. Gayle
W. N. Boynton	

p. 5. March 10th, 1866. Preamble and resolution presented by John White and Edmund W. Pettus, a tribute to
the members of the Bar of Dallas County, who have died
since the commencement of the late war; at the begin-
ning of the War, the Dallas Bar numbered 45 members. Of
these, sixteen perished in the struggle:

Christopher C. Pegues	Robt. H. Lake
Alfred C. Price	Wm. A. Dunklin
John T. Duke	Augustus H. Jackson
Thos. H. Lewis	Henry B. Boynton
Chas. E. Haynes	John F. Womack
Wm. A. Beene	Julius A. Robbins
Alexander W. Ellerbee	John A. Lodor
Wm. T. Gibson	Wm. S. Maples

Cureton Bibles
No title page

James Cureton and Judith Lockett, daughter of Reuben
and Sarah Lockett was married Nov. 12, 1818

Araminta Cureton, dau. of James and Judith Cureton,
was married to Lewis Cammack July 5, 1835

Wm. B. Cureton and Charlotte May, daughter of Francis
and Charlotte May, was married on April 16, 1850

Araminta E. Cureton, daughter of Wm. B. and Charlotte
Cureton, was married to Wm. N. Fike, Dec. 25, 1880

James Cureton was born 1794, October, 21st day

Judith, his wife, was born Dec. 16, 1802

Araminta Cureton, his and her daughter, born Sept. 14,
1819

John Lockett Cureton, born Nov. 22, 1821

Doctor Dickson Cureton, born Jan. 4, 1824

James Crall Cureton, born Nov. 4, 1825

Wm. E. Denson, born Nov. 30, 1832

Edwin W. Cammack, son of Lewis & Araminta Cammack,
born May 25, 1837

Sarah M. Cammack, born Dec. 29, 1838

James C. Cammack, born Oct. 25, 1840

Michael Dickson Cammack, born May 6, 1843

Wm. Baw Cureton, born May 11, 1815

Charlotte, his wife, born Jan. 31, 1815

Araminta Elizabeth Cureton, his and her daughter,
born Jan. 16, 1856

Ira Walton Fike, son of Wm. N. & A. E. Fike,
born Jan. 12, 1882

Rufus German Fike, son of Wm. N. & A. E. Fike,
born Aug. 10 (?), 1886

Julia Edna Fike, daughter of Wm. N. & A. E. Fike,
born June 17, 1888

Wm. Nelson Fike, born May 31, 1850

Judith Cureton, wife of James Cureton
departed this life Aug. 4, 1826, in the 24th year

Doctor D. Cureton departed this life Apr. 16, 1827
in the 4th year of his age

Wm. Cureton departed this life Sept. 18, 1827, in the
62nd year of his age...Our father

John Cureton departed this life June 12, 1839, in the
43rd year of his age, son of Wm. and Margaret Cureton

James Cureton departed this life July 18, 1843,
in the 49th year of his age

Araminta Cammack, daughter of James and Judith Cureton,
departed this life June 17, 1844, in the 25th year of her
age.

Mary Joyce departed this life Nov. 1, 1868,
in the 78th year of her age
Elizabeth May departed this life July 22, 1866, in the
53rd year of her age

Reuben Lockett departed this life April 7, 1829

Sarah Massey, wife of James M. Massey, and daughter of
Reuben and Sarah Lockett, departed this life March 23,
1842.

Jane Ann Massey departed this life May 13, 1842

Dickson Cureton departed this life Dec. 24, 1845,
in the 43rd year of his age

Margaret Cureton departed this life May 20, 1852,
in the 78th year of her age

Cindarilla May departed this life Nov. 11, 1853,
in the 47th year of her age

Martha Donaghey departed this life Oct. 16, 1876, in
the 84th year of her age, being the daughter of William &
Margaret Cureton.

Wm. Baw Cureton departed this life Sept. 30, 1835,
aged 70 years 4 months 9 days

Charlotte May Cureton, wife of Wm. Baw Cureton, departed
this life Sept. 15, 1886, aged
71 years 8 month 15 days

Compiler's note: There is other date of more recent date.

The above Bibles are now in possession of Miss Julia E.
Fike. The following data is taken from a photostatic
copy of an older Bible, formerly in possession of Miss Fike,
which she says she gave to Mr. Thos. K. Cureton, of Urbana,
Ill., and he in return sent her this photostatic copy:

Wm. Cureton departed this life Sept. 18, 1827, the farther
of the under registered

John Cureton, son of Wm. and Margaret Cureton,
departed this life June 12, 1839

Elizabeth Cureton departed this life 1805 June 9.

Chapman Croll Cureton departed this life Aug. 4, 1812

My dear daughter, Mary Cureton, departed this life
July 7, 1756 (?); dyed in the 39th year of her age, being
Wensday.

Susanna Cureton, born March 25, 1761

Martha Cureton born April 29, 1764
Wm. Cureton, son of Wm. Cureton and Martha, his wife,
    born June 10, 1776

Mary Cureton, dau. of Wm. and Martha Cureton,
    born June 9, 1768

*

      "The births and deaths"

Mary Cureton, born Dec. 14 ...

Frances Cureton, born July 26, 1720

Susanna Cureton, born Jan. 29, 1723

Elizabeth Cureton, born Jan. 20, 1726

John Cureton, son of John and Frances, his wife,
    born Sept. 27, 1735

Wm. Cureton, son of John Cureton and Frances, his wife,
    born March 27, 1737

Frances Cureton departed this life Sept. 26, 1747,
    aged 27 years, being Tuesday

Mary Cureton departed this life July 7, 1756,
    aged 38 years, being Wensday

Robbert Harrison, son of Robbert Harrison and Elizabeth,
    hiw wife, born Feb. 13, 1755

Sally Harrison, born June 30, 1757

John Cureton, son of John Cureton and Winifred, his wife,
    born Nov. 13, 1757

James Cureton, son of Wm. Cureton and Martha, his wife,
    born Dec. 17, 1758

Louisa Cureton, daughter of John ... (illegible)

* Omitted at this point by error in typing:
Elizabeth Cureton, dau. of Wm. & Martha Cureton,
    born Feb. 17, 1770

"A register of the ages of Wm. and Margaret
Cureton's children, and also their own ages"

William Cureton, born June 10, 1776

Margaret Cureton, his wife, born Oct. 8, 1774

Mary Cureton, his and her daughter, born Feb. 26, 1791

Martha Cureton, born Oct. 28, 1792

James Cureton, born Oct. 21, 1794

John Cureton, born Nov. 5, 1796

Elizabeth Cureton, born Dec. 30, 179?

Dickson Cureton, born August 3, 1803

Chapman Croll Cureton, born Jan. 1, 1806

Wm. Baw Cureton, born May 11, 1815

Note: All dates should be checked by the original if
possible. The photocopy is not too clear.

Statement of Miss Julia Fike, whose address is Fike's
Ferry Road, Marion, Ala.:

I am the daughter of Wm. N. Fike and his wife, Araminta
Cureton Fike.

The said Wm. N. Fike was the son of German Fike and his
wife, Catherine Smith Fike.

The said Catherine Smith was a daughter of William
Smith, whose wife was a Crow.

The said Wm. Smith was a son of Solomon Smith

The wife of the said Wm. Smith was a daughter of Charles
Crow.

The said Araminta Cureton, wife of Wm. N. Fike, was a
daughter of Wm. Baw Cureton and his wife, Charlotte May.

Wm. Baw Cureton was son of Wm. Cureton and grandson of
another Wm. Cureton.

Dunaway Family of Perry, Marengo and
Dallas and Wilcox Counties.

Jeremiah Dunaway was married to Asenath O'Gilvie on
Oct. 22, 1835, by Levi Parks, M. G., in Perry Co., Ala.

No other male Dunaway is indexed in the Perry Co. Marriage
Record prior to 1863.

There is no record of a Dunaway estate or will in Perry Co.

From Deed Book E, p. 241, Perry Co., Ala.: John C. Flanagan and Mary, his wife, or Perry Co., sold to Jeremiah
Dunaway, land in Sec. 33, T16, R6, by deed dated 26 Nov., 1838.

From Deed Book F, p. 561, Perry Co., Ala.: John Reagh and
Eliza Jane, his wife, sold to Jeremiah Dunaway, of Perry Co.,
Ala., land in Sec. 33, T16, R6, on 10 Feb., 1841.

On 20 April, 1841, Eliza Jane Reagh appeared in person before Robt. S. Cowan, justice of peace in Cherokee Co., Ala.,
and acknowledged that she signed the above deed with her
husband, John Reagh.

From Deed Book M, Perry Co., Ala., p. 329: Jeremiah
Dunaway and Asenath Ann, his wife, of Wilcox Co., Ala., to
D. M. A. Dansby, of Marengo Co., Ala., for $1700.00, land
in Sec. 33, T16, R6. 8th Nov., 1853.

From 1850 Census of Marengo Co., Ala.:

450-450:	Jeremiah Dunaway, farmer,	age 55,	born in Ga.
	Esenith A. "	age 35	"
	Wm. "	13	born in Ala.
	John "	11	"
	Ann E. "	8	"
	Francis M. " (male)	4	"
	Dansby T. " (?)	1	"

From Deed Book G, Dallas Co., Ala., p. 470:

Deed Headed Perry Co., Ala. John P. W. Barfield, to
Jeremiah Dunaway, of Perry Co., Ala., land in Sec. 6,
T15, R6. 14th Feb., 1839. Witnessed by:

> James M. Dunaway
> D. L. Barfield

James M. Dunaway appeared personally before James D.
Craig, Clerk of the County Court, of Dallas County, Ala.,
on 24 June, 1839, and took oath that he saw Barfield sign
above deed, etc.

From Deed Book D, Dallas Co., Ala., p. 336:

I, Jeremiah Dunaway, convey to Mastin Stringfellow, land
in T17, R10, reserving to myself 4 Acres on which my house
now stands, on the Craig's Ferry Road. 16 July, 1837.
Witnessed by:

> James Grumbles
> Reuben Brabham

From Deed Book F, p. 35, Dallas County, Ala.: Jeremiah
Dunaway and Asenath Ann, his wife, of Perry Co., Ala., to
James Hall, a tract of land in T17, R10, and a lot containing four **acres**, at the crossroads where the Cahaba
and Greensboro Roads cross, all in Dallas Co.

Jeremiah and Asenath Ann Dunaway acknowledged their signatures to the above before Isaac R. McElroy, justice of
the peace in Dallas Co., on the same date.

From Will Record B, Dallas Co., Ala., p. 84: Will of
Amos Dunaway, dated 28 April, 1853. I, Amos Dunaway, of
the Village of Orrville...whole estate to wife, Sarah A.
Dunaway. Executor, my brother-in-law, Moody R. Ellis.
Witnessed by:

> John A. Norwood
> James M. Dunaway

Amos Dunaway was married to Lucinda (or Lucretia) Rogers
on 20 Sept., 1848, by John Dennis, M. G., in Dallas Co.,
Ala. See Marriage Record for 1845-65, p. 58.

Dallas Co., Ala. Marriage Record for 1818-45, p. 177:

James M. Dunaway to Julia Robertson
16 July, 1840, by Rev. J. Rives.

Compiler's note: This is th earliest marriage record
book for Dallas Co., and there is no other male Dunaway
indexed in this volume.

Mrs. Moody R. Ellis was evidently a Dunaway, but I do not
find record of this marriage in Dallas Co., prior to 1865.

From Minutes of Probate Court of Dallas Co., Ala., Book H,
p. 519: Nov., 1854. Final settlement of the estate of
Amos Dunaway, dec'd. Balance paid to the widow, who is
the only legal heir.

From Monroe Co., Ala., Marriage Record Book for 1834-80:

p. 297. F. M. Dunaway to E. M. Lambert on 25 Dec., 1868,
by A. J. Lambert, M. G., at the residence of Andrew
Lambert. Bondsman:
M. L. Lambert

p. 231: W. J. Dunaway to Drucilla Lambert, on 13 Feb.,
1862, by A. J. Lambert, M. G., at the residence of
Andrew Lambert. Bondsman

H. M. **Lambert**

Compiler's note: Since the above was typed, I have found
additional Dunaway material in Dallas Co.

No search for Dunaway documents was made in Wilcox or in
Marengo Counties; the search in Monroe was not exhaustive.

See our "Vital Statistics from Cemeteries in Dallas Co.,
Ala." for Dunaway and Ellis inscriptions.

Addenda

From Minutes of Probate Court of Dallas Co., **Ala.**:

Book A, p. 5: John B. Bates was administrator of the estate of Daniel Hutcheson in 1819.

Compiler's note: I found no other papers, but did not make an exhaustive search.

From Deed Book Q, Dallas Co., Ala.: p. 236. 14 April, 1854. Geo. W. Bates and Sarah E., his wife, sold to James C. Taylor, for $50.00 2 acres in the SE corner of the W½ of NW¼ of Sec. 18, T15, R7, to include the house formerly occupied by Mrs. Nancy Worthington. Witnesses:

Jos. C. Chapman
J. M. Mobley

Dallas Co., Ala., Deed Book Q, p. 176. 19 Jan., 1854: Samuel H. Taylor sold to Geo. W. Bates, land lying between J. Holmes and J. Hayes, in Sec. 18, T15, R7. Witnessed by:

A. C. Mobley
C. M. Taylor

From Deed Book Q, Dallas Co., Ala., p. 470: 6 Dec., 1854. John S. Mayes and Margaret A., his wife, to Geo. W. Bates, land in Sec. 18, T15, R7. Witnessed by:

Albert W. M. Ridgway

Dallas Co., Ala., Deed Book U, p. 619. 28 Feb., 1866:

Whereas Margaret A., wife of John S. Mayes, is entitled as one of the heirs of A. C. Mobley, dec'd, to a portion of his estate, and her husband, J. S. Mayes, is indebted to said estate by two promissory notes...for the purpose of paying said debts and others...Margaret A. Mayes has consented that her distributive share of her father's estate may be applied by said John S. Mayes on these debts...in consideration whereof and $1.00 paid him by Geo. W. Bates...said Mayes conveys to said Bates in trust for Margaret A. Mayes, 280 A. in Sec. 23, T15, R7.

John S. Mayes acknowledged his signature to this deed on same date, before Wm. W. Mobley, J. P., in Dallas Co.

Dallas Co., Ala., Deed Book S, p. 411. 3 May, 1859. David M. Bates, mortgage to James Bates, horse, buggy & harness.

Dallas Co., Ala., Deed Book P, p. 74: 3rd Aug., 1852.
A. C. Mobley and his wife, Elizabeth E., to J. P. Strother.
Sec. 10, T15, R7. Signatures acknowledged before A. C.
Jackson, J. P., on Aug. 4, 1852.

Dallas Co., Ala., 10 Feb., 1851. Deed Book Q, p. 50:

John Bates and his wife, M. Jane Bates, of Dallas Co.,
deed to John D. Adams, for $450.00, lot containing 5 A.,
in the town of Fulton, in Dallas Co., Ala. Not witnessed.

Dallas Co., Ala. Deed Book C, pp. 124-5. 3rd Aug., 1831.
A. C. Mobley and Ann, his wife, to Joseph Strother. Land
in Sec. 24, T15, R7. Witnesses:

> F. Vaughan
> Male. Pegues

A. C. and Ann Mobley appeared in person before J. R.
McElroy and James J. Morgan, justices of the peace in
Dallas Co., and acknowledged their signatures to above
deed, on 28 July, 1832.

Dallas Co., Ala., Deed Book L, pp. 315-16. 9th Apr., 1845:

Abner C. Mobler and Ann, his wife, deed to Joel E. Matthews.
They acknowledged their signatures in person on 15 April,
1845.

From 1850 Census of Perry Co., Ala. David M. Bates,
aged 25, mechanic, born in S. C., was living with the
James Goocher family in Pinetucky Beat, House No. 7.

Perry Co., Ala. Will Book A, p. 52. Will of Albert Bates.
Not dated. It names:

> Brother Jeremiah Bates   Brother Pleasant Bates
> Sister Rebecca Hood   Sister Rhoda Bates
> Each of these, $1.00. Balance to wife, Sarah J.; if
> she should be in a state of pregnancy, she is to get
> one-third, and the child the balance.

Executors, David Weaver and Wm. A. Melton
Witnessed by James Goggans, John Ford, W. O. Beckley.
Recorded 27 March, 1834.

From Perry Co., Ala., Marriage Record for 1820-39.
License No. 562: Albert Bates to Sarah Jane Melton,
24 Nov., 1831, by James W. Cosby, J. P.

Perry Co., Ala. Marriage Record for 1820-39:

No. 819. A. E. Lockridge to Sarah Bates on 28 Dec., 1834,
      by George Everett, M. G.

No. 57. Burrell Taylor to Betsy Bates on 5th May, 1822,
      by Charles Crow, M. G.

From 1820 State Census of Conecuh Co., Ala. Copies from
the Ala. Historical Quarterly, Vol. 6, pp. 346 ff.:

    Wm. Bates: 2 males over 21   1 female over 21
            5 males under 21 3 females under 21

Same reference lists John Barge, over 21, alone.

Torrence lists Bates wills prior to 1800 in the following
Virginia Counties: Albermarle, Amelia, York, Bedford,
Essex, Fairfax, Halifax, Madison, and Brunswick. The
majority of these are in York Co.

From 1860 Census of Dallas Co., Ala., p. 39: (In Selma)

Wm. M. Ridgway	age 47	born in Ga.
S. W. Ridgway	45	"
B. M. "	17	born in Ala. female
Wm. G. Bates	28	born in S. C.

From 1860 Census of Lexington Beat, Dallas Co., Ala.:

Martha E. Lyles	30	born in Ga.
Sarah "	14 or 16	born in Ala.
J. S. " male	10	"
Clark Lyles	8	"
B. A. Lyles female	6	"
W. T. Lyles male	4	"

Also living in the above family: C. S. McGuire, male,
aged 21; and H. McGuire, male, aged 18, both born in Ala.

From 1860 Census of Dallas Co., Ala., p. 43:

    Harrell's Beat, P. O., Fort's:

H. G. Ridgeway	age 33	male born in Ala.
E. E. "	27	female "
T. E. "	7	male "
Mary E. "	3	"
E. F. "	1	female "

Index of Personal Names

Bates
  Mamie England 44
  Martha E. 41, 45
  Martha J. 45
  Mary D. 44, 45
  Murphy 42
  Nannie A. 41, 43, 44
  Pleasant 99
  Prentice R. 44, 45
  Rhoda 99
  Robt. 44, 45
  S. E. 41, 43
  Sallie 41, 42, 43
  Samuel 41, 44, 45
  Sarah 43, 100
  Susan 45
Beck, Abner 77
Beckley, W. O. 99
  Waller O. 87
Beene, Wm. A. 89
Belcher, Obadiah 72
Belk, Augy Myram 27
  Brittain 27
  Darling 27
  H. J. 27
  Mary 27
  M. Z. 27
  Sarah 27
  Wm. 27
Bell, Elijah 49
  Robt. 38
  Joel 57
Bennett, Bowen 19
  Mary 28
Benson, Gabriel 4, 66
Bethea, Mrs. 29

Billingsley
  Cyrus 58, 59
  Eliza 59
  Elizabeth 59
  Isaac 58, 59
  Mary 59
  Thos. 58
  Wm. 59
Birdsong, Alex'r 18, 19
Blackburn, J. L. 60
  Sid W. 70
Bland, Eliza 54

Bledsoe, Moses 28
Boggan, Mary C. 51
Bolling, Wm. Ransome 82
Bonds, C. C. 17
Bondurant, J. H. 14, 18
  Mary 83
  Thos. 83
Boney, Jos. D. 40
Bonner, Wm. Jr. 22
  Wm. Sr. 22
Borden, Ann M. 35
  Thos. R. 35
Borroughs, B. 67
Boutwell, Dixon 56, 57
Bowers, Nancy 52
Boyd, Isabella S. 88
  John 60
  Samuel B. 88
Boyd, Susan H. 88
  Wm. 22
Boyles, John W. 69, 70, 71
  Louisa J. 69
  Mary 69
  Nancy M. 69
Boynton, Henry B. 89
  W. N. 89
Brabham, Reuben 96
Brackenridge, Jos. 9, 10
Brantley, Jno. E. 22
Brazelton, A. J. 67
  Fannie 88
  Rebecca 67
Brazelton, T. V. 67
Brewer, Ann C. 63
  Wm. 63
Brooks, Oliver C. 7
Brown, Alex'r W. 41, 42
  C. Ella 41, 42
  Margaret B. 51
  Wm. ? 79
Browning, Wm. 20, 21
Bruce, John B. 13, 14, 15, 17
Bryant, Ann 87
  Wm. Monroe 87
Buck, Wm. 29
Buckaloo, Richard 10
Burge, Martha 51
  Patsy 50

Burks, Wm. 9
Burr, W. S. 89
Burris, Wm. 59
Burroughs, Mary 58, 59
Burrows, Dr. 10
Burton, Louisa 18
Burwell, Wm. M. 21
Bussey, Harmon 22
Byrd, Wm. M. 15

Callahan, Jacob 19
Calaway C. C. 37
Cammack
    Araminta 90, 91
    Edwin W. 90
    Jas. C. 90
    Lewis 90
    Sarah M. 90
    Michael Dickson 90
Camp, Martha F. 51
Campbell, Isaac N. 8
Carpenter, Jubal 84
    Simeon 33
Carson, Adam 40
    John 37, 63
Carter, Benj. D. 22
    Samuel D. 20
Casey, Thos. 87
Catling, Jno. D. 20
Chambers, Ann 39, 40
    J. B. 57
    Jos. B. 38, 39, 40
    Wm. G. 23
Chaney, Chas. 26
    Sarah 26
    Wm. 26
Chapman, John H. 76
    Jos. C. 98
    H. H. 89
Childress, John W. 79
Chiles, David R. 31
    Elizabeth 61
    Henry 61
    Thos. T. 31
    Walter 38
Christopher, Doctor 38
Clark, Richard 40
    Wm. 18
    Isham 25
    Jane 25

Coats, Chas. 80
    J. G. 61
    Jas. G. 64, 80
    John 38
    Laura 61
    W. W. 62
Cocke, Jack F. 40
    Woodson 40
Cockroft, Ann 54
Coleman
    Augusta A. 61
    A. W. 51
    B. A. 51
    Chas. 60
    D. W. 51
    Elijah L. 47, 48
    G. W. 51
    Jesse W. 50, 51
    J. W. 51
    Jno. F. 51
    Jno. G. 32
    L. E. 51
    T. E. 51
    T. B. 51
    Theodore 51
    Wiley 78
    Wm. B. 82
Collier, John 18
Compton, J. C. 89
Cone, Wm. 72
Connell R. O. 29
    Robt. O. 30
Constantine Elizabeth 37
Cook, Olive 18
Cosby, C. A. 1
    Jas. W. 28, 99
Covington, Louisa A. 51
Cowan, Robt. S. 95
Cox, Nixon 8
Craig, Jas. D. 80, 96
    Jas. W. 24
    Joe Bates 45
    John J. 24
    John W. 24
    Martha 45
    Robt. 80
    Sallie 80

Eubanks, Wm H. 29
Evans. A. B. 51
  Abner, Jr. 71
  B. S. 51
Everett, Geo. 100
Ezelle, Nannie Adele 45
Falconer, Alexander 32
Farrington, Edward F. 23
          26, 27
  Mary 26
Faulk, Wm C. 29, 30
Fellows, W. H. 89
Field, Henry 38, 39, 40
  Mary J. 38, 39, 40
Fike, A. E. 91
  Araminta 90, 91, 94
  Catherine Smith 94
  German 94
  Ira Walton 91
  James M. 4
  Julia Edna 91,92,94
  Rufus German 91
  Wm. N. 90, 91, 94
  Wm Nelson 91
Fishburn, Rebecca B. 85
  Thos. J. 85
Fisher, Geo. D. 27
  Green A. 27
  Wm Sr. 27
Flanagan, Jno. C. 95
  Mary 95
Flowers, John L. 80
Fluker, Ann 61
  Cibell 61
  Elizabeth 61
  Dr. 10
  Hardy C. 61
  Laura 61
  Minerva E. 61
  Nancy 61
  Wm 61
  Wm L. 61
Ford, A. P. 5
  Alexander P. 5
  Benj. 28
  Carlos 5
  Chas. 5
  John 99
  John M. 5, 6

Ford, John S. 5, 6
  Keziah F. 5
  Martha 5
  Mary 5
  Pressley 6
  Sarah M. 5
  Simeon H. 5
  T. J. 18
  Wm 4
  W. M. 67
Fountain, A. F. 18
  Catherine 26
  Wm F. 25
Fowler, Martha E. 36
Freeman, King 19
  Robt. 19
  Sarah 19
Frost, Mrs. A. D. 44
  Clara 44
  M. M. 44
Fuller, Alfred 4
  Robt. Royston 44
Gaines, Ann 20
  Edmund P. 35
  Francis 35
  Geo. S. 20
Gamble, Catherine 54
  James 39
  John H. 39
Garrison, E. W. 1
Gary, Harvey S. 67
Gayle, Matt 7
  Geo. W. 89
George, James 24
  James G. 33
  Matilda M. 24
  Stewart 9
Gibson, Abbie
  Anna Maria 86
  Mason J. 67
  Sam'l A. 86
  Wm 82
  Wm T. 89
Gildersleeve, John 12
Gilmer, Jas. Jr. 24
  Samuel H. 24
Gilmore, H. M. 62
  Stephen M. 56

Hendrick, John 79
Henry, Ausban 22
Herrin, Harriett 54
Higginbotham, Blakely 27
Hightower, Raleigh 18
    Thos. 9
Hill, Jas. N. 15
    Louisa 18
    Mary 14, 15
    Nancy A. 13
Hillier, Abram 22
Hobbs, C. M. 40
Hogan, David 20
    Wm
    Maj. Wm C. 23
Hogue, David 76
    Susan 76
Holbrook, Bettie 6
    Mary 6
Holland, John 20
Holley, James 19
    Sarah 19
Holman, M. C. 29
Holmes, J. 98
Holsten, Jas. 8
    Margaret 8
    Nancy 8
    Wm 8
Holt, Hiram 22
Hood, Rebecca 99
Hopkins, Hardy 84
    Mary 84
Horton, Stephen 80
Howard, John 87
Howell, Lewis 9
    Wiley 9
Howie, Mary 88
    Wm 88
Huckabee, Gray 35
    Martha A. 35
Huddleston, Jos. C. 7
Hughbanks, Caleb 84
Hurt, H. H. 88
Hutcheson, Daniel 98
Hutton, T. M. 33
Hughey, Cary 75
    Cassaline 75
    James M. 75

Hughey, Jefferson 75
    John 74
    Lucinda M. 75
    Polly 74
Hudson, Sallie 80

Idom, J. M. 36

Jackson, A. C. 99
    Andrew 12
    Augustus H. 89
    Columbus Marion 86
    David 79
    Edward 59
    J. K. P. 17
    John 18
    Jno. C. 19
    Shield 17
    Woody 19
Jamison, Robt. 88
Jeffries, Jno. M. 61
Jemison, Henry 35
    Humphrey 73
    Samuel 73
John, A. C. 24
    Aly W. 24
    J. R. 89
    Jos. F. 42
Johnson, B. W. 20
    E. O. 51
    Edward 20
    Geo. C. 89
    Lewis 82
    Mary S. 86
Johnston, Elizabeth 57
    Thos. M. 37
Jones, Gray B. 11
    James R. 15
    John C. 19
Joyce, Mary 91

Morrisett, Caroline 34
    Edmund P. 34
    Fannie B. 34
    Francis S. 34
Morrisette, Geo. G. 34
    James 34, 35
    James D. 34, 35
    John 34, 35, 39, 40
    Lalula 34
    Maud 34

    May 34
    Robinson 34
Morton, Joseph W. 1
Morse, Wm L. 26
Mosby, Ann 61
    James L. 61
Mounger Wm H. 15, 16
Munroe, T. C. 3
Myers, Asbury 82
    James G. 82
    Martha 82

Nave, Jesse B. 66, 69, 70
Neighbors, Allen 1
    Sam'l 1
Nelms, Samuel H. 9
Nettles, Amos A. 21
    John 21
Nelson, John 36
Newberry, Benj. F. 29
    Martha A. 29
Nolen, J. 10
Norwood, Jno. A. 96
Nuffer, C. B. 62
    Jno. A. 62

O'Gilvie, Asenath 95
Oliver, Lucinda 73
    M. W. 66
O'Neal, Betsy 10
Owens, Mrs. Julia A. 51

Packer, David 39
Painter, Charlotte 57
    John 56, 57
    Richard J. 57
Panther, Nancy 57
Parker, Asa 29
    James 9
    Sherod 9
Parks, Levi 95

Pate, Jno. F. 27
Patton, Betsy 75
    Elizabeth 36
    James 36
    James K. 36
    Joseph 82
    Powhattan E. 36
    Samuel 36, 37
Paul, Mary 54
Payne, Daniel W. 60
    Dilliard 60
    Hiram 60
    James M. 60
    John B. 60
    Mariah W. 60
    Mary 60
    Nancy A. 60
    Thos. 4
    Wm Y. 60
Pearson, Leonard 9
    Penelope 69
Peck, Frederick 37
Peeples, Jesse H. 13
Pegues, Christopher C. 89
    Male. 99
Permenter, Mariah 54
Perry, Robt. 72
Perryman, Alex'r 39
Pettus, Edmund W. 89
Pharr, E. H. 85
    Geo. Matthews 85
    Ida Lindsay 85
    Martha Robins 85
    Mary 85
Philen, Catherine 26
    Chapman R. 26
    Eliza Ann 26
    Elizabeth 26
    Fereby 25, 26
    Harrison 26
    Jackson 26
    Jane 26
    John 26
    Joshua 26
    Manassah 25
    Martha 26
    Mary 25
    Peter 25, 26
    Riley 26
    Sarah 26
    Sidney 25
    Susan 26

Philen, Wesley 26
  William 25, 26
Phillips, H. M. M. 32
  Maj. John 32
  Lawrence D. 81
  Mrs. Martha G. 82
  Wm S. 7
Pickens, E.ekiel 24
Pierce, Abram 7
  Wm F. 31
Pippin, Eldred 71, 78
Pledger, Elizabeth E. 49
Pool, J. K. C. 9
Pope, Alex'r 87
  Anderson 12
  Brittain T. 17
  Jackson 12
  Sarah J. 12
Porter, Frederick 81
  H. 18, 20
Portis, Solomon W. 22
Powers, Julia T. 32
  W. J. 82
Price, Alfred C. 89
Primm, Henrietta A. 37
  John B. 37
Pritchett, Christopher 56
  Jeremiah 11
  Robt. 10, 11
Puckett, Mary 60
  Richard 60
Pryor, Martha 2, 3
  R. Q. 2, 3
Purnell, Wm T. 85

Raiford, Hanson 7
Rankin, Wm 20
Rainer, Thos. G. 24, 48
Ralls, Catherine 29
Rauls, Julia 29
Raines, M. E. 43
Ragsdale, Lucinda 74
Radcliff, John 83
  Richard 33
Reeves, J. 43
Read, Briant 22
  Elias 22, 23

Read, Elizabeth 22, 23
  Levina 22, 23
  Marion 22, 23
  Wm H. 22, 23
Reed, Dr. Alex'r 86
  Clarissa 11
  Mrs. Cornelia 51
  Wm 11
Reel, Robt. J. W. 83
Reagh, Eliza Jane 95
  John 95
Rembert, James M. 19
Rencher, Mary Ann 81
Ridgway, Albert W. M. 98
  B. M. 100
  E. E. 100
  E. F. 100
  H. G. 100
  Mary E. 100
  S. W. 100
  T. E. 100
  Wm M. 100
Rikard, Mrs. Elizabeth 29
Ringgold, Thos. 9, 14, 16
Rinaldi, Jno. W. 37
Rice, Elizabeth 74
Richardson, Hopkins R. 32
Roan, C. T. 88
Robards, Edmund W. 35
Robbins, Julius A. 89
Roberson, Bartram 7
Robertson, B. 69
  Tilford 64
  Julia 97
  Thos. M. 69
Robins, Andasia 85
  Henrietta 85
  J. 86
  Jno. L. B. 85
  Littleton 35, 36
  Martha 35, 36
  Mary S. 36
  S. F. 36
  Samuel W. 36
Robinson, Bartram 7
Rogers, Lucinda 96
  Lucretia 96

Willingham, Martha 50
   Samuel M. 50
   Willy 50
Willis, J.P. 81
Wilson, Geo. 61
   James P. 40
Winn, H.J. 47
Witeker, James M. 24
Withers, Frances 60
Wisdom, John 28
Wolf, John J. 88
Womack, John F. 89
Wood, P.G. 89
   Stephen C. 72
Woolf, Thos. J. 17
Wootley, Reason 54
Whitted, James 22
   Moses 22
Worthington, Mrs. Nancy 98
Wyatt, Wm N. 66, 67
Worthington, Nancy 98

Yarborough, Alfred 10
   Elizabeth 18
   Sarah S. 81
Yeats, James 79
Young E.A. 1
Youngblood, Isaac 85

ALABAMA NOTES

Volume 2

Table of Contents

Bird - Sample data from Marengo Co.

From Marriage Record A, pp. 49-50:

pp. 49-50 License for Robert Sample to marry Martha Bird,
dated 28th August 1823. Ceremony on 4th Sept. by Geo. N.
Steward, J. P. Security on bond: John Sample.

pp. 128-9. Marriage of James Bird to Pinkey Ford, solemnized 22 Jan. 1822 by M. Porter, J. P. Security on the bond:
Robert Sample.

pp. 82-3: Alexander Sample to Mary Pistole, on the night of
Feb. 20th 1825, by James Yarborough, M. G. Security:
Robert Sample.

p. 232. Daniel Bird to Minerva Goodbread on 26 Jan. 1831
by Thos. McGee _ _. Security: Burrell McClendon.

Note: The marriage of Wiley Duren to Brunetta Bird is
not indexed in this volume, nor in the volume for 1836-51,
which follows this one.

Estate of Abraham Bird

From Minutes of Orphans' Court, Book A-B:

p. 11. 9th Oct. 1828. Thos. Ringgold, Judge, presiding:

Jonathan May applied for letters of administration
on the estate of Abraham Bird, dec'd. Jesse W. Bird and
Robert Sample, two of the legatees of said estate, as-
sented to his appointment. Bond for $3000.00.

The following were appointed to appraise this estate:
Josiah Skinner Sr., Wm Quinney, James Renfrow, Daniel
Curtis and Wm H. Banks.

Jonathan May, as administrator of Abram Bird, is allowed
to sell the stock of cattle and furniture and hogs, they
being subject to great expense in keeping them up;
also to sell the crop now on the plantation.

p. 169. 16 Aug. 1830. Jonathan May, admr., allowed 5%
of the sales and monies collected as compensation for his
services.

pp. 169-70. 18th Aug. 1830. Came Jonathan May, admr., of the estate of Abraham Bird... the heirs have had due notice of the final settlement; and also for bringing into hotchpotch the advances made by the deceased in his lifetime. By acknowledgment of Robert Sample, he has received $160.56¼ in advance; Jesse Bird $50.00 in advance; and the following are the legal heirs of said estate:

Robert Sample and his wife Martha; James Bird; Jesse Bird; and Daniel Bird, who have all attained to the age of 21 years; and Harriett Bird, Abraham Bird and Wm Bird, all minors over 14 years of age, and Brunetta Bird, a minor under 14 years.

p. 170. 18th Aug. 1830. Final Settlement. The admr's account shows $3293.35½ in notes due on Negroes, land, and advances made to the heirs in the lifetime of dec'd, and in ready money. Court ordered that this be equally divided among the heirs aforesaid. Commissioners appointed to make the division: Nathan Smith, John Boid, Elisha Lacy, Austin Lacy and Wm Quinney.

p. 170. 18 Aug. 1830. In open Court, Harriett Bird (age 19), Abraham Bird, (age 17), and Wm Bird (age 15), children of Abraham Bird, dec'd, made choice of Daniel Bird to be their guardian; and Jonathan May was appointed by the Court to be guardian of Brunetta Bird, aged 11, a minor of Abraham Bird, dec'd.

p. 172. 20 Sept. 1830. Daniel Bird filed his bond for $2400.00 with Robert Sample, James Bird, Henry Bates, & John Browning as his securities -- bond as guardian of Harriett, Abram and Wm Bird, children of <u>William</u> Bird, dec'd. (Note obvious error.)

p. 175. Nov. 1830. Jonathan May, admr. of Abraham Bird, dec'd, filed a petition praying for a sale of the SE¼ of Sec. 34, Township 18, Range 3, East, to which the deceased had an incomplete and very imperfect title. Notice of sd. petition being acknowledged by the heirs and guardian, who appear to waive all exceptions, and consent to said sale, it is ordered that the title of sd. deceased be sold to the highest bidder at the Court House in Linden on 1st Mon. in Jan. next; and the Court appointed the following comrs. to make this sale:

B. P. Whitlow and John Rains

pp. 321-22. Sept. term of Court, 1836, 5th Sept.:

Jonathan May, admr. of Abram Bird, produced receipts
showing that each of the following has received the
amounts due them as heirs of Abram Bird:

    Robert Sample, in right of his wife Martha,
        formerly Martha Bird

Daniel Bird

    Ethelred Quinney, in right of wife Harriett,
        formerly Harriett Bird

    Wiley Duren and his wife Buretta,
        formerly Buretta Bird

And Jonathan May is released from further liability as
admr. and gdn.

Estate of William Bird

From Minutes of Orphans' Court, Book A - B:

p. 286. 2nd Nov. 1835. Wm Bird, a minor, has died,
and no person has administered his estate. Court
ordered that citations issue to his next of kin, to
administer before the next term of court, or the
administration will be given over to the sheriff.

p. 372. Nov. 1837. E. Quinney, admr. of the estate
of Wm Bird, dec'd, petitioned to distribute the said
estate among the following:

Jesse W. Byrd, Daniel Bird, Abraham Byrd; Robert
Sample and his wife, Wiley Duren and wife. Some or all
of these are non-residents. Publication to be made in
the Tuscaloosa Intelligencer, that the parties may be
present at Court on 1st Mon. in Feb.

From Minutes of Probate Court, Vol. for 1840:

p. 110. March 1841. Ethelred Quinney, admr. of Wm.
Bird, dec'd, is ordered to make a settlement on 12th
April next.

Note: Nothing else about this estate is indexed in
      this volume.

      There is no Sample estate in Vol. A-B, nor in
      the volume for 1840

Marengo Co., Ala. Deed Record A, pp. 133-4:

27 Jan. 1824. Abraham Bird purchased of Mark Anthony
Frenage, the SE¼ of Sec. 30, T13, R3E, and in payment gave
his note payable March 1st 1826, for $160.00. Witn.:
Martin Wells and John Curry.

Deed Record D, p. 452. 29 Sept. 1836. Robt. Sample &
his wife Martha sold to Solomon Rhodes, land in T17, R4E.

Compiler's note: This name also spelled Semple, Semples.

Deed Record I (eye), pp. 260 - 71: 17 May 1842, Robt.
Sample and Martha, his wife, sold to James Greene and
Joshua A. Wade, deacons of the Baptist Church of Christ
at Shiloh, in Marengo Co., for $5.00, 2½ A. in Sec. 15,
T13, R3E. Witn.: S. S. Hosea, Chas. Raley (or Barley).

From Deed Record M, pp. 422-3: 4th Jan. 1849. Robt. T.
Sample and wife Eliza A., and David Espy, sold to
Arthur M. Lewis, all of Marengo Co. land in T16, R one E.

From Deed Record K, p. 109. 7 Oct. 1843. Sarah Sample,
Catherine Boykin, Turner Trim and Martha his wife, all
of Marengo Co., Ala.; Wisdom Trim and Laury his wife of
Sumter Co., Ala., -- all heirs of the estate of Wm N.
Sample of Marengo Co., Ala., dec'd., sold to Robt. T.
Sample of Marengo, for $1000.00, all their title to
certain lands in T16, R2E. Signatures acknowledged be-
fore John W. Smith, J. P. same day.

Marengo Co. Tract Book, p. 280: Robert Sample entered
land from the U. S., on Nov. 21, 1825, by certificate
No. 1719, in Sec. 30, T17, R4E. In the same neighborhood
were Jonathan May and Wm Quinney.

Also from the tract book, p. 107: Wm N. Sample entered
land in T16, R2E, in 1833.

Compiler's note: The above may not be all the entries
in the Tract Book under these names; since the tract
book is not in Alphabetical order, but is arranged by
townships and ranges. Hence it is necessary to locate
the land first in deed books, then find the names in
the tract book.

In the Minutes of Probate Court, Book D, there are 7 documents relating to the estate of Wm N. Sample.

From Final Record, March, 1845. The will of Wm N. Sample was filed 6th Oct. 1843 by Robt. T. Sample

From Will Record A, pp. 243-4: Will of Wm N. Sample, dated 8th June 1843: All property to only son, Robt. T. Sample. He is to provide for his mother. One cow to Laury Trim. After his mother's death, proceeds to be divided equally among heirs.

From Marriage Record for 1836-51:

p. 355: Marshal H. Byrd to Caroline S. Moore. License dated 26 March 1845. No minister's return. Byrd's Bondsman was D. C. Anderson.

Compiler's note: Also indexed in this volume: J. B. Sample, R. T. Sample, and Henry A. Sample.

From Marriage Record for 1818-36:

p. 238: Etheldred Quinney to Harriett Bird on 5 May 1831, by Eli Davis, M. G. Bondsman: Wm Quinney

From 1830 Census of Marengo Co.: The only Bird listed in Daniel.

The following Samples are listed in 1830 Census:

Alexander, Robt., Wm N., and Joseph.

Philip Goodbread is also listed in 1830 Census.

Peter Bird is listed in 1830 Census of Bibb Co., Ala.

Isaiah Bird is listed in 1816 Census of Monore Co., Ala., (then in Miss.), and in 1830 Census of Perry Co.

No Bird listed in 1830 Census of Wilcox, Clarke, Greene, Autauga or Covington.

Hugh Bird and Elijah Bird are listed in Lowndes Co., Ala., in 1830 Census.

Hendrix - Oliver Family of Perry Co., Ala.

From 1860 Census of Perry Co., Ala., p. 2, Radfordsville Beat, House No. 16, Family No. 16:

    David Hendrix,   age 38   born in S. C.
    Margaret S. J. Hendrix age 29   born S. C.
    James T. Hendrix   age 4   b. Ala.
    Charles   "   2   "

p. 14, Radfordsville Beat. 12 June 1860
    House and family No. 99:

    William Hendrix   age 43 Gen'l. Supt. b. Mass.
    Althea V. "   38 wife   b. Ala.
    Martin T. "   18   "
    A. Q. B.   "   13 (male)   "
    Donna W.   "   8 (female)   "
    Murrell W. "   6   "
    Roswell   "   3   "
    Lizzie Parker   17 visitor   b. Mass.

p. 23, Pinetucky Beat. House and family No. 160:

    Wm S. Hannah   43   b. S. C.
    Mary O.   "   12   b. Ala.
    Emily G. "   9   "
    W. T.   "   3   "   male
    Sophronia Watson 40   "   widow
    Laura   "   13   "
    Thos. D. "   8   "
    Lemuel   "   11   "

p. 91. **Eastern** Division of Marion Beat.
    House and family No. 628.

    M. W.   Oliver   age 45   born in Tenn.
    C. L.   "   39   "   S. C. wife
    W. C.   "   16   b. Ala.   female
    C. L. Jr. "   14   "   "
    M.   "   12   "   "
    Emily   "   10   "   "
    Alexander "   8   "   male
    Mary   "   6   "   female
    Sophronia "   4   "   "
    Murel   "   3   "   male
    Catherine "   4/12   "   female

House and family No. 629:

>Emily T. Oliver age 23 born Tenn. living alone
>Next item: Valuation of estate of Lucinda Oliver

House No. 630: Elam Parish Family, and living with them:

>A. Q. Bradley age 52 Physician b. S. C.
>Ann G. " 21 female "

House No. 748, p. 109, Eastern Div., Town of Marion:

>Samuel Parker age 26 Physician b. Vermont
>Laura L. " 20 wife b. Ala.
>Wm H. " 6/12 "

In Perryville Beat, living with family of
Dr. A. S. Pickering:

>D. Parker age 25 Physician b. Vermont

From Perry Co., Ala., Marriage Record for 1840-51:

License No. 1723: Wm S. Hanna To Mary V. Oliver
23 Dec. 1845, by Reese Frierson ___.

From Perry Co. Marriage Record for 1851-63:

Lic. No. 637: Samuel Parker to Laura V. Hendrix on
24 March 1859, by P. B. Lawson

Compiler's note: P. B. Lawson, a lawyer in Marion,
also served as "pastor" of the "Christian" Church.

From Perry Co. Marriage Record for 1832-39:

License No. 1089: M. W. Oliver to Catherine L. E.
Bradley. License dated 7 Jan. 1839. There is no
minister's return showing date of ceremony.

License No. 112: Wm Hendricks to Althea V. Oliver.
License dated 27 Feb. 1831. No minister's return.

From Will Book A, Perry Co., Ala., pp. 24 - 26:

Will of Thos. M. Oliver, dated 4th Nov. 1826 and
recorded 15 Nov. 1826, mentions:
1. Son, Murrell W. Oliver
2. Dau., Emily T. Oliver
3. Dau., Sophronia D. Oliver
4. Dau., Atha B. Oliver
5. Dau., Mary Virginia Oliver
6. Don, Thos. H. J. Oliver
7. Wife, Lucinda Oliver

Executors, friends Edwin D. King and Edward Oliver; &
in case either fails to qualify, Gabriel Benson.

Witnessed by: Anderson West
               G. R. or C. R. West
               Sample Orr

Compiler's note: Apparently, all the children were
                  minors at this time.

Inscriptions from Marion Cemetery:

   Thomas M. Oliver   born May 31, 1796
                         died Nov. 13, 1826
                         aged 32y 6m 13d

   William Oliver, father of T. M. Oliver,
                    d. Apr. 18, 1827, aged 85 years

   Thomas A. J. Oliver, son of T. M. & Lucinder Oliver,
                     b. Nov. 27, 1825
                     d. May 27, 1843
                     aged 18y 5m

From Minutes of Probate Court of Perry Co., Ala.:
Book B, p. 162: Feb. term of Court, 1835: Lucinda Oliver
vs John Barron, admr. of Wm Barron, dec'd. (This is a
petition for title to land.)

"It appearing to the satisfaction of the court that the
sale of the land in the bond and petition was fairly made
by Wm Barron in his lifetime, and that said bond was duly
executed by Wm Barron; it is therefore ordered that John
Barron as admr. of Wm Barron, execute to Lucinda Oliver
title in fee simple to following described lands: 15 A.
in N. E. Corner of E½ of SE (or SW) ¼ of Sec. 18, Township 19, Range 8, agreeably to the corner now made by
Hanna, the County Surveyor, including Lucinda's improve-
ments on the said 15 A.

From Minutes of Probate Court, Book E, p. 163:

April 19, 1847. Came Lucinda Oliver, admx. of estate of
Thomas M. Oliver, dec'd, and filed her accts. for a
final settlement of said estate. She is released as admx.

Compiler's note: There is no list of heirs here.

From Deed Book O, pp. 554-5:

29 April 1859: Murrell W. Oliver and Catherine L., his
wife; and Wm S. Hanna and <u>Nancy</u> V., his wife; * sold to
William Hendrix, for $100.00, their interest in a tract
of land known as part of the mill tract of Hendrix, Oliver
& Co., except the timber trees growing on said land, and
right of way to get to them, and the old mill and fixtures
now standing on said land; to wit: E½ of NE¼ of Sec. 8,
and W½ of NW¼ of Sec. 9, all in T20, R9, containing 160 A.

Compiler's note: There are no witnesses to above deed,
but the makers acknowledged their signatures on same day,
before David Gentry, J. P.

From Deed Book O, pp. 718-22:

6 Feb. 1860. Lucinda Oliver; Murrell W. Oliver, and
Catherine L. E. Oliver, his wife; Wm S. Hanna and <u>Mary</u> V.
his wife; Emily T. Oliver; and Sophronia D. Watson, all
of Perry Co., Ala., for $425.00, convey to Wm Hendrix....
17 A. on the Fikes Ferry Road in Sec. 18, T19, R8, as shown
by the plat attached, with the exception of the undivided
interest in said land of Althea V., wife of Wm Hendrix,
who is equally interested therein with the other heirs of
T. M. Oliver, deceased, and who is entitled to a share of
the purchase money thereof, and whose rights are not in-
tended to be conveyed by this conveyance ... and I,
Catherine L. Oliver, wife of M. W. Oliver, in consideration of $1.00 paid me by Wm Hendrix, release my dower
rights in the above - described premises. ***

Signatures to above deed were acknowledged on 11 Feb.
1860, before L. A. Weisinger, J. P.

* Also referred to as Mary V. Seed deed on pp. 718-22.

** The plat or map mentioned is on p. 721.

From Deed Book F, pp. 483-97:

Compiler's note: There are 13 deeds on these pages,
all involving members of the Hendrix - Oliver family. I
have summarized two as examples:

p. 483. I, M. W. Oliver, administrator de bonis non,
with the will annexed, of Thos. M. Oliver, dec'd, by virtue of an order of the Probate Court of Perry County,
proceeded on the 5th of Dec. 1860, to sell at public auction on the premises of the decedent (Thos. M. Oliver),
lands belonging to his estate, lying in Sec. 18, T19,
R8, on both sides of the Fikes' Ferry Road, bounded on
the west by the lands of said Wm Hendrix, and on the east
by lands purchased by E. T. Oliver at said sale -- in
all 48 A., which was struck off to Wm Hendrix for $886.62.
Dated 28 Dec. 1861.

p. 488. 28 Dec. 1861. I, M. W. Oliver, executor of the
will of Lucinda Oliver, deceased, by virtue of an order of
the Probate Court of this County on 5 Dec. 1860, to sell
lands belonging to the late Lucinda Oliver, at public
outcry, on the premises of Thos. M. Oliver, dec'd ....
sold some of these lands to James Underwood.

Compiler's note: The other deeds are similar to this one
and to other members of the family.

From Will Book B, Perry Co., Ala.:

Will of Lucinda Oliver, dated 4th April 1860, mentions
a son, Murrell W. Oliver, daughters Emily T. Oliver,
Althea V. Hendrix, and Sophronia D. Watson; grandchildren
Mary C., Emma C. and Wm T. Hanna, who are to get what
their mother, Mary V. Hanna would have got.
Witnessed by:
                    S. H. Fowlkes   A. O. Bradley

Probated July 18, 1860.

The will of John Tubb, dated 17 Sept. 1835, and recorded
in Will Book A, pp. 73-76, mentions among other heirs,
a daughter, Lucinda Oliver. This John Tubb was a soldier
of the Revolution.

Minutes of Probate Court, Book L, p. 30⁵:

Sept. 13, 1866. Pinckney B. Lawson is appointed administrator of the estate of Wm Hendrix, dec'd. He
produced in court a written waiver of the right to administer on said estate, signed by Althea V. Hendrix,
Martin T. Hendrix, and Laura H. Parker, the widow and
children of deceased. Lawson gave bond for $50,000,
with Althea V. Hendrix, Martin T. Hendrix, and Laura H.
Parker as his securities. The court appointed the following to appraise the personal property: Samuel H.
Fowlkes, W. B. Lawson, and John Howze.

From Minutes of Probate Court, Book M, p. 62:

p. 62. Aug. 29, 1867. P. B. Lawson, admr. of estate of
Wm Hendrix, filed a petition to sell the land for division among the heirs.

p. 86. October 14, 1867. Samuel H. Fowlkes and M. W.
Oliver testified that the sale of the land is necessary
for a division. Mentions minor heirs.

p. 137. 13 Jan. 1868. Lawson reported land had been
sold.

pp. 171-2. March 30, 1868. P. B. Lawson made a final
settlement of his administration on the estate of William
Hendrix. Martin T. Hendrix was appointed by the court
to act as guardian ad litem of the minors interested in
this settlement. The administrator charged himself with
$15,852.81; and credited himself with $4,190.49; leaving
a balance due the estate of $11,662.32.

Lawson produced vouchers as evidence that he has paid
advancements to the distributees of said estate, who are:
Althea V. Hendrix, the widow; Martin T. Hendrix; Laura H.
Hamner; Bradley Hendrix; Donna Hendrix; Murrell Hendrix;
and Roswell Hendrix -- in all $8797.50; Leaving a bal-
ance of $2864.82 in the hands of said administrator,
who now asks that this be treated as a "Partial" instead
of a "final" settlement.

p. 256. Aug. 15, 1868. The admr. filed another petition
to sell more land. "Such heirs as live in this State
are of full age and have had notice..."

p. 284. Oct. 14, 1868. Hearing of above petition to sell land. Mrs. Laura V. Hamner, one of the heirs who is not a resident of this State, having been "Brought into Court" by publication in the Marion Commonwealth.

p. 342. Dec. 19, 1868. Murrell, Donna and Roswell Hendrix are mentioned as "infant" heirs of this estate.

pp. 390-92. Mar. 12, 1869. P. B. Lawson, admr. of Wm Hendrix, made report of sale of land: John Howze bought the ½ interest in 380 A. Hendrix had owned in T19, R4; also 265 A. east of Cahaba River, known as the Bolling Tract; also 20 A. lying 2 miles E. of Marion .... at 80¢ an acre for all but the 20 A. near Marion, for which he paid $180.00 an A.

Martin T. Hendrix, as guardian of Donna, Roswell, and Murrell Hendrix, purchased the ½ interest that Wm Hendrix had in Lot. No. 9, in Marion, with the building thereon, known as the Howze and Hendrix corner, bounded N. by Green St., East by Washington St., South by the Fiquet lot, and West by E. Duncan's livery stable lot, for $6,200.

M. T. and Bradley Hendrix bought 470 A. at $2.15 an A., in T20, R8.

Fifty shares of stock in the Perry Insurance and Trust Co., also sold at auction, was purchased by people not connected, apparently, with the family; except 20 shares purchased by M. T. Hendrix as guardian of Donna, Murrell and Roswell Hendrix.

From Minutes of Probate Court, Book M, pp. 411-14:

April 13, 1869: Distribution of this estate made to:

1. The widow, Mrs. Althea V. Hendrix. 2. Laura H. Hamner, wife of James Hamner, and dau. of dec'd. 3. Martin T. Hendrix 4. Bradley Hendrix 5. Donna Hendrix, whose gdn. is M. T. Hendrix 6. Murrell W. Hendrix, whose gdn. is M. T. Hendrix 7. Roswell Hendrix

---

From Minutes of Probate Court, Book L, pp. 155-6:

Jan. 5, 1866. Murrell W. Oliver made final settlement and distribution of the estate of Thos. M. Oliver, dec'd. Money divided into 5 equal shares and distributed to:

Murrell W. Oliver; Sophronia D. Watson; Wm Hendrix for his wife, A. V. Hendrix; Emily T. Oliver; and to Wm S. Hanna as gdn. of Mary O., Emma C. and Wm T. Hanna.

Mahan of Bibb County

From Minutes of Probate Court of Bibb Co., Book F:

p. 8. Nov. 12, 1855. Petition of Jesse W. Mahan and Anthony Mahan, administrators of the estate of Edward Mahan, deceased, to sell 2 slaves belonging to said estate.

pp. 19-20. Dec. 3, 1855. Petition of Jesse W. and Anthony Mahan to sell the real estate of Edward Mahan for distribution among the heirs. Notice has been given to the non-resident heirs by publication in the Montevallo Herald; Benj. Stevens to act as gdn. ad litem for the minor heirs.

Edward M. Carleton appointed commissioner to take the testimony of Green B. David and James P. Carson, which testimony sustains the facts set out in the petition. Description of the land, on Mahan's Creek, in Township 24, Range 12, part in Bibb and part in Shelby Co.

From Administrators' Records, Book D:

p. 353. March 10, 1856. Jesse W. Mahan, one of the administrators of the estate of Edward Mahan, filed an account of sale of real estate and personal property. Apparently J. W. Mahan bought all the land for $425.00. Among the purchasers of personal property were: J. W. Mahan, Alfred Galaway, Joseph Ferrington, James Carson. The 1855 cotton crop was sold to P. J. Weaver in Selma. No list of heirs given here.

From Administrators' Accounts, Boo I (eye):

pp. 92-93: 16 March 1859. Final settlement of the estate of Edward Mahan by both administrators. Heirs named:

1. Anthony Mahan, residing in Bibb Co., Ala., Over 21
2. James   "   "   in Texas   "
3. Jesse   "   "   in Bibb Co., Ala.,   "
4. Aquelaus   "   "   in Texas   "
5. Wm C.   "   "   in Bibb Co., "   "
6. Edward   "   "   in Texas   "
7. Elizabeth, wife of Chas. Huffman, both of full age, and residing in Texas
8. Catherine, wife of Thos. E. Meroney, both of full age, and residing in Shelby Co., Ala.

9.   The heirs of John S. Mahan, dec'd, to wit, his dau.,
Nancy, wife of Chas. J. Steward, said Nancy being a minor
and said Charles of full age, and both residing in Bibb
Co., Ala.

10. The heirs of Robt. Mahan, dec'd, to wit: Emily Harvey,
wife of G. B. Harvey, both of full age, and residing in
Miss.

11. The heirs of Nancy Childress, dec'd, to wit:
     a.   Mary, wife of Wm Burns, both of full age and
          residing in Shelby Co., Ala.
     b.   Elizabeth, wife of James Smith, both of full
          age and residing in Miss.
     c.   Frances M. Childress, of full age, and residing
          in Miss.
     d.   Catherine, wife of John Lyles, a minor who
          resides in Bibb Co., Ala.
     e.   John Childress, a minor residing in Bibb Co.
     f.   Wm Childress, a minor, residing in Bibb Co.
12. Mary M. Large, wife of Wiley Large, who is under 21
and resides in Bibb Co., Ala.

     and Mary Mahan, widow of said Edward Mahan, dec'd,
     who is of full age and resides in Bibb Co., Ala.

From Bibb Co. Marriage Record, 1837-50:

p. 43.   Charles A. Huffman to Elizabeth Mahan on 5th Feb.
         1836 by H. Carleton, J. P.

p. 18.   Thos. Maroney to Catherine Mahan on 1st March
         1835 by John Garner, J. P.

         "Feb. 26, 1835. I hereby authorize the Clerk
         of the County Court of the County of Bibb to issue
         marriage license for Thos. Maronia. (Signed:)
                                   Edward Mahan"

         "Anthony Mahan deposeth and maketh oath that
         Edward Mahan whose name is assigned to the within
         certificate authorized the same as his own act..."

p. 27.   Wm Burness to Mary Childres on 31 Dec. 1843,
         by Joshua West, M. G.

From Marriage Record E. (1850 - 1868_:

p. 34.   Wm Meahan to Martha J. Temple. License dated:
         3rd March 1852. No minister's return.

p. 85.   Charles J. Stewart to Nancy R. Mahan
on 19 January by H. P. Griffin ___ ___.

"Jan. 14, 1854. To Probate Judge of Bibb Co.,
Ala. This is to certify that Charles J. Stewart
has by consent of parties concerned obtained
leave to unite in Matrimony with Nancy R. Mahan.
(Signed) Joseph A. Blake, Gdn.:

p. 392.   Wm Childress to Nancy E. Maroney. License
issued 16 May 1866. No minister's return.

p. 162.   Wiley Large to Mary E. Mahan on Oct. 2, 1856,
by N. J. Norris, M. G.

From 1830 Census of Shelby Co., Ala.

    John Mahan:
    1 male 15 - 20   1 female under 5
    1 male 40 - 50   1 "   5 - 10
                          1 "   10 - 15
                          1 "   30 - 40
                          1 "   50 - 60

From Minutes of Probate Court of Bibb Co., Book E:

p. 571. Oct. 1st 1855. Came Jesse W. Mahan and Anthony
Mahan and asked for letters of administration on the
estate of Edward Mahan, late of Bibb Co., who has been
dead more than 40 days. They gave bond for $6500.00 ea.
with Geo. W. Moreland and Cornelius D. McCrimon (?) as
securities.

Ezekiel G. Smith, Joseph Ferington and Green B. Davis
were appointed to appraise the estate of Edward Mahan.

pp. 582-3. Oct. 22, 1855. Description of land owned.
List of heirs same as that on pp. 13 - 14 of this type-
script, except as follows:

    Wm C. Mahan was then of Henry Co., Ala.
    Thos. D. Marona instead of Thos E. Meroney
    Elizabeth, wife of James S. Smith
    Frances M. Childers, residing in Shelby Co., Ala

Catherine Chil<u>ders</u>, under 21, residing in Shelby Co.,
            Ala.
Mary M. Mahan, under 21, residing in Bibb Co., Ala.,
    being a half sister to the full heirs, being a
    daughter of Edward Mahan by his last wife, Polly.

From Minutes of Probate Court, Book C:

pp. 12-13: Came Bird Griffin and Jesse Mahan and
applied for administration on the estate of John Mahan,
dec'd. They gave bond for $6000.00 with Samuel Stanley
and Henley G. Snead (?) as securities. Oct. 1840

Appointed to appraise this estate:

    Henry P. Brodnax   Julius Goodwin   Samuel H. Bogle

p. 17. Dec. 1840. Came Martha Mahan, widow of John
Mahan, dec'd, late of Bibb Co., Ala., and applied in
proper person for guardianship of Thos. J. Mahan, infant
orphan child of John Mahan, dec'd. She gave bond with
Bird Griffin and Lindsey Rucker as her securities.

p. 25. Feb. 1841. Bird Griffin filed an account of
sale of property of John Mahan, dec'd.

p. 74. Feb. 1842. Samuel H. Bogle and Julius Goodwin
filed an account of the sale of land of John Mahan, dec'd.

p. 143. June 1843. Final settlement of estate of John
Mahan by Bird Griffin, admr. Heirs of Mahan are his
widow, Martha, now Martha Blakey, consort of Joseph A.
Blakey, and two orphan children, to wit: Thos. J. Mahan
and Nancy Mahan.

p. 192. Feb. 1844. Bird Griffin, admr. of estate of
John S. Mahan, dec'd, petitioned for sale of Lot No. 23
in Town of Montevallo, formerly belonging to said Mahan.
There are two legatees, Nancy and Thos. J. Mahan, minor
heirs of said John S. Mahan; James Griffin is guardian
of their persons and estates. Joseph A. Blakey, in
right of his wife, Martha, late widow of said John S.
Mahan .... etc.

pp. 278-9. March 17, 1845. Final Settlement of estate
of John S. Mahan by Bird Griffin and Jesse W. Mahan.

There are three heirs to this estate:

Martha Blakey, late Martha Mahan; Nancy Mahan and
Thos. Jefferson Mahan.

From Minutes of Probate Court, Book D:

pp. 12-13: 9 Jan. 1847. James Griffin, gdn. of
Thos. Jefferson and Nancy Mahan, minor heirs of John S.
Mahan, dec'd, reported that Thos. Jefferson Mahan had
died, leaving Nancy Mahan his sole heir. James Griffin
then resigned as gdn. of Nancy Mahan, and Joseph A.
Blakey was appointed her guardian. Blakey gave bond as
gdn. with Sebourn Aycock and Wm Wood as his securities.

As gdn., James Griffin paid Jos. A. Blakey for a coffin
for T. J. Mahan, $5.00; and Paid J. C. Campbell for the
burial expenses, $7.12.

From Deed Book F, p. 63:

16 Oct. 1845. Edward Mahan, for love and affection, to
my wife, Polly, and my daughter, Emiline Mahon, a tract
of land in Bibb and Shelby Counties, on the waters of
Mahan's Creek, bounded on north by lands of Sumner &
Mink, on east by Hoffman's lands, South by Mahon's Creek,
west by the road leading from Montevallo to Selma, leaving
said road near the dwelling and running to Mahan's Creek
near Mahan's old mill, including the dwelling house and
well and the apple orchard on the west side of the road;
also a Negro girl named Mary, about 14 years old, also
all the bedding and household furniture and kitchen furniture; also a good horse or mare, two cows and calves,
one sow and pigs, and sufficient pork for one year's
consumption ... I appoint David Ward trustee for this my
deed of gift. They are to take this property after my
death.

Witnessed by James P. Dennis and Wm Cocke.

From Deed Book F, p. 64:

6 Sept. 1854. Edward Mahan to his daughter, Elizabeth
Hoffman, deed of gift. Land and a Negro. Trustee,
Thos. Marona. Witnessed by James Mahan and Lewis Miree.

From Deed Book F, p. 65:   6 Sept. 1854.

6 Sept. 1854.   Edward Mahan, by deed of gift , to his
daughter, Catherine Maroney, land and a Negro boy.
Trustee, Charles Huffman. Witnessed by James Mahan &
Lewis A. Miree.

From Deed Book G:

pp. 171-?. James Mahan sold to Edward Mahan Sr., for
$50.00, land in T24, R12E, on 16 April 1854. (This deed is
apparently made in Bibb County, Ala., and refers to James
Mahan as "of Bibb Co.", but it is witnessed by James
Woodruff, who acknowledged his signature before Wm H.
Moore, clerk of the Probate Court in Itawambia County,
Miss., on 17th Sept., 1850).

p. 258. 29 Nov. 1851. Edward Mahan, deed of gift to
his son, Jesse Mahan, land on Mahan's Creek.
Witnessed by John W. Mardis and Stephen Splawn.

From Minutes of Orphans' Court, Book D:

pp. 223-4: 19 Sept. 1849. Came Susannah, widow of
James Mahan, dec'd, in her own person, and relinquished
her right to administer the estate of her deceased hus-
band; and the court appointed Peter DeShazo and Edward
C. Seals administrators. They gave bond for $32,000, with
Wm L. Prentice (?) and Jacob Perry (or Peavy) and Geo.
W. Morland as their securities. The court appointed the
following to appraise this estate: Richard Woods, James
Mink, Stephen Splawn, and Jonathan Wone (?).

pp. 226. 29 Sept. 1849. Edward C. Seal resigned as admr.

From Minutes of Probate Court, Book E:

pp. 12-13: Feb. 13, 1852. Final settlement of the
estate of James Mahan by Peter DeShazo. Heirs named:

The widow, Susannah   Mary, wife of Peter DeShazo
Ruth, wife of John Patterson
Elizabeth, wife of Geo. W. Moreland
Elvira, wife of Wm Garner
Desdemona, wife of Edward C. Seal

Compiler's note: See our Volume 1 of this series for
                  notes on Mahan of Perry Co., Ala.

Abston Family of Dallas, Perry and Bibb Counties

No Abston is listed in the 1820 Census of Dallas Co.,
as this is given in Volume 6 of the Ala. Hist. Quarterly.

The 1830 Census of Dallas County lists:

Elijah Abston Sr.:
1 male 20 - 30   1 female 15 - 20
1 male 60 - 70   1 female 20 - 30
                                  1 female 50 - 60
Elijah Abston:
2 males under 5   1 female under 5
2 males 20 - 30   1 female 20 - 30

Allen Abston
1 male under 5   1 female under 5
1 male 5 - 10   1 female 20 - 30
1 male 20 - 30

From Deed Book B, Dallas Co., Ala., pp. 289-90:

1st June 1830. Israel Jessop and Mary his wife, sold
to Elijah Abston, for $150.00, 80 A. in T16, R8. Israel
and Mary Jessop appeared personally before Horatio Gates
Allen and acknowledged their signatures to above deed,
on 4th June 1830.

Compiler's note: The above deed is not indexed.

Deed Book E, Dallas Co., Ala., p. 399:

5th March 1832. John Cleckley, formerly of Dallas Co.,
but now of Shelby Co., Ala., sold to Elijah Abston of
Dallas Co., 80 A. in T16, R8. Witnessed by Thos. Rucker
and W. R. DeShazo.

Lucy Cleckler, wife of John, relinquished her dower
rights in above land on 10th of March, before Thos.
Tucker and W. R. DeShazo, justices of peace in Bibb Co.,
Ala.

Dallas County Marriage Record for 1845-65: p. 171:
June 7, 1855. Wm H. Platt, Rector of St. Paul's Prot.
Epis. Church, married Jos. J. Abston to Louisa J. Jones.
Done in presence of the family of the bride, Thos. Black,
J. Howard and wife, _ ? _ Curtis and others.

From Abstract of Minutes of Probate Court, Vol. 1:

pp. 696-700: Dallas Co., Ala.   p. 696:   Feb. 13, 1843.
Estate of Elijah Abston, dec'd.   The widow relinquished
her right to administer said estate, and Hamblin Kirkland
is appointed admr.   He gave bond for $4000.00.

Sept. 1845. Hamblin Kirkland cited to appear and make
new bond. He failed to appear; his letters of adrm. are
revoked; he is cited to appear and make his final settlement.

p. 697. April 1846. On final settlement, it appears
that the estate is indebted to Hamblin Kirkland in the
sum of $51.44.

Nov. 1846. John F. Conoley is appointed administrator
of the estate of Elijah Abston. He gave bond for $2500.
Conoley petitioned to sell Elijah's land to pay the debts
of the estate. Petitioner represents that Elijah Abston
late of Dalllas Co., died in the year 184_ , intestate,
and that the personal property has been sold by the
former administrator, and same is insufficient to pay
the debts. Deceased owned 160 A. of land in T17, R9 &
R10. His heirs are:
            William Abston, a son, of full age
            Elizabeth Abston, a daughter)
            John Abston, a son   ) these 3 are
            Mary Ann Abston, a dau.   ) minors

and the widow, Nancy, who is entitled to dower in said lands.

Estis Whitted is appointed guardian ad litem to represent the minors at the hearing of this petition.
Publication in the "Selma Reporter".

p. 699. March 1847. The admr. reported to the Court
that on 28 Dec. 1846, he sold the land to Robert Ellison
for $1120.00.

p. 700. Nov. 1845.* There remains $644.23 to be divided
among the four heirs. Each received $159.69 and the
admr. filed their receipts. but the receipts are not
recorded here.

* Compiler's note: I observe a discrepancy in dates.

From Index to Deeds, Perry Co., Ala., Book L:

Elijah Abston and Wife sold to Robt. Moseley, in 1833, land in T18, R9. Deed Book B, p. 347.

Elijah Abston and wife sold to Paschal B. Traylor, land in T18, R9, in 1830. Deed Book B, p. 432.

Note: These are the only deeds recorded in the name of Elijah Abston prior to 1870.

From Perry Co., Ala., Tract Book, p. 21:

Elijah Abston "entered" land in T18, R9, direct from the U. S. Govt., in 1830.

Elijah Abston Jr. "entered" land in T18, R9, in 1832.

No male Abston marriage is recorded in Perry Co. between 1819 and 1863.

From 1850 Census of Bibb Co., Ala.:

304- 04. Wm. R. Abston, age 20, born in Ala.
         Mary   "   22 (?) b. in N. C.
         Wm.   "   3/12 b. in Ala.

307 - 07 Olive Abston   age 55 b. in S. C. female
        John   "   17   b. in Ala.
        Elizabeth Magaha 23   b. in Ala.
        Jos. G. Magaha   2 (or 3) b. Ala.
        Millissa Abston 17   b. Ala.

312 - 12: David Abston, age 16, living with a Lee
            family.

Compiler's note: a client asks for information on Hugh Jones, wife, Lydia White, of Wilkes and Greene Counties, in Ga. He was father of Joseph White Jones (1785-1855) and wife, Rebecca Hightower, and grandfather of Hugh Jones (1809-64), wife Genetta Woolley, both of Bibb Co., Ala. If anyone has this information, please contact the compiler.

Fuller - Harbour Family of Perry County

From Marriage Record of Perry Co., Ala., for 1840-51:

No. 1492. Wm Harbour to Lucinda Nolly (or Nally),
on 12 Oct. 1843 by L. P. Ramsey, J. P.

No. 1646. Samuel P. B. Fuller to Delana Heard. This
license is dated 4 Feb. 1845. Ceremony by Geo. Everett,
M. G., date not shown.

"This is to certify to the clerk of the county court
that S. P. B. Fuller is at liberty (to) obtain marriage
license. A. Fuller".

Compiler's note: S. P. B. Fuller apparently left no
will or estate in Perry Co. Descendants say he did not
die here.

From Orphans Court Record, 1823-32:

p. 35. Nov. 5, 1824. Elizabeth Harbour and Isaiah
Harbour appointed admrs. of the estate of Talman Harbour,
late of this county, dec'd. Court appointed the following to appraise the estate:

Wm Calloway   Thomas Barnett   Benjamin Pearson
Parker Clark   Obed Lovelady

p. 238. Sept. 1831. Isaiah Harbour, one of the admrs.
of Talman Harbour, petitioned court for a sale of
Talman's lands, since these could not be equitably
divided among the heirs. Land described as follows:
NW¼ of Sec. 32, T20, R10, patented to Talman Harbour by
the U. S. Gov't. Heirs of Talman Harbour are:

The widow, Elizabeth, and Nancy Sarah Mary and Jemima
who have intermarried, Nancy with Elijah Skelton; Sarah
with James Varner (or Varnell?); Mary with John Warren;
and Jemima with Michael Hemitor. Also that Thos. Abner
John David and Wm Harbour are over age 21; and that
Elijah Barsheba and Calaway Harbour are under 21; and
all reside in Perry Co., except Elijah Skelton (or
Shelton) who resides in County of Jefferson (State?)
and James Varnum (?) who resides in St. Clair Co. (in
Ala?)

p. 239. Same date, Sept. 1831. Elizabeth Harbour is
aptd. Guardian to defend the rights of Elijah Bashua
and Calaway Harbour, minors of Talman Harbour, dec'd,
in the hearing of Isaiah Talman's petition to sell the
land. She is the mother of these minors. Isaiah is
given leave to take the depositions of Thos. Barnett
and Obed Iovelady, as to the necessity of selling the
land.

p. 256. Feb. 1832. Isaiah Harbour bought the land
for $1550.00

Same volume, p. 42. Feb. 1825. Elizabeth Harbour is
chosen by Abner Harbour, John Harbour, David Harbour
and Wm Harbour, as their guardian, they being minors
over 14 years of age; and the Court also aptd. her gdn.
of Elijah Harbour, Barsheba Harbour, and Calloway
Harbour, minors under 14.

From Minutes of Probate Court, Book B:

p. 28. Dec. 1832. Isaiah Harbour, admr., and Elizabeth
Harbour, admx., of the estate of Talman Harbour, distributed $4549.66 among the following heirs, equally:

    The widow, Elizabeth, and
    1. Isaiah Harbour
    2. Elijah Skelton (Shelton) in right of wife Nancy
    3. John Warren in right of wife Polly
    4. James Varnum in right of wife Sarah
    5. Michael Hemeter in right of wife Jemima
    6. Abner Harbour   7. John Harbour
    8. David Harbour   9. Wm Harbour
    10. Robert Bishop in right of wife Bershaby
    11. Elijah Harbour 12. Callaway Harbour

The last two are minors whose guardian is Elizabeth
Harbour.

Estate of Elizabeth Harbour

From Minutes of Probate Court, Book B:

p. 192. Aug. 1835. David Chandler aptd. admr. of
the estate of Elizabeth Harbour, dec'd. The Court
aptd. the following to appraise her estate: Reuben
Edwards, James Edwards, Thomas Oaks, Reuben Bennett.

From Minutes of Probate Court, Book B:

p. 261. Aug. 1836. The admr. of the estate of Elizabeth Harbour applied for a final settlement. Publication in the Alabama Mercury.

p. 268. Sept. 1836. Joshua B. Crow claimed that
Elizabeth Harbour, in her lifetime, sold him the tract
of land on which she then resided, a quarter-section.

p. 300. Jan 1837. The Court ordered David Chandler,
admr. of Elizabeth Harbour, to give Joshua B. Crow title
to the SW$\frac{1}{4}$ of Sec. 21, T19, R9.

p. 305. Jan. 9, 1837. Final distribution. Each of the
heirs of Elizabeth Harbour received $187.75. Heirs are:
(Punctuation as in the original)

Nancy Sary Polly Thomas Isaiah Abner Maria (or Mina)
William David Elijah Barsheba Calloway and John.

p. 210. Nov. 1835. Elijah Harbour appointed gdn. of
Wm C. Harbour, a minor.

Estate of Wm Harbour

Perry Co., Ala., Minutes of Probate Court, Book L:

p. 317. Sept. 27, 1866. D. H. Smith granted letters of
administration on the estate of Wm Harbour, dec'd, late
an inhabitant of this County, who died in this County
more than 40 days ago. Smith gave bond for $5000.00 with
Ephraim Q. Heard, Joseph Airely and E. T. Harbour as his
securities.

p. 380. Nov. 29, 1866. Came D. H. Smith, admr. of Wm
Harbour, praying that dower be assigned to Lucretia, the
widow of said William. Land in T19, R10.

From Minutes of Probate Court, Book M:

p. 36. June 10, 1867. 160 A. of Wm Harbour's lands
are allotted to Lucretia as her dower. Commissioners
who were appointed by the court to allot her dower were:

A. J. B. Suttle   John W. Suttle   A. G. (or A. C.) Guyse
            John W. Melton   A. J. Mahan

David H. Smith is administrator.

From Minutes of Probate Court, Book N, p. 137:

May 9, 1870. Final Settlement of the estate of Wm Harbour by D. H. Smith, admr. G. W. Watters served as guardian ad litem of the minor heirs. The expenditures of the admr. exceeded the amount he received as admr. The heirs received nothing; no list of heirs.

Compiler's note: There are about 9 Harbour deeds prior to 1840.

From 1850 Census of Perry Co., Perryville Beat:

House and family No. 25:

Samuel P. B. Fuller	age 22	born in Ala.
Delany "	22	"
Jesse S. "	4	"
Thos. A. "	2	"

Plantersville Beat, House & Family No. 58:

Alfred Fuller	age 66	born in N. C. farmer
	val of real estate $8800.00	
Susannah "	age 50	born in Ga.
Joseph A. "	21	born in Ala.
Lexington Y. Fuller	17	"
Blake J. "	15	"
Cynthia J. "	13	"
James M. "	11	"

and living with this family, Samuel Daniel, upholsterer, age 32, b. in N. Y.

Also listed in Plantersville Beat in 1850 is

Samuel Fuller	age 25	born in Ala.
Delena "	27	"
Samuel W. J.	3	"
Thos.	1	"

Perryville Beat, House and Family No. 23:

William Harbour	age 40	born in Ga.
Lucretia "	30	"

William, age 14, Nancy Jane, age 12; Elisha T., 10; Christopher age 6; John R., age 4; Ezekial, age 3 --- all born in Ala.

Harris - Watts Family

From Monroe Co., Ala., Marriage Record for 1833 - 1908:

p. 41. Thos. R. Watts to Mary Tiller on 7th Feb. 1838,
by H. Schroebel, M. G. Bondsman: Jesse O. Rawls.

p. 82. Vincent Watts to Martha Ann Harris
Jan 19, 1843. Bondsman, R. S. Watts

p. 229. Vinson T. Watts to Frances Myrick
on Oct. 13, 1861

Monroe Co., Ala., Deed Book A, pp. 367-71: Deed of
trust from Thos R. Watts and wife Mary H. to John L.
Marshall. Lots No. 250 and 251 in Claiborne, on Monroe
St., known as The Tavern or Washington Hotel. Dated:
24 Aug. 1838.
Witnessed by James B. Harris and John W. or M. McClure.

Monroe Co., Ala., Inventory A, p. 338: The Court aptd.
comrs. to lay off the dower of Mrs. Amanda Harris, being
one-third of the real estate of her former husband,
Richardson Foster. Her present husband is Chas. F.
Harris. Dated April 24 1828.

Compiler's note: There may be other Watts - Harris
papers in this volume, which has no index.

Monroe Co., Ala. Order Book No. 1, p. 284: Feb. 1844:
Thomas R. Watts is gdn. of Sarah Jane (Or Mary Jane)
Watts, a minor. (No index to this volume either)

From Wills and Deeds, Book A, pp. 355-6:

30 Nov. 1836. Deed of Mortgage from James B. Harris of
Simpson Co., Ky., to Joseph Lindsey of Monroe Co., Ala.,
to Lots. No. 250 and 251 in the Town of Claiborne, known
as The Tavern premises, fronting on Monroe St., being
the premises conveyed to James M. Lindley by Ward Taylor
by deed dated April ___ 1836. (Signed) Jas. B. Harris.
Witnessed by J. C. Dumas, Stephen Steele.

James B. Harris Personally acknowledged his signature to
the above on 3 June 1838, before James Cauldfield, J. P.
in Monore Co., Ala. Thos. R. Watts was a party to one
of the promissory notes mentioned in the above deed. I
found no other deed in name of James B. Harris, prior to
1850.

Dallas Co., Ala., Deed Book A, p. 339:

Charles Watts, a sargent of Capt. Joseph J. Clinch's
Co., 7th Reg. of Infantry, who enlisted 21 Sept. 1814
to serve 5 years, is hereby honorably discharged from
the Army of the U. S., his time of service having ex-
pired. Said Charles was born in Winchester Co., Tenn.,
is 19 years old, 5 ft. 8 in. high, dark complexion,
dark eyes, dark skin, and by occupation when enlisted,
a farmer. Given at Ft. Scott, Ga., 20 Sept. 1819.
Signed: J. J. Clinch, Capt. 7th Inf.
        W. N. Bronaugh, Lt.

From Min. of Orphans Court of Dallas Co., Ala.:

Book D, p. _?_. Oct. 9, 1837. Came John Watts and
asked to be appointed guardian of Elizabeth, Celia, and
Frances Watts, minor heirs of Charles Watts, late of
Ky., dec'd. He gave bond with Jeremiah Watts and Thos.
Watts as his securities.

Book D, p. 1. Jan 26, 1836. Came Jeremiah Watts, son
and heir of Mrs. Hannah R. Raburn, deceased, and asked to
be appointed administrator of the estate of said dec'd.
He gave bond for $15,000.00 with Thos. Watts and John
Sorrell as his securities.

Philip Milhous, James Hunter, Abram Matthews, Abner
Stone and Thos. Hardin were appointed to appraise the
personal property belonging to Hannah's estate.

Same Vol., p. 68. Nov. 1836. To the Judge of the County
Court of Dallas Co., Ala.: Your petitioner, Jeremiah
Watts of Butler Co., Ala., respectfully represents unto
your honor that sometime in January 1836 Hanna R.
Raburn of Dallas Co. died and that he (Jeremiah) was
appointed administrator of her estate .... and that she
owned the NW$\frac{1}{4}$ of SW$\frac{1}{4}$ of Sec. 20, T15, R11, and that said
land cannot be fairly divided among the heirs without a
sale thereof. The heirs are:

1. Thomas Watts   2. Vinson Watts   3. John H. Watts

4. Josiah Watts   and 5. Jeremiah Watts (the admr.)

who are the sons of Hannah Raburn now living ...

6. Thos. R. Watts; Margaret, wife of James Harris; Jesse Watts; John B. Watts; Rumsey S. (or L.) Watts; Keziah, wife of Wm Earnest; Elizabeth A. Watts; Celia Watts; and Frances Watts -- all children of Charles Watts, now dead, another son of Hannah R. Raburn

7. Polly, wife of John Sorrell; Celia, wife of Samuel Ansley; John Watts; Vinson Watts, Ludwell Watts, and Agnes Watts, children of Finetty (or Finetly) Watts

8. Starling Ansley; John Ansley; Pamela (Ansley), wife of David Sears; and Elizabeth Ansley -- who are the children of Elizabeth Ansley.

of the above-named heirs, the following live without the limits of this State: viz:

All the children of Charles Watts, except Thos. R. Watts, who live in Kentucky; and

John W. Ansley, Elizabeth Ansley, and David Sears with his wife Permelia, who live in Georgia.

Permelia Sears, Margaret Harris, and Keziah Earnest are "femmes covert".

The following are minors: Elizabeth A., Celia, and Frances Watts.

Same Volume, p. 161: Oct. 1837. Final settlement & distribution of the estate of Hannah R. Raburn. Amount for distribution: $12,814.40, which was divided as follows:

1. One-sixth to John H. Watts
2. " to Thos. Watts
3. " to Vincent Watts
4. " to Josiah Watts
5. " to Jeremiah Watts
6. " to the heirs of Charles Watts, to be divided into 9 equal parts and paid to:

   Thos. R. Watts; James Harris and his wife, Margaret; John Watts; Rumsey Watts; William Earnest and his wife Keziah; Elizabeth Watts; Celia Watts and Frances Watts.

Compiler's note: This document does not mention the Ansley's or the Sears.

From the 1850 Census of Dallas Co., Ala., Cahaba Beat:
House and Family No. 589:

    M. J. Harris   age 49   female   born in Ga.
    Josaphine B. Harris, age 10   "   Ala.

From old catalogs of Judson College, Marion, Ala.:

For the year ending July 7th 1853, Josephine Bell
Harris is listed; name of parent or guardian is not
given; address is Dallas County, Ala. In the year ending 1855, Josephine Bell Harris is still "of Dallas Co."
In the catalog for the year ending July 1856, her address is
given as Marion, and Mrs. R. Wiley is named as guardian.
In the catalog for the years 1859 and 1860, her name is
still listed as Miss Josephine Bell Harris; her address
is given as Mississippi. In the catalog for the year
ending June 1861, she is listed among the alumnae as
Mrs. Cotten; address, Miss. (Carthage added in pencil).

Compiler's note: I infer that her mother, Margaret Jane,
must have died 1855-56.

Will of Thos. Watts, from Will Book A, Dallas Co., Ala.:

p. 174. 27 Sept. 1838. Mentions wife, Sarah; a son,
Simeon Andrew Watts; a dau., Julia Ann Watts; a son,
Edward T. Watts. Some land in Lowndes Co., Ala.
Witnessed by James Pylant, Jesse Pylant,
              Margaret Pylant; Reuben Saffold.
Proved, Oct., 1840.

From Dallas Co., Ala., Marriage Record for 1818-45:

p. 303. Henry J. Crocheron to Miss Julia A. Watts on
      12 Feb. 1841, by Robt. Carson, O. M. G.

p. 183. Edward T. Watts to Louisa M. Todd, on
      10 Dec. 1840, by Jesse Hartwell, M. G.

Dallas Co,, Ala., Deed Book E, p. 80: Thos. Watts Sr.
of Dallas Co., Ala., sold to Thos. Watts Jr., living on
Mush Creek in Dallas Co., land described as S$\frac{1}{2}$ of Sec.
18, T16, R9. This deed witnessed by Edward Watts,
John Terry, and Thos. H. Watts. The wife of Thos. Watts
Sr., is not mentioned.

The deed which shows purchase of this piece of property
is as follows:

Dallas Co., Ala., Deed Book E, pp. 79-80. State of
South Carolina. We, Thos. Lee and James Jervey of the
City of Charleston, trustees of the individuals at pre-
sent composing the Alabama Co., of South Carolina, sell
to Thos. Watts Sr., the S½ of Sec. 18, T16, R9, in Dallas
Co., Ala.   12 Nov. 1835

From same Vol. pp. 207-9: 7th April 1836: Thomas
Watts Jr. and Sarah, his wife, sold to Thos. Craig,
the S½ of Sec. 18, T16, R9,   349.20A

Thos. Watts and Sarah, his wife, appeared personally
before James D. Craig, Clerk of the County Court of
Dallas Co., Ala., on 10 Sept. 1836, in Cahaba, and
acknowledged their signatures to this deed.

From 1860 Census of Dallas Co., Ala.:

Town of Selma, house no. 565, family No. 663:

Edward T. Watts	age 45	farmer	born in Ga.
Louisa M. "	35		"
Ella T. "	16		born in Ala.
Althea C. "	11		"
Wm. W. "	10		"
James "	3		"
Murry "	1		"

From Perry Co., Ala., Marriage Record, 1820-32:

p. 14, No. 27: Robert Smith to Ruthy Hunter on
                9 Aug. 1820, by Chas. Crow, M. G.

Will of Mrs. Ruthy Wiley from Will Boo B, Perry Co.,
Ala., pp. 64-69:

Mentions: Daughter, Mary Ann Tarrant; daughter, Sarah
R. Holman; son John S. Smith; son Moses Wiley;
grandson, Joseph W. Smith. Executor, John S. Smith

Dated: 8th Jan, 1859. Withessed by F. A. Bates
                                        J. G. Huckabee

Proved by John G. Huckabee and F. A. Bates on
          17 Sept. 1859.

Elliott - Maroney - Mahan - Nabors
of Shelby County

Compiler's note: My notes on these families are not
as well organized as I should like them to be. This is
due to the fact that the records of Shelby are very hard
to get at; and not in sequence; and I took them as I
could find them.

From Deed Book A - E (transcribed)

p. 76. Autauga Co., Ala. Peyton Bibb, admr. of James
Sanders Walker, dec'd, of Autauga Co., Ala., sold to
Abraham Neighbors of Shelby Co., Ala., the E½ of NE¼ of
Sec. 8, T21, R3W, on 6th March 1826.

Peyton Bibb acknowledged his signature to the above deed
before Joab Lawler, Judge of the Shelby Co. Court.

p. 77. Abraham Nabors sold the east half of theabove
tract to Wm Crowson.

p. 172. David Crowson and Penelope, his wife, of
Shelby Co., Ala., sold to Andrew Harkins of same, all
his title and claim to land in T22, R2W, being the farm
Richard Crowson owned at the time of his death.
Dated 8 Aug. 1827. Witnessed by: Thos. Payne, J. P.
James Edge, J. P., Henry W. Wilson, Wm West and
            Thos. L. Bailey

p. 176. Thos. Crowson and Mary, his wife, of Shelby
Co., sold to Andrew Harkins, all their title and claim
to the farm owned by Richard Crowson in his lifetime.
Same witnesses as above.

p. 463. 1st June 1827. Moses Crowson and Martha, his
wife, sold to John Lawley, land in T12, R3W, 29 A., conveyed to Moses Crowson by U. S. patent recorded in
the land office at Tuscaloosa, Vol. 2, p. 310.
Witnessed by Richard C. Ryans, John Nabors.

Moses Crowson acknowledged his signature to above deed
before Leonard Tarrant, Judge of the County Court, on
same date.

p. 467. 25 Jan. 1828. Moses and Martha Crowson sold
more land to John Lawley.

p. 480. Perry Co., Ala. Aaron Crowson of Perry Co.,
Ala., sold to John Mahan of Shelby Co., Ala., his
interest in the farm which Richard Crowson owned at the
time of his death. Dated 16 Nov. 1830.
Witnessed by James W. Corley (?) J. P. in Perry Co., &
by Samuel Murry, J. P.

p. 481. 24 Aug. 1827. Elias Pitner and Sarah, his wife,
sold to John Mahan of Perry Co., Ala. Witnessed by:
Thos. Payne, James Edge, Henry H. Wilson.

(Rhoda Crowson, wife of Aaron, joined in the deed on
page 480; date of her signature is 16 Dec. 1831)

pp. 482-3. 19 Nov. 1828. Wm Crowson and Catherine, his
wife, sold to John Mahan, also of Shelby Co., their
claim to the farm owned by Richard Crowson in his lifetime.
Witnessed by Thos. Payne and Thos. H. Arnold, J. P.'s.

p. 484. Not dated. Asa A. Billingslea and Margaret H.,
his wife, deed to John Mahan, the farm Richard Crowson
owned in his lifetime.

p. 485. 17 Nov. 1828. John Crowson and Annis, his wife,
to John Mahan, their claim to the Richard Crowson farm.

p. 253. Robt. Fulton and Hulda, his wife, of Shelby Co.
sold to Andrew Harkins, their title to the farm Richard
Crowson owned in his lifetime. Dated: 8 Aug. 1827.
Witnessed by Thos. Payne, J. P. James Edge, J. P.
Henry H. Wilson, Wm West, Thos. L. Bailey

p. 286. 4 Aug. 1829. Wm Ellett to Bryant Rushing.
On Waxahatchie Creek.

p. 639. 19 March 1834. Allen Elliott of Shelby Co.,
and Margaret, his wife, to Kenneth L. Morrison of
Richmond Co., N. C., ... Witnessed by Wm M. Johnson, Clk.

p. 646. Samuel Fulton and Elizabeth, his wife, to
Joseph Hancock, land in T22, R3W, patented to John
Parson(s) and conveyed by Parsons to David Fletcher,
and by said Fletcher to Samuel Fulton. 29 Oct. 1833.
Test.: Joseph Noble, Wm Pitts.

p. 19. Bill of sale from Joseph Hale to Amos Elliott, for a Negro man named Garrett, 50 years old, and a Negro woman, Charlotte, wife of said Garrett, both slaves, for $600.00. Witnessed by John Cary, and Ann Hale.

Joseph Hale acknowledged his signature to the above bill of sale before Joab Lawler, Clerk of the County Court, on Dec. 1st, 1823.

Also on 28 May 1823, Joseph Hale sold Amos Elliott tin Stills for $170.00.

p. 20. Joseph Hale sold to Amos and William Elliott, all his title, legal right, and interest in certain live-stock, household and kitchen furniture. Not dated. Witnessed by John Carey (?) and Ann Hale. Joseph Hale acknowledged his signature to this deed on 1st June (?) or 1st January 1823.

p. 21. Joseph Hale sold to Wm Elliott for $500.00 a Negro woman 21 years old. 28 Oct. 1822. Witnessed by: Ann Hale, John Carey

p. 21. 31 Oct. 1824. Bond of James Nabors as Tax Assessor and Collector of Shelby Co. Securities: Martin and Green McLeroy. Approved April 5, 1824, by Thos. W. Smith, J. C. C.

p. 77. Abraham Nabors to Wm Crowson, 6 March 1826.

p. 197. Arthur Nabors and wife Sally, to David Mere-dith, on 11 Feb. 1828.

p. 212. 25 June 1825. James M. Nabors, Sheriff of Shelby County, sold lands belonging to Jacob Vanderbilt, to satisfy his creditors, who are:

> Thos. W. Smith, surviving partner of Warren & Smith
> Loftin Quinn

James W. Smith bought the lands.

Compiler's note: There are numerous other deeds in this volume in the name of James M. Nabors, Sheriff. It seems unlikely that these would contain family data.

p. 227. 5 Feb. 1829. Roda Maroney sold to Sarah Mc-Clain, for $2000.00, seven Negro slaves. Names and ages of the Negroes are given. Roda acknowledged her signa-ture to this document before Levi Lawler, on 16 Feb. 1829.

p. 228. To John Murphy, Governor of Ala. Bond of
Abraham Nabors, Assessor and Tax Collector of Shelby
County, for 1829. Securities:

Henry Couch   Samuel W. McClanahan   Jonathan McDavid

p. 549. 16 Feb. 1829. Samuel and Allen Nabors to
Thomas Arnold. Witnessed by Thos. Arnold, Benj. Wilson.

p. 101. Patent from U. S. to Thos. Lindsey. Land in
T22, R2W, 160 A. 10 April 1824. James Estill, clerk of
the County Court.

From Deed Record F - G, transcribed:

p. 150. Richard W. Crowson, of Talladega Co., Ala.,
sold to John Mahan, his claim to the farm Richard
Crowson owned in his lifetime. Dated 3 Nov. 1835.

p. 732. 31 Dec. 1840. Amos Elliott and Nancy, his
wife, to Ewel S. Harrison. Witnessed by Samuel Wallace
and John Elliott. Noel Mason, Clerk of County Court.

p. 191. 18 Aug. 1837. Indenture between John Lovelady
of the first part, and James M. Nabors and Wm J. Peters
of the second part, and Daniel E. Watrous of the third
part. Whereas, John Lovelady is indebted to the Branch
Bank of Alabama at Montgomery, for $550.00 and Nabors
and Peters are his securities for said debt ... Deed of
trust to Watrous, to indemnify the securities.

p. 211. 27 April 1819. Elizabeth Lucus and J. (or T.)
Underwood, sold to John Crowson, 4 Negroes for $1600.00.
Witnessed by Benj. Frost and William Blevins.
Signatures attested by Benj. Frost before George Phillips
chief justice of the Orphans Court of Shelby Co., Ala.,
on 12 Nov. 1819.

p. 5. 31 March 1834. Harrison V. Nabors of Montevallo,
in Shelby Co., Ala., mortgage to J. and W. Camerson,
now of Jefferson Co., Ala. Witness: John Edmondson.
Harrison V.Nabors acknowledged his signature to above
before Wm Cameron, J. P., in Shelby Co., on 12 May 1834.

Compiler's note: This volume is transcribed from an
older record. It would be advisable for persons
wanting photostatic copies to get these from the older
record, which was not accessible at the time I made
these notes.

Shelby Co., Ala., Minutes of Probate Court, 1852-56:

p. 21. The heirs of Mary Haney, dec'd, vs. B. F.
Randall, admr. of Amos Elliott, dec'd. Motion for
judgment "nunc pro tunc". Came the parties by their
attorneys, and it appearing to theCourt that on the
final settlement of the estate of Amos Elliott, the heirs
of Mary Haney were in right of their mother entitled to
$204.11, and it also appearing that $100.00 of this has
been paid ... Court ordered that the balance be paid to
said heirs, namely: (Dated 1852)

    J. J. Bains and his wife, Louisa; Thomas Davis and
his wife Martha; Charles W. Haney; John W. Haney; Mary J.
Haney; and William Haney.

p. 71. 23 Dec. 1852. Ordered by the Court that notice
be issued to L. F. Elliott, alias Dock Elliott, constable, to execute new bond as such.

p. 74. 3 Jan. 1853. L. F. Elliott, constable, having
failed to execute new bond, his office is vacated ...

p. 71. 23 Dec. 1852. Ordered that William Elliott, gdn.
of Farren Elliott, minor son of Amos Elliott, dec'd,
have special leave to sell and transfer land warrant No.
8407 to him as gdn. aforesaid, on 17 June 1851, and his
acts in sale of same are ratified by Court.
J. M. McClanahan, Judge.

p. 232. 10 Jan. 1854. Came Bennett M. Elliott, admr.
of the estate of Joseph M. Brinker, dec'd, and petitions
for a sale of real estate belonging to said Brinker, in
order to make distribution among the heirs. Notice of
hearing of this petition to issue to Lavinia (?) S.
Brinker, the widow of dec'd. Samuel H. Johnson aptd.
gdn. ad litem of the minor children of dec'd, to represent them at the hearing. Names of these children:

    Wm J. Brinker   Martha L. Brinker   Ann E. Brinker

p. 233. 17 July 1854. Parthenia Elliott tendered his
resignation as admr. of the estate of Cornelius Elliott,
dec'd, and Hudson W. Nelson, Sheriff, by virtue of his
office, is appointed administrator of Cornelius, in his
stead.

p. 234. 20 July 1854. H. W. Nelson, as administrator de bonis non of the estate of Cornelius Elliott, filed petition for sale of the real estate.

p. 268. Above petition is granted. No list of heirs.

p. 397. Sept. 17, 1855. H. W. Nelson, apptd. admr. in chief of the estate of Cornelius Elliott, gave bond for $2000.00 with Jno. N. Cahill and W. F. Bevill (?) as his securities.

Same volume, p. 90. 6th March 1853. Blassingame Nabors filed his accounts for a partial settlement of the estate of Allen Nabors, dec'd.

p. 104. 9th May 1853. Blassingame Nabors filed his accounts for a final settlement of the estate of Allen Nabors, Wm H. Moore appointed gdn. ad litem to represent the minor heirs of said Allen; namely:

Sarah, William, Hugh and David Nabors.

pp. 199-200. April term 1854. Blassingame Nabors made distribution of the estate of Allen Nabors to the following heirs: The widow, Ann, and children:

     1. Eliza, wife of M. L. Bealer)
     2. Sara, wife of ____ Lee   )   Children and
     3. James Nabors   )   heirs at law
     4. William Nabors   )
     5. Hugh Nabors   )
     6. David Nabors   )

Compiler's note: Correction: The name of Hugh Nabors should be listed before that of William, above.

p. 309. 1st Jan. 1855. Blassingame Nabors filed the receipts of the heirs of Allen Nabors for their shares of his estate. Ann Nabors gave receipt for herself; also for the four minor children, namely, William, David, James and Hugh; also for Sarah Lee. All the receipts were witnessed by James P. Allen.

p. 73. 3 Jan. 1853. Caroline M. and Ezekiel T. Nabors are appointed administrators of the estate of James M. Nabors, dec'd.

From Minutes of Probate Court, Shelby Co., Ala.:
Book for 1852-56:

p. 248. Caroline M. and Ezekiel T. Nabors, admrs. of
the estate of James M. Nabors, petition to sell the
real estate. John H. Nabors, one of the legatees, is
a non-resident of this State. Wm G. Perry is aptd.
to represent the minor heirs of Nabors at the hearing
of this petition. Minor heirs are: Nancy C., Matilda
F., Paralee R., Louisa J., and James M. Nabors.

p. 263. 24 Sept. 1854. Hearing of above petition.
French Nabors and G. Galloway made oath that it is
necessary to sell the land, which is in T24, R12E.

p. 312. 3 Jan 1855. Caroline M. Nabors aptd. gdn.
of her minor children: Nancy C., Matilda F., Paralee R.,
Louisa J., and James M. Nabors.

Shelby Co., Ala., Will Book K:

p. 18. Benjamin F. Randall, admr. of the estate of
Amos Elliott, dec'd, filed the receipts of the 17 heirs
for their shares of said estate:

1. Amos H. Elliott, one of the children of Amos Elliott
   Jr., dec'd. $50.00. June 9th 1854 (or 1851)*

2. C. B. Elliott (by A. M. Elliott), one of the ch.
   of Amos Elliott Jr., dec'd. $50.00.
   9th June 1854 or 1851.

3. George Elliott   9th June 1854. $202.09

4. Frances Nelson, in right of his wife, $202.09

5. Simpson Nelson, in right of his wife, $202.09
   (by his attorney in fact, Francis Nelson)

6. Nancy and Starling Baker for $200.00, the share of
   Jefferson Elliott, one of the minor heirs. (This
   receipt signed by Francis Nelson.)

7. Rec'd of B. F. Randall, admr. of Amos Elliott, dec'd,
   $200.00, the distributive share of Miley (?) Elliott,
   one of the minor heirs of said estate. Signed:
   Nancy and Starling Baker, by Francis Nelson.
   9th June 1854.

*Bad handwriting. Can't be sure whether the date is
1851 or 1854. This is true for all these receipts.

8. Jan. 15, 1850 (?). Receipt of Jonathan Clowar
    for his portion, $200.00

9. 19 May 1851 or 54. John Elliott's receipt for
    $200.00, as one of the heirs at law.

10. Montivallo, Feb. 22, 1854 or 1851. Recieved of
    B. F. Randall, admr. of Amos Elliott, $100.00.
    (Signed) George Haney in right of his wife, Mary,
    as a portion of her legacy. (Allen Elliott's name
    signed below George Haney's.)

11. John Rogers in right of his wife, Jane, $202.09.

12. Nancy Baker gave receipt for their share, due the
    widow. Witness: Willis Ellit.

13. Receipt of John Elliott for $2.09 (sic).

14. Receipt of Amos and Elizabeth Merrill, dated
    9th June 1851 or 1854.

15. Receipt of Hardy S. Melson or Nelson, for $202.09,
    dated 9 June 1854 or 51.

16. William Elliott's receipt for $202.09, same date.

17. Allen Elliott's receipt, $202.09, same date.

18. Allen Elliott, one of the minor heirs of Chas.
    Elliott, dec'd, $202.09.

19. Miles (?) Elliott, receipt by Wm Elliott, for
    $202.09. June 9, 1854 (?)

20. J_____ Elliott $202.09, June 9th 1854, receipt.

Compiler's note: There are 20 receipts instead of the
17 mentioned above.

S. Leaper witnessed several of the above receipts. He
himself gave a receipt for $50.00: "Received of B. F.
Randall, admr. of Amos Elliott, in full of my fee in
said estate, for collecting and fees in preparing
settlements."

Compiler's note: I have listed the amount each heir
received, since this helps to determine the relationship of the heirs to deceased; which is nowhere stated.

Shelby Co., Ala., Will Book K.   Estate of Cornelius
Elliott:

pp. 424-30. These are papers relating to the petition to sell land, filed by Hudson W. Nelson, admr.
Description of land to be sold: Heirs named:

The widow, Parthena Elliott, and children:

1. Narcissa K. Elliott, over 21, res. in
   Shelby Co.

2. S. J. (or S. G.) Elliott, over 21, res. in
   Shelby Co.

3. Joshua W. Elliott, over 21, Shelby Co.

4. Mary Ann, wife of Willis G. McClinton,
   over 21, res. in Shelby Co.

5. Johns (or Jabus or Jabez) Elliott, who res.
   in Louisiana. (I think Jabez)

6. Elizabeth J., wife of Alisander J. Moore; also
   a non-resident of this State.

7. Martha Elliott, a minor, not a res. of Ala.

8. Louisa Elliott, between the age of 14 and 21,
   who res. in Shelby Co. with her mother.

One witness testified that Josaphine, wife of Alexander
J. Moore resides in Louisiana. One document states
that Martha, under 21, resides in Louisiana. Another
witness thought Martha was of age.

Another witness testified that Cannon and Jefferson
Elliott, heirs of Cornelius, res. in Shelby Co.

Compiler's note: If there was a date on this document,
I failed to record it. Estimate: Prior to 1852.

Also from Will Book K: p. 53. Bond of Blassingame
Nabors as gdn. of the estate of Blassingame H. Nabors,
minor of Allen Nabors. Security: Ira Nabors. Dated:
13 Feb. 1852.

p. 54. 24 March 1852. Bond of Ann Nabors as gdn. of
James M., Sarah A., Hugh, Wm M. and David A. Nabors,
minor ch. of Allen Nabors, dec'd. Securities: David
Meredith and Wm H. Moore. James M. and Sarah A. are
over 14 years.

Shelby Co., Ala., Final Record 3 (1894).
Estate of James L. Elliott:

p. 28. To Hon. John S. Leeper, Judge of Probate: The
petition of C. C. Elliott to be appointed administrator
of the estate of James L. Elliott, who died at Vincent,
Ala., 9th Feb. 1894, leaving no will; but he left an
estate in this County worth about $4000.00. His heirs
are his widow, Mrs. J. L. Elliott; J. E. Elliott and
C. C. Elliott, all of Vincent, Ala.; and Mrs. D. N.
Kidd, wife of D. N. Kidd, of Harpersville, Ala.; all
the heirs are over 21. The petitioner, C. C. Elliott
is also an heir.

p. 30. List of open accounts belonging to this estate
includes the name of C. M. Elliott.

List of notes and mortgages includes one of C. B. Elliott Jr.
due 15 Oct. 1888, and one from W. T. (?) Elliott. Appraisal of this estate made by G. W. Clements, C. F. Elliott, and
W. H. Kidd, on May 2, 1894.

Also from Final Record 3, Estate of French Nabors:

pp. 248-57. French Nabors died at Montevallo on
29 June 1896. The widow, Sarah E. Nabors and son-in-
law, E. S. Lyman, were appointed admrs. Other heirs
named are:

1. F. May Lyman, wife of E. S. Lyman, Montevallo

2. French Nabors Jr.

3. Lewis N. Nabors

4. Burr Nabors, a minor over 14, Birmingham, Ala.

5. Welton Nabors, minor over 14, Montevallo.

Also from Final Record 3:

pp. 455-7: 10 Feb. 1896. James McGowen's petition to
be appointed gdn. of Willie and Mary Elliott, minor
female children of Hugh W. and Virginia Elliott; both
of whom are over 14, and have a living father who is
not a proper person to act as their guardian, on account of his health and mental condition.

Same volume, p. 527. 11th Nov. 1898. J. R. Taylor's
petition to be appointed guardian of W. A. Elliott,
whose father died leaving a widow and several children.
Said minor has an estate in her own right, and J. R.
Taylor is a friend and neighbor.

From Final Record 4 (1899), p. 421. 14 Oct. 1903.
B. H. Smothers' petition to be appointed admr. of est.
of Maggie Elliott, who died in April 1900. No list of
heirs in this document.

From Will Book E, Estate of Amos Elliott:

p. 266. 15 Feb. 1849. Wm G. Bowden Judge of Probate,
Starling C. Baker and Nancy (Elliott) Baker, his wife,
relinquished their life-time estate in the personal property of Amos Elliott, dec'd. Amos left a will. This
estate appraised by:

        John W. Teague   Wm Strain   George Farr

p. 267. Slaves belonging to this estate were purchased
by:

        Starling Baker   Hardy Nelson   Leonard Bullock
            William McPherson   Kennon Wells   Marshall Smith
                        Green Elliott

B. F. Randall, admr. (Handwriting here is plain).

pp. 267-8: In return for the above relinquishment of
Starling and Nancy Baker, the other heirs agree to let
her *bid off* at the sale, without cost, a Negro woman,
Bias, and her child. This agreement signed by:

    Willis Elliott   William Elliott   Allen Elliott
    John Rodgers   J. S. Clowers   G. M. Elliott
    G. W. Elliott   Hardy Nelson   S. (?) S. Elliott
    Amos Merrel (?)   Francis Nelson

p. 478. 6th Sept. 1850. Bond of Starling and Nancy
Baker as gdns. of Jefferson and Willie (?) Elliott.
Security: John C. Hannah.

p. 529. 29 March 1851. James M. Finley, admr. of
Amos Elliott, dec'd, reports that no property belonging to said estate has yet come into his hands.

Shelby Co., Ala., Will Book E:

p. 276. 3rd April 1848. Rec'd of Blassingame Nabors, guardian for my wife, Elizabeth, formerly Elizabeth Teague, the full amount due. Signed: James Baker.

pp. 487-92. Papers relating to estate of Allen Nabors. The minors are: James, age 19; Sarah, age 16; Hugh, age 12; William age 10; and David, age 8.

p. 492. Court appointed Chas. B. Elliott commissioner to take evidence as to the title to lands of Allen Nabors.

From Will Record H, pp. 766-70. Dates from 1862 to 1864. Mary Elliott, and James L. Elliott were admrs. of the estate of William Elliott. Heirs named.

The widow and: Bennet W. Elliott; William Elliott; John P. Elliott, James L. Elliott; Elizabeth, wife of Chas. F. Elliott; Ann Perry, dec'd; Martha Ann E. Brinker, wife of Calvin Thom___ (evidently something omitted here.)

J. V. R. Perry is guardian of Ann Perry's children. The oldest heir is 49; age of youngest heir not known.

pp. 904-5. Bond of Amos Elliott, as general guardian for Shelby Co. His securities: (Dec. 30, 1864)

    A. A. Sterrett   H. S. Nelson   J. T. Leeper
                J. L. Elliott
Napoleon B. Mardis, Judge of the Probate Court.

Will Book H, pp. 397-706: Papers relating to the minors, David, William, Hugh, Louisa J., James M., and Parolee R. Nabors.

Compiler's note: I did not read all of these. One of interest:

p. 401. 11 April 1860. E. T. Nabors, admr. of estate
of J. M. Nabors, dec'd, represents that decedent owned
eleven shares of stock in Ala. & Tenn. Railroad, valued
at $25.00 each, and he asked the Court to allow him to
sell these for distribution among the heirs, who are:

1. John H. Nabors, residing in Arkansas
2. Catherine, wife of W. G. Perry, Shelby Co., Ala.
3. Ezekiel T. Nabors, Pascagoula, Miss.
4. Fannie, wife of W. B. Phillips, Baldwin Co.,
   Ala.
5. Parilee, under age, res. in Union Co., Ark.
6. Louisa Nabors, under age, Pascagoula, Miss.
7. James M. Nabors, Shelby Co., Ala.

French Nabors acted as agent for these heirs; and he
testified that the facts set forth are true.

From Will Record D, Shelby Co., Ala.:

p. 103. 27 Dec. 1841. Bond of Parthena Elliott as
guardian of the estate of Elizabeth J., Jabez P.,
Narcissa R., Sylvanus J., Joshua W., Martha W., and
Louisa C. Elliott, minor heirs of Cornelius Elliott,
dec'd. Securities, Charles McDonald, James Stedham.
Charles R. Gibbs, Judge of the County Court. Noel
Mason, Clerk. Witnessed by Martin Jennings, J. P.

p. 104. May 13, 1842. Parthena reported that no portion of this estate had yet come into her hands.

pp. 134-5. Will of Amos Elliott. Oct. 18, 1842.
Names wife, Nancy Elliott. Description of lands. At
death of wife, lands to be equally divided between the
five youngest sons, namely: George M., Jefferson B.,
Wiley J., John and Green Elliott. The balance of the
estate (Negroes, stock, etc.,) to be equally divided
among all my children, namely:

William Elliott, Jenny Rodgers, Polly Haney, and the
share of my two sons that are dead, Amos and Charles
Elliott, to go to their children: Parralee Elliott,
Nancy Elliott, Sarah Ann Elliott, Elizabeth Merrell &
Mahala Clowers; and the five youngest sons named above.

Will witnessed by John W. Teague   Mary Teague.

p. 135. Will of Amos Elliott proved by John W. Teague on Nov. 4, 1842. Allen Elliott resigned as executor on Nov. 26, 1842. On Dec. 19, 1842, William Elliott also resigned as executor.

p. 135. 17 Feb. 1843. Bond of Nancy Elliott, ad admx. with the will annexed of the estate of Amos Elliott. Securities on the bond:

　　　Elisha Nelson　　　Green Elliott　　　Amos Merrell
　　　　　　　Sarah Elliott　　　Allen Elliott

p. 168. Appraisal of estate of Amos Elliott, made by Francis Sims, John Ray, and John W. Teague, on March 23, 1843

p. 169. Nancy Elliott bought for herself an old Negro man belonging to the estate, for $50.00.

pp. 273-5. 2 May 1842. Parthenia Elliott, widow of Cornelius Elliott, petitioned to have her dower in his lands set apart to her. Lands in T20, R2E.

Maroney Data

Shelby Co., Ala., Will Book B, dated from 1819, has no index. Items found in passing:

p. 1. Inventory of the estate of Isaac Meroney. Mentions a note on John Meroney.

Another old Book, dating from 1819, without any title or binding:

p. 4.: Will of Isaac Maroney, dated 12 Nov. 1811 (or 1814 or 1816.) "I appoint John Howard and Rhody, my wife, executors." Mentions sons and daughters, but not by name.
Witnessed by Mary Ayettott and Mary Person.

January Term, 1819. "Presented for probate, and found insufficient, and of course rejected. Henry Avery, Register."

Compiler's note: I think the date of this will must be 1816, and that it must have been recorded first in another County, and copied into Shelby records later.

Same Volume:

pp. 5-7: 25 Jan. 1819. Bond of Rhoda Maroney as
administratrix of estate of Isaac Maroney, dec'd.
Security: Jesse Wilson.

pp. 8-9. Inventory of estate of Isaac Maroney, made
by Bennett Ware, Benjamin Taylor, Richard Crowson, and
Jesse Wilson, 27 Feb. 1819.

pp. 17-19: 26 July 1819. Bond of Rhoda Maroney as
guardian of Emily Moore. George Phillips, chief justice
of the Orphans' Court. (Compiler's note: There are
several reports made by Rhoda as guardian of Emily. One
dated 1825, says that Emily is residing with her mother,
Polly Byrum, wife of Alden Byrum. One of the reports
mentions money received by Rhoda Maroney as gdn. of
Emily M. Maroney.)

p. 284. 4th Aug. 1829. Bond of Moses Crowson as gdn.
of Rhoda Maroney, minor heir of Isaac Maroney, dec'd.
Securities, Charles Mundine and Isaac Johnson.
Leonard Tarrant, Judge of the Orphans' Court.

pp. 284-5. Bond of Moses Crowson, who has heretofore
been appointed gdn. of Rhoda Maroney, minor heir of
Isaac Maroney, dec'd. and is desirous of moving to
Tennessee; also of removing said ward and her effects
to Tennessee. Dated 9 Dec. 1830. Securities:
Bartholomew Maberry and David Fletcher.

p. 285. 1st Feb. 1830. Bond of John Mahan as gdn. of
Martha Crowson, minor heir of Richard Crowson, dec'd.
Securities: William Johnson and William Baker (?)

p. 286. Aug. 24, 1831. Ephraim Hill came into Court
and made a settlement with John Mahan as gdn. of
Martha Crowson, who has married said Ephraim.

p. 25. Dec. 1, 1830. Edward Mahan offered his
resignation as guardian of Richard and Martha Crowson,
minor heirs of Richard Crowson, dec'd.

p. 27. 1st Feb. 1830. Bond of John Mahan as guardian
of Richard Crowson, minor heir of Richard Crowson. His
Securities: Wm Johnson, Wm Baker.

p. 408. 23 Dec. 1839. Bond of John A. Maroney as gdn.
of his children. John A. Maroney has been apptd. gdn.
of Matilda Rhoda, Hannah Thomas Mary and Isaac, minor
heirs of Hanna Frost, dec'd. Securities: John Frost,
Alexander Hill. (Punctuation as in the record.)

From another old book, without title, called just "B":

p. 26. 26 July 1819. Bond of Rhoda Maroney as gdn.
of Emily Moore. Security: Alden Byram
Signatures witnessed by Henry Avery.

p. 44. 4 Dec. 1822. Bond of John Maroney as gdn. of
Nancy Holsombeck, orphan of Abraham Holsombeck, dec'd.
Securities: Wm Davis, Robt. McLean. Maroney was also
gdn. of Hiram Holsombeck.

pp. 106-8: 2 Nov. 1826. Inventory of Richard Crowson
estate. John Crowson, admr., James Estill, clerk of
the Court.

p. 146. 1 Oct., 1827. Bond of Hugh Wiseman and Chas.
Elliott as admrs. of estate of John Wiseman, dec'd.
Securities: Green Berry Seale, Samuel McLanahan.

From Shelby Co. Marriage Record for 1849-59:

p. 274. Charles B. Elliott to Engline Fulton
          on 13 Dec. 1846 by Jordan Jones, J. P.

p. 313. Elijah L. Fulton to Martha A. Nabors
          on 4 Feb. 1858 by Jas. P. Allen, J. P.

From old Bond Book A, 1841-60: pp. 9-10:

14 Oct. 1841. Bond of Samuel Fulton as constable of
Capt. Nelson's Beat. Securities: David Fulton, and
Asa A. Billingslea.

Shelby County Marriage Record, 1885-91: Charles B.
Elliott Jr. to Rima Freeze. 8th Feb. 1885, by
W. W. Kidd, M. G.

From Will Book K, (1851-54) p. 19: Rec'd of Benj. F.
Randall, admr. of estate of Amos Elliott, $50.00, in
full of my distributive share of said estate, as one of
the children and heirs of Amos Elliott Jr., who was an
heir of said Amos Elliott, dec'd. Dated 9 June 1851
(or 1854 ?). Signed: C. B. Elliotte
                              per A. M. Elliotte

same page: Similar receipt from Amos H. or M. Elliotte.

Shelby Co., Ala. Minutes of Probate Court, 1861-8:

p. 459. 20 Sept. 1866. On application of D. W. Caldwell
and A. M. Elliott, who allege that they are creditors of
Charles F. Elliott, dec'd, it is ordered that Titus
Strong, the general administrator for the County, be
appointed admr. of the estate of Charles F. Elliott ...

From Minutes of Probate Court for 1872-86:

p. 64. Came James J. Nabors, one of the admrs. of the
estate of John Nabors, dec'd, and reported that Andrew H.
Nabors, who purchased some of the land, on 17 Oct. 1870
and 27 March 1871, has fully paid for same.

Minutes of Orphans Court, 1818-29:

p. 101: Oct. 1826. Sally Crowson, relict of Richard
Crowson, dec'd, relinquished her right to administer
the estate of said Richard, and asked that John and
William Crowson be appointed. (Compiler's note: Other
Crowson papers in this volume.)

p. 161. March 1829. Distribution of the estate of
Richard Crowson. Sally Crowson got 1/5. Each of the
following heirs got $116.65:

William Crowson   David Crowson   Aaron Crowson
Mary Sims   Rebecca Mahan   Sarah Pitner
John Crowson   Thos. Crowson   Rachel Crowson
Hulda Fulton   Nancy Billingslea   Joshua W. Crowson
Richard Crowson   Peggy Billingslea   Martha Crowson

From Minutes of Probate Court for 1868-72:

p. 574. Dec. 30, 1872. John W. Nabors and James J.
Nabors made final settlement and distribution of the
estate of John Nabors, dec'd. A. A. Sterrett acted as
guardian of the minor heirs (gdn. ad litem).

In his lifetime, John Nabors had made advancements to
Hugh, James, John, Jane and William Nabors. His estate
was distributed to:

    James Nabors   John Nabors   William Nabors
    A. H. Nabors   Sarah Nabors
    James and Margaret Howard   Willis & Mary Ozley
    James T. & Mary Nabors whose guardian is Daniel
          McLeod
    Columbus, Sarah, Catherine, Henry, Thomas & Zilla
        Nabors, whose gdn. is John Nabors.

p. 73. Nov. 18, 1868. James J. & John W. Nabors
report the death of John Nabors, and ask the Court to
appoint them **executors,** as sons of deceased.

Gravestone inscriptions contributed by client:

John Nabors, b. Oct. 21, 1808, d. Oct. 31, 1868
Elizabeth H., wife of John Nabors
         b. Oct. 5, 1807, d. Oct. 15, 1868
C. B. Elliott   Oct. 30, 1822   Nov. 20, 1895

Deed Book A - E (transcribed) Shelby Co., Ala.:

p. 77: 24 Nov. 1825. Christopher Butler and Mahala,
his wife, sold to Littlepage Sims, land in T20, R3W.
This deed witnessed by Benj. May, Thos. Lee, and
Charles Mundine.

Shelby Co., Ala., Will Book E;

pp. 49-50: Will of William Lovelady, dated Dec. 1,
1845, names wife, Rachel; dau., Lydia Lovelady; son,
Elijah Lovelady; (dau. ?) Polly, wife of Ransom Davis;
son, John Lovelady; son, Henry Lovelady; son, David Lovelady; son, Wm Lovelady; son, Joseph Lovelady; Rhoda,
wife of John Fulton; James Lovelady. Executor:
Edmund King. Witnessed by:

    Edmund King   George D. Shortridge   Peyton G. King

Proved 30 Dec. 1846 by Edmund and Peyton King.
D. W. Prentice, J. P.   E. G. Lawley, Clerk.

From Will Book E, pp. 225-6: Winston Co., Miss.
Feb. 3, 1845. Randolph C. Canterberry is appointed
gdn. of Mary, Benajah B., Catherine and Margaret Lindsay,
all of Winston Co., Miss., and all minors under 14,
and heirs of Elijah Lindsay, late of Shelby Co., Ala.

p. 281. Bond of John W. Nash as gdn. of Elijah Lindsay, minor heir of Elijah Lindsay, dec'd. Security:
Richard T. Crowson, Abraham Nash. 27 June 1845.

Shelby Co., Ala., Will Book H, p. 926:

Will of Noah Haggard: Entire estate to remain in
possession of my wife during her lifetime.

Daughter Lucy E. Wood and son Samuel to have property
to make them equal to what my former children have had
from me.

Executor, son, Henry O. Haggard.

Dated 25 Oct. 1853. Witn.: James Gregory,
F. B. Allen and French Nabors.   Filed 15 Jan. 1866

Notices issued by the Judge of Probate to the following
persons, that a paper purporting to be the will of Rev.
Noah Haggard has been filed, and that they can appear
on the 2nd Mon. in May and contest same if they think
proper. All notices dated 9th April 1866.

1. Alamath Woods and Susan R., his wife;
2. Willis Woods and Lucy E., his wife
      (Service acknowledged by all four)
3. H. O. Haggard (Service acknowledged by T. W. Haggard)
4. Sarah Dobyns (Service acknowledged by Sarah A. Dobyns)
5. Mr. M. M. Thirman (or Ikerman) (Service
      acknowledged by M. M. Ikerman)
6. J. W., John D., Martha J., Sarah E., W. H. C.,
      James M, and Elizabeth McColough.* (Service Acknow-
      ledged by James W. and John D. W. McColough.)

*Correction: Elizabeth E. McColough.

Lolly of Shelby Co., Ala.

Shelby Co., Ala., Minutes of Probate Court, 1852-56:

p. 141: 28 Oct. 1853. Came Elizabeth Lolly, relict of
Henry Lolly, and filed her petition for dower in lands
he owned at the time of his death, in T22, R3W. Hudson
W. Nelson has been appointed admr. of said estate. (he
is Sheriff of the County.) Heirs named:

> The widow and:
>
> 1. Andrew Lolly
> 2. Mary A., wife of John Lucas
> 3. Elenor Holsomback, wife of Derrick Holsomback
> 4. Margaret, wife of John Holsomback
> 5. Nancy, wife of Abram Lucas
> 6. Louise Lolly
> 7. Joseph Lolly
> -- all the above are of age and reside in
>   Shelby Co., Ala.
> 8. Miles Lolly)
> 9. Henry Lolly) both und. 21, res. in Shelby Co.

Samuel H. Johnson appointed gdn. ad litem to represent
the minors.

Shelby Co., Ala. Deed Record A-E (transcribed):

p. 47. I, Christopher Lolly, for love and affection,
to my two grandchildren, Bradley and James Lucas, heirs
of my daughter Nancy, wife of George Lucas.
Dated 6th Jan. 1824.
Witness: Joab Lawler, Clerk of Shelby Co. Circuit Ct.

p. 535. Will of Christopher Lolly:

> Dated 1832. Names wife, Catherine; son,
> Christopher; "all my children"; Stepson,
> James Walker to have a child's part.
> Executors: Sons Jeremiah and John Lolly
> Witnesses: Green W. McLeroy, Martin McLeroy
>   and John Rodgers

Deed Record F - G (transcribed):

p. 454: Bond of Elijah G. Lawler as treasurer of
Shelby Co., Ala. Dated 21 Aug. 1839. Securities:

> Noel Mason   John W. Roper (or Rosser)
>   John G. Primm

Fuller of Perry County

Perry County, Ala., Minutes of Probate Court, Book H:

p. 69. Sept. 25, 1867. Benj. H. Watson aptd. admr. of
estate of E. W. Fuller, dec'd. Bond for $1000.00 with
H. B. Campbell, J. B. W. Smith, and J. R. Shelby as his
securities.

p. 92. Oct. 14, 1867. Benj. H. Watson filed petition to
have the homestead set apart in the estate of E. W. Fuller
dec'd, for the two minor heirs, Samuel Fuller, age 20,
and Mary Fuller, aged 18, and members of the family of the
deceased. The estate is insolvent.

The Court appointed commissioners to set part $500.00 worth
of land, including the homestead, for said minors.

p. 98. Oct. 28, 1867. The admr. petitioned to sell the
land to pay the debts of the estate. Land not described.

Minutes of Probate Court, Book N:

p. 268. Oct. 10, 1870. Final settlement of estate of E. W.
Fuller. No list of heirs. The expenses incurred by the
admr., Benj. H. Watson, exceeded the amount he, as admr.,
took in.

From Minutes of Probate Court, Book O:

p. 35: June 6, 1871. Came N. M. Walker, as admr. of the
estate of E. W. Fuller, dec'd, and filed a petition which
alleges that more than 18 months have lapsed since the
grant of letters of admr. on said estate, and he is satis-
fied that said estate is solvent. He further alleges that
the heirs of said E. W. Fuller are his children:

1. Sarah, wife of Wm. Harris, residing in Texas
2. Margaret, wife of A. G. Guise, res. in Miss.
3. Green Fuller, residing in Texas
4. Susan, wife of W. W. Corsby, both res. in Tex.
5. Mary, wife of W. W. Edwards, res. in Miss.
6. Melissa Fuller, res. in Miss.
7. Samuel T. Fuller, res. in Perry Co., Ala. ---
   who are all of age; and the following gr-children:
8. The children of Frances, wife of Benj. H. Watson,
   who is dead, to wit:

John B. Watson, Joab Watson, Sarah E. Watson,
Seeney Susan Watson, Mary T. Watson, and Benj. H.
Watson, all minors and residing in Dallas Co., Ala.

9. The heirs of Judith Harris, dec'd, who was the wife
    of Wm Harris, to wit:
    Wm Harris Jr., Susan Harris, both minors & residing
    in Texas.

The land is in Township 19, Range 10.
N. M. Walker is administrator "de bonis non".
Note: Some discrepancies appear in this record.

p. 99. 14 Aug. 1871. Oath of Geo. W. Pardue, John A.
Fuller and Vincent T. Pierson, that said land cannot be
equitably divided without a sale.

p. 316. Feb. 23, 1872. The admr., N. M. Walker, reported
the sale of the land to James F. Bailey.

p. 323. Feb. 28, 1872. Walker filed accts. for final
settlement of this estate.

pp. 347-9. April 8, 1872. Charles G. Brown appointed
guardian ad litem to represent the minors at the final
settlement. Amount for distribution: $20.72. The heirs
are all named again in this document.

N. M. Walker gave his receipt to the Judge of Probate,
A. C. Howze, for $4.50, the shares of Samuel T. and
Melissa Fuller.

From Perry Co., Ala., Marriage Record for 1820-32:

Elijah W. Fuller to Cenith B. Fuller, 30th Jan. 1829
                by James Goggans, J. P.

From Marriage Record for 1832-39:

No. 966: L. S. B. J. Fuller to Sarah Melton
          on 13 Sept. 1836, by Benj. Ford, J. P.

Orphans Court Record for 1823-32: Page 34.
Oct. 1824. Jesse Fuller aptd. gdn. of John Calbert
Glaze, Elizabeth Cena Glaze, Joseph Green Glaze, Abner
Jutson Glaze, and Samuel Jesse Glaze, minors. He gave his
bond as gdn. with Green Fuller and A. G. Jackson as his
securities.

Compiler's note: Jonathan Glaze, who is listed in the
1830 Census of Perry Co., Ala., might have been the father
of these Glaze minors. I do not find an estate in his name
in the Perry Co. Records. Descendants say he married one
of the sisters of Alfred Fuller.

From 1860 Census of Perry Co., Ala.:

p. 63. Perryville Beat:

```
426 - 26:  John B. Fuller, age 47, b. Ala.
           Sarah E.    "    wife, 42, b. Ala.
           Richard R. P. T. Fuller, 24, b. Ala.
           Geo. W. Fuller  age 18  b. Ala.
           Martha H. Fuller      16      "
           Margaret C.   "       13      "
           Mary C.       "       12      "
           Laura         "       11      "
           James H.      •        7      "
           Robert        "        5      "
           Sarah D.      "      9/12     "
           B. J.         "       22      "
```

pp. 60-61. Perryville Beat:

```
408-8.    Samuel Fuller    age 32  b. Ala.
          Delany    "        33     "      wife
          Jesse     "        14     "      male
          Thos.     "        11     "
          Frances   "         9     "
          Martha    "         6     "
          Susan     "         3     "
          Josephine L. Fuller 4/12   "
```

From 1860 Census of Perry Co., Ala., Heard's Beat, p. 34:

```
239-9.    E. Wm Fuller    age 50  b. Georgia
          Senith B. Fuller    47     "         wife
          Green H.    "       20  b. Ala.   (blind)
          Melissa     "       19     "
          Sarah J.    "       16     "
          Susan T. Fuller     15     "
          Samuel T. (?) Fuller 13    "
          Mary P.          "   10     "

237-7:    William Harris      39  b. Ga.
          Judith B.   "       29  b. Ala. wife
          Wm H.       "        7     "
```

From 1860 Census of Perry Co., Ala., Heard's Beat:

p. 34.   House and family No. 235:

      James R. Fuller   age 30   b. Ala.
      E. H. (?)   "   20   "
      Jesse M.   "   2   "   (male)
      M. A. F. (or T.) Fuller, age 4/12, female, b. Ala.

      House & family No. 233:

      John A. Fuller   age 38   b. Ala.
      Cynthia P.   "   37   "
      Mary E.   "   10   "
      Jesse   "   8   "
      Wm L.   "   6   "
      Sarah A.   "   5   "
      Susan J.   "   3   "
      John   " Jr.   2   "
      Seaborne   "   3/12   "

p. 60.   Perryville Beat:

      House and family No. 405:

      Wm C. Harbour   age 53   born in Ga.
      Lucretia Harbour   35   b. Ala.,   wife
      E. F. (?)   "   19   "   male
      Christopher C. "   15   "
      John R. Harbour   12   "
      Ezekiel   "   10   "
      Bazel   "   8   "
      Mary F.   "   6   "
      Martha   "   2   "
      Middleton Moseley, age 56, boarder, b. Ga.

      House and family No. 404:

      A. G. Guyse   age 28   b. Ga.
      M. E. Guyse   23   b. Ala., wife
      Frances A. J. Guyse   5   "
      Sarah C. Guyse   3   "
      Wm J. H.   "   2   "
      Linander (?) B. Guyse, age 3/12, female, b. Ala.

Also in Perryville Beat: Joel Guyse, age 22 and family;
    and Joel Guyse, age 65, and family.

Rhodes of Perry County

From Minutes of Probate Court, Book I, p. 183:

Nov. 14, 1859. Ingraham Rhodes apts. admr. of estate of
Mary Rhodes, dec'd. Securities on his bond were:
Thos. Rhodes & David Avery.

MPC Book I, pp. 526-7: 10th June 1861. Ingraham Rhodes
divided the estate of Mary Rhodes, dec'd, between himself
and Allen T. and W. F. Rhodes, Ingraham taking half, and
dividing the other half between Allen T. and W. F. Rhodes, of
whom he is guardian.   /See note below./

From Minutes of Probate Court, Book M:

p. 93. Oct. 14, 1867. Final settlement of estate of
Thos W. Rhodes, dec'd. J. F. Monts acted as gdn. ad litem
of the minor heirs. A balance of $18.90 was left for dis-
tribution, to following:

1. To Mary W., wife of W. P. Baldwin $3.98
2. To Ingraham Rhodes; Margaret, wife of Robt. W. Lee;
   John Rhodes; Sarah Ann Rhodes; Susan M. Rhodes; &
   Elizabeth, wife of Frederick Monts, each $2.13.
3. To Joseph F. Rhodes, Elizabeth Rhodes and Alva Lucinda
   Rhodes, each $.71.

From Deed Record B, p. 715:

6 Dec. 1834. Wm. W. Walton and Elizabeth, his wife, sold to
              Presley Rhodes, land in T20, R6.

From Deed Record C:

p. 606. 25 Dec. 1837. Presley D. Roads and Charity, his wife,
sold to Allen A. Smith, land on the Marion-Tuscaloosa Road.
Signatures acknowledged before Geo. K. Chatham, J. P.

p. 611. 1st Nov. 1833. Presley D. Rhodes and Charity, his
wife, to Joseph Jimison.

Note: From Minutes of Probate Court, Book K:

p. 23. Feb. 9th 1863. Thos Rhodes aptd. admr. of estate
of Thos. W. Rhodes, dec'd. Securities on his bond were
R. W. Lee and James H. Madison.

From Deed Record D, p. 613:

5 Dec. 1837. Presley D. Rhodes and Charity, his wife, sold to Bryant Brand, land in T20, R6. Witn. Geo. K. Chatham.

From Deed Record E, p. 89:

21 June 1839. Wm W. Sims of Greene Co., Ala., sold to Benjamin Rhodes of Perry Co., Ala., land in T21, R6. Witn.: John Meggs, Mark Smith.

Wm W. Sims, and Susan (also referred to as Susannah), his wife, acknowledged their signatures to above deed before Henry Sims, J. P., of Perry Co., on 12 June 1839. Recorded 23 July 1839.

From Deed Book I (eye):

pp. 74-5: 3 Dec. 1846. Presley D. Rhodes and Charity, his wife, to Middleton Harrison, land in T20, R7.

p. 343. 2 Aug. 1849. Wm R. Rhodes and Abigail V., his wife, sold to Bryan Avery, land in T20, R6. Witn.: Jacob Rowland, Silas Moore.

Jacob Rowland proved the signatures to above deed on 24 Nov. 1849, before John Cunningham, Clerk of Co. Court.

From Deed Book L:

p. 302. 4th July 1853. Wm W. Stokes, Sheriff of Perry Co., deeded to Isaac S. Hurt, land in T22, R6, that had belonged to Benjamin Rhodes and was sold by the Sheriff to pay damages and cost of a suit in Circuit Court.

p. 328. Benjamin Rhodes sold to J. N. Chadwick, of Greene County, Ala., 80 A. in T20, R6. Witn. J. D. Webb. Dated 21 Oct. 1853.

pp. 542-3. 6 March 1854. Land formerly belonging to Benj. Rhodes was sold by Sheriff to satisfy a debt owed by Rhodes to Isaac S. Hurt. James W. Rhodes bought the land, which is in T21, R6.

p. 653. 5 Sept. 1854. James W. Rhodes and Sarah, his wife, of Perry Co., Ala., sold to Peyton Madison of Greene Co., Ala., land in T21, R6. Signatures of James W. and Sarah Rhodes acknowledged before Wm Shaffer, J. P., on 2 Oct. 1854.

From Deed Book M, pp. 323-4: 3 Feb. 1854. Joel Scarborough
Henrietta M. Scarborough and Josiah D. Rhodes, sold to
Daniel A. Christenberry, land in T21, R7. Signatures to this
deed acknowledged before J. Hall, M. P., same day.

From Deed Book N, pp. 613-4: W. P. Rhodes and Telitha, his
wife, sold to Wm Dunkin, land 15 feet wide, for a private
road, commencing 110 yards S. of the house in which we now
live, on west side of the Marion-Centerville Road, "till
it strikes John Dobbins line." Dated: 19 March 1838.
Signatures acknowledged same day, before R. C. Hodge, J. P.

From Deed Book P, p. 439. Polk Co., Texas. John R. Rhodes
& Elizabeth, his wife, gave quit-claim deed to Andrew P.
Sparks (?), of Perry Co., Ala., "all our title" to land in
T21, R6, being the tract formerly belonging to Isaac E.
Sparks, dec'd; also to some land in T21, R6, "embracing the
land belonging to our mother, Christiana Sparks."
Dated 10th May 1861.

John J. & Elizabeth Rhodes acknowledged their signatures to
above deed on 10th May 1861, before James Warner, J. P. in
Polk Co., Texas.

From Deed Book Q, p. 585: W. P. Rhodes and Telithy, his
wife for 6 bales of cotton weighing 500 lbs. each, delivered
at the nearest ginning house, on or before Jan. 1867, sell
to P. W. Nichols, land in T20, R8, formerly belonging to
James A. Howze, on the Centreville Road.
Deed dated 3 Nov. 1865.

From Marriage Record of Perry Co., Ala., for 1820-32:

License No. 331: Priestley Rhodes to Charity Duckett,
                  8th July 1828 by Wm Clark, J. P.

No. 465: John P. Rhodes to Rebecca Simpson
          28 Aug. 1830. No minister's return.

From Marriage Record of Perry Co., for 1832-39: No male
Rhodes is indexed in this volume.

From Perry Co., Ala., Marriage Record for 1840-51:

No. 1285: John P. Rhodes to Nancy A. Claty on 20 July
           1841 by O. V. Levert, M. G.

No. 1885: John J. Rhodes to Elizabeth Sparks on 21 Jan.
           1847, by Tho. Chilton, M. G.

Perry Co., Ala., Marriage Record for 1851-63:

No. 87. B. M. Rhodes to Elizabeth Carrington on 28 July
1852 by S. R. Freeman, M. G.   /Baptist/

/Compiler's note: This is indexed as B. W. Rhodes/

Same Volume, No. 194: James W. Rhodes to Sarah LaGrone
on 22 Dec. 1853 by John Crowson, M. G.

No. 365: J. M. Rhodes to Mary P. (or D.) Crowson, on
3 Jan. 1856, by Jno. W. Williams, "licensed
preacher". Consent of John Crowson, the
father of Mary.

No. 427: Alva Rhodes to Elizabeth Albert on 4 Dec. 1856
by C. C. Calloway, M. G. Consent of Jacob Bush,
guardian of Elizabeth.

No. 484: Ingraham Rhodes to Mary Allen on 16 Sept. 1857
by John Hall, J. P.

No. 824: T. W. Rhodes to Mary W. Moseley, on 18 Dec. 1861
by H. Talbird, M. G.

From 1830 Census of Perry Co., Ala.: Listed are:

p. 86: John P. Roads   p. 79: Prestley Roads
p. 55: Priestley Roads

From Perry Co., Ala., Marriage Record for 1820-39:

No. 1166: James Simmons to Nancy Rhodes on 17 December
1839 by L. Q. C. DeYampert.

From Perry Co., Ala., Marriage Record for 1839-51:

No. 2006: John Maddison to S. M. Rhodes

No. 1597: James G. Russell to Mahulda S. Rhodes

No. 1923: Joe Scarbrough to H. M. Rhodes

Webb of Perry County

Will of Thomas Webb is recorded in Will Book A, pp 225-7. It mentions:

Wife, Martha
Sons-in-law: L. Q. C. DeYampert
                Dunstan Banks
                Evan G. Richards
Sons: Wm. T. Webb
        John H. Y. Webb
Daughter: Mary F. B. Webb
Son: James Webb
Daughter: Mary D. C. Richards, wife of
            Evan G. Richards
Two youngest sons: Jesse L. and Sidney Webb

Executors: Wm Webb and John H. Y. Webb
Dated: 2 Nov. 1847
Witnessed: John L. Kennedy, H. Webb, Warren E. Kennedy

Perry Co. Marriage Record for 1820-32: No male Webb, or Banks, or Richards, or DeYampert is indexed.

Marriage Record for 1832-39:

No. 704:   Dunstan Banks to Lucretia Webb, on 10th Dec. 1833 by Thos. A. Smith, E.M.E.C.

No. 605:   L. Q. C. DeYampert to Parthena Webb on 10th January 1833 by E. V. LeVert, V. D. M.

No. 837:   Evan G. Richards to Sarah D. Webb. License dated 19th May 1835. No record of ceremony.

Note: No male Webb indexed in this volume.

Marriage Record for 1840-51:

No. 1414:   John H. Webb to Julia A. DeYampert on 11 Dec. 1842 by T. W. Dorman, M. G.

Marriage Record for 1851-63: No Male Webb indexed.

Marriage Record for 1863-66:

No. 996:   W. S. Webb to Margaret J. Sherman, on 26 April 1865, by W. H. McIntosh, Pastor of Baptist Church at Marion.

Perry Co., Ala.

Deed Book A, p. 194. 29 May 1828. Deed of trust from
Thos. S. Ashe and Samuel Strudwick to Thos. Webb and Samuel
Webb. Apparently Thos. and Samuel were securities for Ashe
on a note; Ashe deeded to Strudwick, in trust, to secure
payment on the note, two quarter-sections of land on the
waters of Brush Creek, where said Ashe now lives.

Deed Book A, p. 266. 29 July 1826. Wyatt C. Webb sold to
Anderson West, Lot No. 9, in Town of Marion, E. of Pickens
St. Witn.: Richard B. Walthall, Wm. Stringfellow.

Deed Book A, p. 123: Dunstan Banks of Jasper Co., Ga.,
deed of gift to Elizabeth Haynes of Perry Co., Ala., "for
the natural love and affection he has for said Elizabeth, as
well as for the relationship existing between said Banks and
said Elizabeth....a Negro girl named Mary, aged 7 years.
13 Dec. 1822.
Witn.: M. Phillips, Wm H. Pritchett, John Hill

From Deed Book E:

pp. 152-3: 27 Jan. 1839. Thos Webb, John Boyd, and Wm
Shaffer were appointed by the Court to sell the land belong-
ing to the estate of Wm Wilson, dec'd, at public auction.
Land in T21, R6, sold to John Thomas.
Witn.: Henry Sims, Benjamin Rhodes.

Note: Lambeth Hopkins was administrator of estate of this
William Wilson.

p. 506. 3 Dec. 1840. Thos Webb and Martha, his wife, of
Perry Co., sold to Robt. J. Kennan, Jr., of Tuscaloosa Co.,
Ala., 300 A. in T21, R6, "commencing at Clement's Corner";
"to a stake on W. H. Kennan's line".
Witnesses: Wm Kennan, Woodson H. Kennan.

From Minutes of Probate Court, Book E:

p. 424: Nov. 11, 1848: Came Wm T. Webb and John H. Y.
Webb, who say they are executors of the will of Thos. Webb,
dec'd, and present said will for probate. James D. Webb is
appointed guardian ad litem of the minors concerned.

pp. 428-9: Nov. 20, 1848. Probate of will of Thos. Webb.
Martha Webb, the widow; Evan G. Richardson, in right of his
wife, Mary F. Webb; James Webb; Jesse S. Webb; L. Q. C.
DeYampert, in right of his wife; and Sidney V. Webb, heirs

and distributees under said will, have waived the written
notice required by law, and consent that the executors may
have said will admitted to probate;   and James D. Webb,
gdn. ad litem of Samuel & Sidney Webb, minors and children
of testator, has also acknowledged due service of notice; and
Dunstan Banks and his wife, Lucretia M., formerly Webb,
have also acknowledged due service of notice ... Came
also John S. Kennedy, Warrent E. Kennedy, & Henry Webb,
who testify that they signed said will as witness ...
Executors not required to give bond, as directed by said
will, & also in conformity to an Act of the Legislature
of Alabama., passed at the late session of 1847-48.

Minutes of Probate Court, Book F:

p. 88. Sept. 9, 1850. Wm F.(?) Webb and John H. Y. Webb,
executors, filed their accounts for a final settlement of
est. of Thos. Webb. Notice to be published in "Alabama
Commonwealth". James D. Webb, guardian of the minors.

p. 187. Nov. 11, 1850. No new family data. Fin. Sett.

p. 245. July 14, 1851. Apparently another "final" settlement of this estate. Extrs. discharged from further
responsibility. No new family data.

From Minutes of Probate Court, Book K, p. 45:

April 29, 1863. This day came James Yates and applied for
letters of administration on the estate of Thos. Webb, dec'd.
He entered into bond for $700.00 with J. M. Gayle and A. G.
Tadlock as his securities.

Note: I find no other papers indexed in Re: Yates' administration of this estate.

From Deed Book H, pp. 547-8: 17 Jan. 1848. John W. and
James A. Clement, for $1.00 in hand paid by Thomas Webb,
sold him 4½ A., commencing on the Greensborough Road,
Kennidas Corner, running E. to the half-mile stake, Webb's
line, then S. to the Greensborough Road....
Witnesses: John H. Bishop   H. Webb.

Thomas Webb is listed in the 1830 Census of Perry Co., Ala.

Adams of Marengo County

From Minutes of Orphans Court, for 1840-43:

p. 292. March 1, 1842. Citation to Wm Adams to appear at next term of Court and settle his administration on the estate of Howell G. Adams, dec'd.

Compiler's note: There must be earlier papers regarding this estate, probably in the book that has no index.

From Minutes of Orphans Court, Book E:

p. 147. 21 July 1847. Administration on the estate of Howell C. Adams, dec'd, was granted to Wm Adams in his lifetime; then Wm Adams died, and Wm Burks, Sheriff of Marengo Co., took over the admrn. of said estate. Heirs named:

1. Jordan Anderson and Nancy, his wife
2. Wm H. L. Burton (or Barton), and Constance, his wife
3. Sarah Ann Adams
4. Benjamin Adams

From Marriage Record for 1866-70:

p. 228: J. H. Adams to Miss Roberta C. Powell. License dated 20 April 1869; ceremony June 3, 1869, at the residence of the bride's father, by F. H. Hanson, Minister of the Protestant Episcopal Church.

p. 171. Felix G. Adams to Miss Sarah E. Powell on 19th July 1868, at Dr. Nixon's, by J. D. Cameron, M. G.

From Deed Book C, p. 78: Christopher H. Taylor sold to James H. and Felix G. Adams, 12 April 1834.

From Deed Book V, p. 425. 10th Jan. 1871. Felix G. Adams, and Sarah E., his wife, sold to Roberta C. Adams; all Marengo Co. Felix and Sarah sold Roberta their undivided half interest in 50 A. in T15 & T16, R3E....on the Cahaba-Linden Road.

From Deed Book W, p. 553. 7th Jan. 1877. Felix G. and Sarah E. Adams, his wife, sold to Allie Cook, 10 A. to run full length through the purchase of M. M. Ballow, to the land of Roberta C. Adams, in T16, R3E, bounded by S. E. Fate land, C. B. Cleveland's land purchased of F. B. Jackson, on West by my land, deeded to me by R. C. Adams.

From Deed Book X, Marengo Co., Ala.:

p. 30. ___Dec. 1877. Felix G. Adams and Sallie C., his
wife, all that land deeded from E. A. Ballow to R. C. Adams,
and from R. C. Adams to Felix G. Adams, in T15 & 16, R3E,
except 10 A. formerly sold to Ayle Cook.

Signed: Felix G. Adams
          Sarah E. Adams

Sarah E. Adams appeared before Geo. S. Zeigler, Notary
Public in Colorado County, Texas, on 27 Jan., 1878, and
acknowledged her signature to above deed.

pp. 226-8. 26 Jan. 1880. Felix G. Adams of Marengo Co.,
Ala., and Sarah E. Adams, his wife of Waller Co., Texas,
sold to James H. George of Marengo Co., Ala....
Witnessed by T. S. Reese, M. V. Reese, W. B. Adams,
          and D. D. Yeager.

Sarah E. Adams acknowledged her signature to above on
26 Jan. 1880, in Waller Co., Texas, before T. S. Reese,
Notary Public.

Deed Book V, pp. 56-7: I, Felix G. Adams of Marengo Co.,
Ala., desirous of making some provision for my daughter,
Harriett, wife of John P. Walke, who is in debt, give her
$3000.00, free of control of her husband, and empower him
to use same in a mercantile business in Uniontown or else-
where. Dated 20 Aug., 1868.
Witn. by L. A. Simms and J. H. Adams.

Dallas Co., Ala. Abstract to Minutes of Probate Court,
          Volume 1, pp. 445ff.:

Oct. 17, 1838. Estate of Stephen Morgan, who died in
August, 1838. Administrators are: James J. Morgan, and
Daniel W. Morgan and Sackfield Brewer. Deceased left a wife
Elizabeth, and the following lineal heirs, all residing in
Dallas Co., Ala., except one:
1. James J. Morgan   2. Silas Morgan   3. Daniel W. Morgan
4. Elizabeth, wife of Sackfield Brewer   5. Malinda, wife
of Wm F. Handley   6. Martin Morgan   7. Isham Morgan of
Greene Co., Ala.   8. Asa T. Morgan   9. Eppy Morgan
-- all of age; and 10. Stephen Morgan, Jr. and Malissa
Morgan, who are minors.

Stephen Morgan owned land in T13, R9 on Prairie Creek,
          4 miles S. of Portland, Dallas Co., Ala.

Chapman of Clarke County

From old estate file, Box C:
Estate of Archibald Chapman:

Bond of Samuel Forwood as admr. of estate of Archibald H.
Chapman, dec'd. Security, William Goode.
Dated Oct. 15, 1835.

List of personal property sold by the administrators on
January 20th, 1836. Purchasers include: Gaius D. Wilson,
James Foot (or Fort), John Bettis, John Murphy, William
Boney, Daniel Miller, Edmund Whatley, Wm R. Hamilton,
Guilford D. Green.

Inventory and appraisal of personal property was made on
18 December 1835 by: John Mackey (?), Edmund Whatley,
David Dodwell, and Silas Bryan.

Promissory notes made by Archie x Chapman to Edward Smith
in 1835.

Bill from D. C. & H. Sampson of Monroe County, Alabama, for
articles bought by Archibald Chapman in 1835. Henry Sampson
made oath before Edwin Cater, J. P., in Monroe Co., Ala.,
that this acct. is true, dated Apr. 15, 1836. "The admr.
will please pay this acct. to Wm H. Arthur."

Another bill from Smith and Allen of Monroe Co., Ala.,
attested by James Foster.

Isaac Avrea (?) made the coffin for $10.00.

Note from Archibald x Chapman to Samuel Forwood, payable
Nov. 1st next, dated Dec. 25, 1834. Witn: Wd Robertson.

This file also contains eight numbered receipts and bills,
referring to Wm Coat as gdn. of Caroline and Malinda Webb,
heirs of Henley Webb.

Compiler's note: I can see no connection with the estate
of Archibald Chapman. Perhaps these are just out of place.

From Minutes of Probate Court, 1829-40, p. 237 & 248:

The estate of Archibald H. Chapman was declared insolvent,
by the admr., Sam'l Forwood. No list of heirs. The admr.
is discharged from further liability.

65

Clarke County, Ala., Minutes of Orphans' Court, Book B:

p. 23: 3 April 1830. On petition of Achsah Chapman, late
wife of Amos Robertson, dec'd, the sheriff, John Bouler, is
ordered to set off to her, her dower in lands Amos owned
in T8, R2E.

Report of Giles Chapman as gdn. of Alvira Roberson, minor
heir of Amos Roberson.

p. 24. Giles Chapman was also gdn. of Matilda, Westley and
Sarah Roberson, minor heirs of Amos Roberson.

Clarke Co. Marriage record for 1814-34:

p. 2. Amos Roberson to Axey Pugh, on 10th May 1814, at
the house of her father, Elijah Pugh, by Wm Robinson, J. P.
Axey is under age.

Minutes of Probate Court, Book B:

pp. 284-5: Feb. 4th 1839. At the instance of Stephen
Williamson, it is ordered that citation issue to John M.
Chapman, to appear in Court, and show cause why letters of
administration should not be granted on the estate of
Reuben M. Chapman.

Compiler's note: I read all the papers re: this estate
(eight of them) in this volume, but found no list of heirs.

p. 460. Estate of John M. Chapman declared insolvent.
Payments made to his creditors, of whom John M. Chapman is
the largest. Other creditors who received payments:
S. T. Barnes, S. Williamson, Dr. A. Denney, Miel Ezell.

p. 480. Elijah Chapman, in right of his wife, is an heir
of the estate of Celia Martin, of which John Martin is
the admr.

Compiler's note: The above are all the Chapman items
indexed in this volume B. The old indexes are imperfect;
there may be other items not indexed.

Joseph Chapman of Clarke County

From old estate file G: Estate of Joseph Chapman, dec'd.
                          Administrator, E. Stewart Pugh

27 Dec. 1858.   Commissioners appointed to divide the Negroes
among the heirs.   The comrs. are: John J. Olds, John
Stewart, T. A. Wimbish, Giles Chapman, John Chapman.

There are 20 slaves to be equally divided among:

1. Amelia, wife of E. S. Pugh
2. Eleanor, wife of Norman Martin
3. Nancy, wife of George Fluker
4. Robt. C. May, only heir of Elizabeth May,
   formerly Elizabeth Chapman
5. James C. and Alice Savage, heirs of Mary Savage,
   formerly Mary Chapman
6. Elizabeth Whitlock, Young C. Dunbar, and Caroline
   Dunbar, heirs of Sarah Dunbar, dec'd, formerly
   Sarah Chapman.

Anthony W. Dillard, Probate Judge of Sumter County, Ala.,
appointed Jonathan May legal gdn. of Robert C. May, a minor
heir of Joseph Chapman, dec'd. 23 Dec. 1858. Robt. C. May
is over 14, under 21. Jonathan May made bond with Wm A.
May and John C. Houston as his securities.

Petition of the admr., E. S. Pugh, to Probate Judge Z. L.
Bettis, dated Nov. 19, 1859, names the heirs of Joseph
Chapman:

1. Nancy, wife of George Fluker, of age, residing in
   Clarke County.
2. Amelia, wife of E. S. Pugh, of age, and
   residing in Clarke Co.
3. Eleanor, wife of Norman Martin, of age, and
   residing in Clarke Co., Miss.
4. Robt. May, child of Elizabeth May, formerly
   Elizabeth Chapman. Robt. is under age, and
   resides in Sumter Co., Ala.
5. Elizabeth, wife of Asa Whitlock, and grandchild
   of Joseph Chapman, dec'd, of age, and resides in
   Marengo Co., Ala.
   Young C. Dunbar and Caroline A. Dunbar, who are
   heirs after the manner of Elizabeth Whitlock, who
   is their sister. They reside in Freestone Co.,
   Texas and are under age.
6. James C. Savage, of full age, a grandchild of

Joseph Chapman, dec'd, being a child of Mary
Chapman Savage, dec'd, who was a dau. of Joseph
Chapman, dec'd; and Alice A. Savage, sister of
James C. Savage, who is a minor and resides in
Clarke Co., Ala.

Chapman deeds from Clarke County

Deed Book A, p. 169: Wm Chapman and Partheny, his wife
to Harriett Dade, a lot in Clarksville. Jan. 16, 1822.

p. 219. 12 July, 1822. Another deed from Wm Chapman and
Parthena, his wife, to Harriett Dade.

p. 264. Wm Chapman and Partheny, his wife, to James Mixon
a lot in Clarksville. 29 May 1822.

p. 85. Wm A. Robinson, Clerk of the Inferior Court of Clarke
County, to Wm Chapman, lot in Clarksville. 6 June 1821.
Witness: James Savage, Clerk of Circuit Court of Clarke Co.

Compiler's note: Similar deeds on pp. 86, 87, 88 -- all to
lots in Clarksville.

From Deed Book C:

p. 329. 21 Oct. 1834. Washington Co., Ala. Wm Chapman of
Washington Co., Ala., to Joel Bell of Clarke Co., Ala., Lot
No. 10 in Coffeeville, except 50 front feet to the depth of
said lot, which has been deeded to Luther Spencer and is
now claimed by the heirs of James Larkin, dec'd. Witn:
Henry J. Y. Moss, Chas. L. Lane. On 3 Jan. 1838, Chas. L.
Lane, J. P. of Washington Co., Ala., certified that he was
present and saw this deed signed.

p. 257. 21 Oct. 1838. Joshua Chapman and Elizabeth, his
wife, of Clarke Co., Ala., sold to Robert Bumpers, Sr.,
land in T8, R2E. Signs. Ack. before John A. Coate, J. P.
in Clarke Co., same day.

p. 289. 15 Jan. 1834. Elijah Chapman and wife Elizabeth, to
Obediah Smith, land in T8, R2E. Witn.: Alexander McMillin,
Giles Chapman.

Lt.-Gen. Joseph Hardee
Dallas County

From Will Book C, pp. 74-77:

I, Wm J. Hardee, of the City of Selma...

1. To wife, Mary Lewis Hardee, the house and lot situated
   on the corner of Dallas and Lapsley Streets, extending
   from Lapsley to Mitchell Streets, with all the appurte-
   nances and furniture in said house, and all the mules,
   horses and other personal property which I have or hereafter may have on my wife's "Hermitage" and "Ash" plantations in Hale Co., Ala.

2. To dau., Bessie Hardee....

3. To three daughters....

4. My orange grove on Indian River in Florida, not being
   at present in condition to bring its value, I desire it
   not be sold for 2 or 3 years ... And as my western Texas
   lands will probably enhance in value greatly, I desire
   they may not be sold at all, if they can be equitably
   divided and taken in kind by my devisees ...

Lastly, I appoint Thos. B. Roy of Selma my executor.

Dated: 16 June 1871.

Witnesses: W. M. Brooks, J. R. Satterfield.

Codicil, dated 29 July 1873, witnessed by A. P. Young and
Jon Haralson: To Miss Ann Dummett of St. Augustine, Florida,
the house and lot owned by me on the corner of St. George
and St. Francis Streets, in St. Augustine, to hold during
her natural life.

Both will and codicil probated on Nov. 22, 1873. The codicil
was proved by Augustus C. Young.

From Abstract of Minutes of Probate Court, Vol. 4, p. 719:

In the matter of the probate of the will of Wm J. Hardee:

Comes T. B. Roy and filed a petition to probate and record the will of Wm J. Hardee, dec'd. Mrs. May Lewis Hardee is the widow, and his only children and next of kin are: Anna Hardee Chambliss, wife of N. R. Chambliss; Sallie Hardee Roy, wife of petitioner; and Bessie Hardee. All are over 21 and reside in this County.

From Deed Record JJ:

p. 95: May 20, 1871. Wm J. Hardee bought from Jonathan Haralson and Wm T. Morgan, extrs. of Isaiah Morgan, for $8,200, a lot in Selma on corner of Dallas and Lapsley Sts. 90x320, known as the Dr. Morgan House.

p. 576. Jan. 15, 1872. Mary Lewis Hardee, wife of W. J. Hardee, bought from the Morgan estate, a lot adjoining the one described above. The deed mentions T. B. Roy as having been the original purchaser.

p. 576. 13 Jan. 1872. Joh'n Haralson, executor of the estate of Isaiah Morgan, deeded to Mrs. Sallie Hardee Roy, wife of T. B. Roy, a lot 78x160 on Lapsley St.

From the Parish Register of St. Paul's Episcopal Church, in Selma:

List of communicants, 1867, Easter Sunday:

Gen. W. J. Hardee, Mrs. Mamie Hardee, Mrs. N. R. Chambliss, Miss Eliza Hardee, Miss Sallie Hardee.

Communicants, Whitsuntide, 1869: Gen. W. J. Hardee, Mrs. N. R. Chambliss, Miss Sallie Hardee, Miss Bessie Hardee, Mrs. W. J. Hardee.

Marriage: Thos. B. Roy to Sallie F. Hardee, on Tuesday, April 18, 1871, at 11 A. M., at Gen. W. J. Hardee, by S. (or L.) M. Byrd.

Burials: Nov. 8, 1873. Lt.-Gen. W. J. Hardee, buried in Selma, age 57 (?).

April 10, 1875: Mrs. W. J. Hardee, buried in Selma.

Baptised Dec. 22, 1868: Willis Hardee Chambliss, age 10 years, Parents: Maj. N. R. & Anna Chambliss. Sponsors: Gen. W. J. Hardee and Mrs. Hardee; Miss Sallie Hardee.

From Southern Argus, a newspaper published in Selma, Ala.,
issue of Nov. 14, 1873: Obituary of Wm Joseph Hardee:

Wm Joseph Hardee, born in Camden Co., Ga., 1815; entered
West Point 1834; graduated 2nd Lt. 1838; made captain of
dragoons 1844; fought through Maxican War, attaining rank
of Lt.-Col.; made commandant of cadets at U. S. Military
Academy, and instructor in tactics in 1856; book on tactics;
resigned and tendered services to Confederate States;
appointed Brig.-Gen., 1861; rose during War to Lt.-Gen.;
returned to private life in this State at the termination
of hostilities in 1865; died at Wytheville Va., en route
to his home in this City, Nov. 6, 1873.

From Selma Argus, March 20, 1878: On Saturday night, in
Summerfield, George Mixon was shot and killed by Dr.
Woolley. On Sunday Dr. Woolley appeared before Magis-
trates Court, and after a full hearing, was dismissed, the
Court holding his act self-defense.

Issue of March 27: Mr. Callen, who has the contract for
sprinkling Broad Street, has erected pumps at the artesian
basin, at the corner of Broad and Alabama, which throw out
100 gallons of water a minute.

Issue of March 27: In our issue of yesterday, we announced
that at the time of going to press, the magnificent iron
steamer, John T. Finnegan, had not arrived. The mystery
was solved about daybreak yesterday, as the captain as-
sured us he was only delayed by his contract for trans-
ferring to Selma, one-half of "ye ancient Citie of Cahaba".
No Selmian seemed anxious to acknowledge a quondam resi-
dense in the Pompeii of Alabama; consequently the "Exile
of Eden" was asking "who frew dat lars brick fust?"

May 22. Messrs. H. C. Graham, W. P. Molett, Lewis Johnson,
B. P. Moseley, Chas. Lenoir, J. A. Harwood, & John D.
Moseley are delegates from Lexington Beat to the County
Convention.

June 23. Rev. L. M. Bird, beloved pastor of St. Paul's
has declined a call to Grace Church in Memphis.

Packer - Powell of Monroe County

From Wills and Deeds, Book A, pp. 195-7: Will of
Robert Packer. Persons mentioned:

Wife, Elizabeth, during her lifetime, and children:

1. David   2. Samuel   3. Thomas   4. Mary

5. Susannah 6. Robert   7. James   8. John

Estate not to be divided until sons David and Samuel
are 21.

Executors, sons David and Samuel, and son Thomas as soon
as he comes of age.

Signed: Robert Packer
          David Packer
          Samuel Packer
          Thomas Packer

Witnessed by: Honor Powell
                John Powell Sr.
                John Powell Jr.

Dated 29 Sept. 1823.

Proved by Honor Powell and John Powell Jr., on 3 Nov.
1823.

Compiler's note: Records of Monroe Co. Court House were
burned about 1833 -- all of them, so far as I can ascer-
tain. So any document dated 1823 must have been brought
in and recorded again after the fire. Hence the unusual
way in which the above will is signed.

The will of Robert Packer is also recorded on pp. 492-4
in same volume. This one is dated 1828.

From Order Book 1, p. 74: May 6, 1839. On application
of Samuel and David Packer, administrators of the estate
of Robert Packer, dec'd, the court appointed John L.
Johnston, Wm Peebles, David H. Bell, Leroy A. Kidd, and
Jesse T. Odum to divide Robert Packer's real estate among
the following heirs:

David Packer, Samuel Packer, and Ann Packer Mary Jane
Packer James Packer Legal heirs of Thos. Packer, dec'd
James Powell in right of his wife Ann formerly Ann
Packer Robert Packer James Packer and John Packer and
Joseph Packer.
Note: Punctuation as in the original.

From Order Book 1, p. 175: On June 6, 1842, David and
Samuel Packer were cited to appear and make a final settlement as executors of the will of Robert Packer, dec'd.

p. 207. At the January term of court, on application of
David Packer, surviving executor of Robert Packer, dec'd,
final settlement is postponed.   (1843)

p. 226. March 6, 1843. David Packer, as surviving executor of Robert Packer, dec'd, made a final distribution of
the estate to:

1. David Packer
2. Heirs of Samuel Packer, dec'd.
3. Heirs of Thos. Packer, dec'd.
4. John W. Foster in right of his wife, Mary,
    formerly Packer
5. James M. Powell in right of his wife, Ann,
    formerly Ann Packer
6. Robert Packer
7. James Packer
8. John Packer
9. Joseph Packer

Each heir received $136.42.

Compiler's note: Joseph Packer is not mentioned in the
will of Robert Packer. This may be an error in copying
(the court's, not mine); or Joseph may have been a post-
humous child.

From Inventory A, pp. 491-3: March 8, 1843. This document
names the Negro slaves allotted to each of the heirs of
Robert Packer, who are:

Lot. No. 1 to James Packer   No. 2 to Joseph Packer
     No. 3 to Thos. Packer   No. 4 to John Packer
     No. 5 to Mary Packer   No. 6 to Samuel Packer
     No. 7 to Robert Packer   No. 8 to David Packer
              Lot No. 9 to Ann Packer

Ann's share of the Negroes included: Nedd and Hetty, his
wife, and Jess their child; old Rachel, Harry, Abigail
and (McGee) Mary. Document dated March 17, 1829.

Note: The will of Robert Packer is the first item recorded under his name in the Index to Deeds, 1833-1908.

The Tract Book shows that Robert Packer entered or
patented land in Monroe Co. on Aug. 5, 1819, certificate
No. 52, directly from the U. S. Govt. James Powell
patented land on same date.

From Order Book No. 1, p. 548: Estate of Robert Packer,
dec'd, Sept. term of court, 1846. Whereas on 6 March
1843, a judgment was rendered against David Packer as
executor of the will of Robert Packer, dec'd, in favor of
James M. Powell, in right of his wife, Ann (alias
Susannah), formerly Packer, one of the legatees under the
will aforesaid, for the sum of $156.95, and it now ap-
pears by the receipt of said James M. Powell, dated 23
January 1841, that he then received all that was due her
from the estate of said Robert.

Compiler's note: I think this merely means that James M.
Powell and Susannah gave David Packer a receipt for their
part of her father's estate. The "alias" just means that
Ann Packer Powell was sametimes called Susannah... and
sometimes Anna.

I do not find record of an estate in the name of any older
Packer, naming this Robert Packer, who died about 1823, as
an heir. I do not believe that the name of Robert's father
will be found in Monroe County Court records.

I do not find in Monroe Co., a record of the marriage of
Susannah Packer and James M. Powell. I searched not only
the index, but searched page by page for the appropriate
years.

From Deeds and Wills, Book A, pp. 519-20:

August 12, 1839. James M. Powell and Anna, his wife,
sold to Samuel Packer, Lot No. 4 of land allotted to
James M. Powell in right of his wife, Ann, formerly Anna
Packer, as their dividend of land belonging to the estate
of Robert Packer, dec'd.

Note: The last item on the preceding page helps to fix the date of marriage of James M. and Anna Packer Powell.

From Inventory B, pp. 562-3: Nov. 28, 1859:

Susannah Powell, administratrix of the estate of James M. Powell, deceased, petitioned the Court to allow her to sell the personal property for division among the heirs who are:

1. Lucy Ann Powell
2. Mary Frances, wife of G. W. Nettles
3. James F. Powell
4. Duncan W. Powell
5. Robert Powell
6. Ella J. Powell

All these are under 21.

From Inventory B, pp. 563-4: Nov. 28, 1859. Petition of Susannah Powell for her dower in the lands belonging to the estate of James M. Powell, who died on the 19th of July 1857. His heirs are named again.

In the above document, Susannah represents that she has been legally married to the deceased and has never relinquished her dower rights in said land, etc.

Also from Inventory B, pp. 564-5: Nov. 28, 1859. Susannah Powell, admx. of James M. Powell, filed a petition to sell his land. The heirs are named again.

From Wills and Deeds, Book E, pp. 581-2: No date.

Susannah Powell, admx. of James M. Powell, dec'd, obtained from the court an order for sale of the lands of said estate, on Jan. 9, 1860; and she bought in said lands herself; and is authorized to make title to herself. Filed for record, July 29, 1861.

Compiler's note: There are other papers relative to this estate, but they add no family data relevant to this problem.

From Deeds and Wills, Book A, p. 486:

24 April 1837. James Powell and Frances Ann, his wife, sold some land to Duncan McCasky.

From Order Book 1, p. 88: Jan. 22, 1840. David Packer, admr., and Mary Packer, admx. of Thos Packer, dec'd, represent to the Court that said Thos. Packer died in the fall of 1838, leaving his widow, Mary, and three minor children, all under 14, namely:

>   Mary Jane Packer
>   Ann Packer
>   James Packer

From Order Book No. 2, p. 101: Dec. 1848:

James M. Powell, **administrator** of Samuel Packer, reported a balance to be divided among the following heirs:

>   William P. Packer
>   T. Judson (or Hudson ?) Packer
>   Samuel B. Packer

The Court appointed the following gentlemen as commissioners to divide the property of Samuel Packer among his three heirs:

Elijah Powell   James Welch   David Packer   Abram Godbold

Compiler's note: There is a large amount of Powell data in Monroe County. John Powell died about 1834 and left an estate there; Sarah Powell died about 1827; and Honor Powell about 1841, both leaving estates. There may be others.

The will of John Powell, recorded in Wills and Deeds, Book A, pp. 168-9, mentions:

1. Dau., Ann Nettles   2. Son Elijah   3. Son James
4. Dau., Elizabeth   5. Dau., Eliza Davis 6. Dau.,
   Martha Gates   7. Dau., Clarissy Ann 8. Dau.,
   Amelia Ann   9. Son John   10. Son Pinckney
11. Dau., Louisa   12. Son William

Executors, **son** Elijah and son John, when he comes of age 18. Extr. to take my minor children to the Choctaw Purchase and enter 80 A. of land for each.

Will dated Sept. 20, 1834. Witnessed by:

>   John Morrisett, David Packer, Wm B. Sanders.

Proved 19 Jan. 1835.

Pace of Clarke County

From Probate Record A:

p. 148: Clarksville, 1st Mon. in Sept. 1824.
        Edward Kennedy, Judge, presiding. Letters of
administration issued to Wm L. Thornton as admr. of John
Pace, dec'd. Bond given, with Wm B. Wills, Stephen Pace,
and James M. Pace as securities. The Court appointed to
appraise this estate:

William Murrell   William Pace   T. C. Gholson

p. 150. 1st Mon. in Oct., 1824. Inventory filed.

p. 278. 4 Dec. 1828. Wm L. Thornton cited to appear and
show cause why the estate of John Pace should not be
settled.

From Probate Record B, p. 286: Inventory of estate of
John Pace filed 5th Oct. 1824. Total value, $214.27½.
He also owned one quarter-section of land, valued at $200.

Compiler's note: This is all I found re: this estate.

Estate of Burrell Pace

From Minutes of Orphans Court, Book B:

pp. 472-3: 7th Sept. 1840. Joseph P. Portis, Judge.

Thos. B. Pace appointed admr. on estate of Burrell
Pace, dec'd. Bond for $1000.00.

Reuben Cox, Lewis Julian, Wm L. Thornton, Eli S.
Thornton and John York appointed to appraise this estate.

From Record of Guardians, Estates and Wills, 1832-39:

pp. 505-6: Estate of Burrell Pace, Sale took place on
12 Oct., 1840. Purchasers: Dempsey Pace Jr., Henry A.
Toland, William Sellers, James L. White, James David,
John U. (or V.) Cassity, J. W. Thornton, James Cox,
Stephen McCollo, Thos. Jarvis.

List of accounts due the estate before his death:

    Thos. Martin, Andy Martin, John V. Cassity, Sarah
    Cassity, Levi Thornton.

H. A. Toland made the coffin for $4.00.

From Minutes of Orphans' Court, Book C, p. 154:

Final settlement of estate of Burrell Pace by Thos. B. Pace, the admr. Payments were made to the creditors only. No list of heirs.

Estate of Richard Pace

From Probate Record F:

p. 360. Bond of Wm J. Pace as admr. of the estate of Richard Pace, dec'd, in amt. of $2000.00 with Dempsey Pace and Mrs. Susannah Pace as his securities. 5 Sept. 1849. Witn. by Marion White.

p. 366. Inventory and appraisement filed by E. S. Thornton, A. A. Turner and G. W. Mitchell. Sworn to before Thos. B. Pace, J. P., on 15 Sept. 1849. Land in Sec. 16, T10, R1W, and Sec. 26, T10, R2W.

From Minutes of Orphans Court, Book F:

p. 23. 29 July 1850. Wm J. Pace gave additional bond as adms. of Richard Pace, with Thos. J. Pace, Susan Pace and Ann Pace as his securities.

p. 129. 30 April 1851. The admr. filed his accts. for a final settlement on March 17, 1851. Mentions "John Cramner in right of his wife" -- evidently she was one of the heirs.

p. 132. Susannah, widow of Richard Pace, petitions for her one-third dower in the lands he owned. 30 Apr. 1851.

p. 144. 9 June 1851. Wm J. Pace, admr., petition to sell land of Richard Pace. Names the minor heirs, Mary Ann and Amelia Pace. Citations to the legatees.

pp. 265-6: 31 March 1852. Final Settlement and distribution. D. Daffin, gdn. ad litem of the minors. Balance for distribution: $781.00. Heirs names:

1. Susannah Pace, the widow 2. Wm J. Pace, the admr.
3. John Cramner for his wife, Nancy (Or Cranmer)
4. Ann Pace (of age) 5. Thos. J. Pace, (of age)
6. Mary Ann Pace, payment to her gdn.
7. Amelia Pace, payment to her gdn.

Clarke County: Wm Pace Estate

From Probate Record A:

p. 184. July 10, 1826. Wiley Ethridge aptd. admr. of
estate of William Pace, dec'd. Bond for $1200.00 with
Richard Pace and Aaron B. Cooper as his securities. The
following were aptd. to appraise this estate.

James Kirkpatrick   Wm L. Thornton   Dempsey Pace

From Probate Record C:

pp. 103-4: Account of sale of the property of William
Pace, on 30 Sept. 1826. Purchasers:

Drucilla Pace   Fredrick (?) Pace   William Sellers
    Burrell Pace   Daniel Henderson   Richard Rainwater
Wiley Ethridge   James Thornton   Rebecca White
    James B. Earl   William Barns   Jessee Cooper
Dempsey Pace   Thos. Pace   Harris Tilman   Levi L. Red
    John Baughman   James Slater   Wm H. Foster
Wm B. Hancock   Jessee Hyde   Josiah White   Sarah Dungan
                    Darsek (?) White

p. 174. 24 July 1826. Report of James Kirkpatrick,
Abner Turner, Wm L. Thornton, Dempsey Pace and James
Thornton, who had been aptd. comrs. to divide the estate
of Wm Pace among the legatees, seven in number.

Frederick Pace   Elizabeth Etherdge   Richard Pace
    Susannah McCullar   Burrel Pace   Anny McCullar
                    Dempsey Pace

The widow received one-fifth before any of the above
received a share.

The above report sworn before Wm Chapman, J. P.
Joel Bell, Clerk of the County Court.

From Deed Book K, pp. 553-4: 13 Feb. 1867. A. J. Pace
sold to J. Foscue & Co., the undivided half of Lot No.
10 in Coffeeville, on the corner of Broad and River Sts.
Wife of A. J. Pace is not mentioned.

From Deed Book K, p. 552. 13 Feb. 1867. M. S. York &
wife, Adaline, sold this same lot to L. M. Williams and
A. J. Pace.

Clarke County: Another Wm Pace Estate

From Minutes of Probate Court, Vol. B:

pp. 149-50. 1st Dec. 1834. Wm H. Hamilton, Judge.
Groce Scruggs aptd. admr. of estate of Wm Pace, dec'd.
Bond for $1500.00. Appointed by Court to appraise said
estate:

    A. E. Ledyard   Wm M. Hewitte   Reuben Cox
       H. R. Williams   John W. Figures

p. 190. 1st Mon. in Dec. 1835. Ordered by Court that
the securities of Gross Scruggs, as admr. of estate of
Wm Pace, be discharged, as <u>Groce</u> Scruggs is now dec'd,
and Thos. Pace has been aptd. admr. of est. of Wm Pace.

p. 238. 1st Jan. 1838. Court aptd. following comrs. to
divide the personal estate of Wm Pace between the widow
and heirs of said estate:

    Horace R. Williams   John W. Figures   Austin E. Ledyard
       Micajah Harris   Reubin Cox

p. 247. 5 March 1838. Thos. B. Pace, admr. of Wm Pace,
filed an account of the division of Wm Pace's property
among the heirs; and Thos. B. is discharged from further
liability. There is no list of heirs in this record.
Thos. B. Pace was appointed guardian of Harriett A. Pace,
minor heir of Wm Pace, dec'd.

From Record of Gdns., Wills and Estates, 1832-39:

pp. 155-8: Sale of the property belonging to Wm Pace's
estate took place Dec. 31, 1834. Groce Scruggs, admr.
Purchasers include:

    Groce Scruggs   R. Pace   Thos. Pace   D. Pace Senr.
      D. R. Pace   D. Pace   Mary Pace

p. 204. 1st Feb. 1836. Thos. Pace, admr. of Wm Pace,
filed list of notes and accounts belonging to the estate
on 8th Dec. 1835. Among others are these:

Thos. Pace, Dempsey Pace, John Pace, Alfred R. Pace,
    Mary E. J. Pace, Richard Pace.

From Record of Guardians, Wills and Estates 1832-39:

p. 342. Jan 8, 1838. Division of estate of William
Pace. Two heirs only: Mrs. Mary J. Parks and Harriett A.
Pace, whose guardian is Thos. B. Pace.

/Compiler's note: These are all the Pace estates I found
up to 1864./

Pace deeds from Clarke County

From Deed Record C:

pp. 389-90: We, William Pace and Sarah Pace
             Dempsey Pace and Lilly A. Pace
             Thos. Pace and Gincy A. Pace
             Richmond Pace and Harriett Pace
             Robert Small and Mary Small
             and Jesse M. Pace,
heirs of John Pace, dec'd, late of Clarke Co., Ala., sell
to James L. White, for $160.00, the SW¼ of Sec. 32 in T10,
R1W, 159.87¼ Acres, except the graveyard, 20 ft. square, of
John Pace. This deed is dated 30 Nov. 1838, and signed as
above, except:

                Sara x Pace
                Lilla Ann x Pace
                Thos. J. Pace
                Jincy A. Pace
                Harriete P. x Pace
                R. J. (or R. L.) Small
                Mary A. Small
                Jesse M. Pace

p. 300. William Pace and Sara, his wife, acknowledged
their signatures to above deed on 31 Nov. (sic) 1838, before Cainan Pistole, J. P., in Marengo Co., Ala.

p. 390. Newton Co., Miss. 18 March 1839. Personally
appeared before G. W. Parris, Judge of Probate for Newton
Co., Miss., Dempsey Pace, Thos. Pace, Richmond Pace,
Robt. Small and Jesse M. Pace, and acknowledged their sig-
natures to above deed; also their wives, Lilla A. Pace,
Gincey A. Pace, Harriett Pace, and Mary Small.

/Compiler's note: John Pace entered this quarter-section
of land, direct from U. S. Govt., in 1815. See Clarke Co.
Tract Book./

From Deed Record C;

p. 502. Frederick Pace and Mary, his wife, sold to Thos.
B. Pace. 18 Feb. 1841. Witness: Joel Bell, J. P.

p. 537. 30 July 1841. John Pace and Martha A., his wife,
to Thos B. Pace.

p. 193. 4th March 1838. Deed of trust from Frederick
Pace to Austin Ledyard. Witness, James A. Howze and
Lewis Julian, J. P.

pp. 195-6: 17 March 1838. Richard Pace is in debt to
Thos. S. Franklin...deed of trust to Austin E. Ledyard,
Witnessed by H. R. Williams and H. H. Turner.

From Deed Record E:

p. 223. 2 Jan. 1847. Thos B. Pace, admr. of est. of
Michael Misendahl, dec'd, sold to Hezekiah Crenshaw, land
in T12, R1E.

pp. 321-2: Bond of Thos B. Pace as district assessor
for 1848, District 3, dated 14 Sept., 1848. His securities were: C. C. Figures and T. G. Christmas.

From Deed Book Q, p. 308: 23 April 1874. Andrew J. Pace
and his wife, Kittie, sold to Henry Pace. Land in T10, R1W.

From Clarke Co., Ala., Marriage Record for 1814-34:

p. 46: Stephen Pace to Martha Stringer. License dated
Sept. 10, 1817. No minister's return. Parties of age.

p. 67. Dempsey Pace to Mary Yarborough on 16 July 1818
by Natt Christmas, J. P. Parties of age.

p. 178. Richard Pace to Susannah Jarvis on 27 Nov. 1823.
No minister's return. Parties of age.

p. 219. Burwell Pace to E. Thornton. License dated
Aug. 26, 1827. No minister's return.
"By consent of parents."

p. 247. Alford Pace to Mary Ann Deas on 5 Jan. 1832
by Wm Chapman, J. P.

p. 220. Wm Pace to Mary Andrews on April 24, 1824,
by John Hanes, Clerk of Co. Court.

From Marriage Record for 1834-65:

p. 336. Burrell Pace to Cynthia Lloyd on 11 April 1864
by M. S. York, J. P. Parties are of age.

p. 5. Dempsey Pace to Rebecca White. License dated
6 Dec. 1834. No return.

p. 25. John Pace to Martha A. Bell on 8 Dec. 1836 by
A. Sale ____.

p. 107. James A. J. Pace to Margaret Bumpers
on 25 Dec. 1864 by Joel Bell, J. P.

p. 184. Wm B. Pace to Emily Bonner on 25 Nov. 1852
S. Forwood, J. P.

p. 213. James G. L. Pace to Maria Hearon. License
granted on affidavit of A. Sellers that Maria
is over 18. "License returned not executed;
Cause: The lady left."

From Clarke County Tract Book: The Assignees of
Stephen Pace "entered" SW¼ of Sec. 28, T10, R1W, in the
year 1819. Certificate No. 649.

Will of Alonzo L. Norwood of Marengo Co., Ala., recorded
in Clarke Co., Ala., in Probate Record L, pp. 116-7:

I, Alonzo Norwood of Marengo Co., Ala., ... Wife,
Caledonia, sole legatee ... I have executed a letter of
attorney to E. W. Keene (or Keese) of Marengo Co., em-
powering him to sell my perishable property, to pay my
debts to H. C. Grayson, of Clarke Co., Ala. Said
Grayson is appointed executor.

Dated 22 June 1861. Witn.: Gray Little, Robt. Hasty.

Proved 19 Jan. 1864, by Gray Little.

Pace Marriage Records from Marengo County

Marriage Record for 1818-36, p. 217: Wm Pace to Sarah
Yarborough on 7 April 1830 by William Fluker.
Bondsman: Edward Williams.

Marriage Record for 1836-51, p. 436: Thos. J. Pace to
Martha Spencer...Bond only, dated March 1851 (or 1857).
Security: Geo. Cunningham.

Pace Deeds from Marengo County

From Deed Book C, p. 501: 2 June 1835. Cainan Pistole
and Milly, his wife, to William Pace of Marengo Co., Ala.,
land in Sec. 12, T16, R1E. Signatures acknowledged on
19 December 1835 before Asa Robinson, Clk.

From Deed Book D:

p. 174. _____ McRoberts to William Pace. Land in
T17, R5E. 4th Jan. 1836.

p. 194. William Pace and Sarah, his wife, to Nathan
Yarborough, land in T16, R1E. March 12, 1835.
Witnessed by Jessee Boykin, James Yarborough.

Estate of Silas Pace, Marengo County

From Minutes of Orphans' Court, Book A-B:

p. 50. 21 November 1825. Came Margaret Pace and on
giving bond for $800.00, is appointed administrator of
the estate of her deceased husband, Silas Pace.

Court appointed following to appraise estate of Silas
Pace: Wm Barton, Jeremiah Washam, William Fowler, Moses
Murphy, Clifford Fulford.

p. 140. November 1829. William Barton, one of the
securities on the bond of Margaret Pace, has clandestine-
ly removed with his property from this State, and the
other security is about to remove ... Margaret must give
new bond.

p. 149. December term, 1829. Margarette Pace failed to
come into Court when summoned, and Henry Chiles, coroner,
is appointed administrator of estate of Silas Pace.

/Note: This book has no index. There may be other
papers re: estate of Silas, which I did not find./

More Pace Deeds from Marengo County

From Deed Book D:

p. 248. 17 May 1836. Richard E. Pace and Mary, his
wife, to James Wood, land in Sec. 12, T17, R5E. Signatures of Mary and Richard E. acknowledged before John
DeLoach, Notary Public, of Perry Co., Ala., on 17 May
1836.

p. 255. 22 Aug. 1836. Williamson Milbern and Prucy, his
wife, of Sumter Co., Ala., to William Pace of Marengo Co.
Land in Sec. 12, T16, R1E.

p. 363. Richard E. Pace, and Mary, his wife, of Marengo
Co., Ala., to William R. Sturdivant, of same, land in
Sec. 12, T17, R5E. Signatures acknowledged in Perry Co.,
Ala.

From Deed Book H, p. 412. 7 Dec. 1840. William Pace
and Sarah, his wife, to James Yarborough, land in T16,
R1E. Witnessed by James Hildreth and Cainan Pistole.

From 1850 Census of Coffee County, Ala.
House and family No. 285:

```
Nancy Pace, age 50 born in Georgia
Nathaniel Pace      age 20   b. Ga.
Nicholas      "           18     "
Sarah E.      "           12     "
John W. Harper            28   b. in Scotland
Willy Williams           35   b. in Ga.
Jesse Troutman           28     "
```

From 1850 Census, Clarke Co., Ala:

House and family No. 163:

```
John Pace         age 44   b. in S. C.
Martha    "            29       "
Francis  "            12   b. in Ala. (fem.)
Robert                11   b. in Ala.
Hamilton"              9       "
Ophelia  "             7       "
John      "            6       "
Laura     "            4       "
Charles  "             1       "
Mary      "          2/12      "
```

From 1850 Census, Clarke Co., Ala., House & Family
No. 586:

Dempsey Pace	age 40	b. Ga.
Rebecca "	34	"
Mary "	14	b. Ala.
John "	10	b. Ala.
Martha "	7	"
Betty "	3	"
W. H. White, male, aged 30, b. in Ala.		

House & Family No. 185:

Susannah Pace	aged 52	b. in Va.
William "	25	b. in Ala.
Ann "	24	"
Mary "	16	"
Amelia "	12	"
Thomas "	20	"

House & Family No. 186:

James Pace	29	b. Ala.
Margaret Pace	25	"
Nathan "	2	"

House and Family No. 190:

Dempsey Pace	74	b. S. C.
Marcy "	50	b. N. C. female
Betsy "	23	b. Ala.
George and Jackson Pace, twins, aged 17, b. Ala.		
Joseph Pace	12	b. Ala.
Sarah Pace	10	"

House & Family No. 239:

Martha Pace	50	b. S. C.
Emily "	14	b. Ala.
Asbury Harrison	23	b. S. C.
Martha "	18	b. Miss.

House & Family No. 239:

Thos. B. Pace, age 47, born in S. C.; Betsy Pace
age 33, b. in S. C.; Hardy Pace, age 11; William Pace,
age 10; Austin Pace, age 7; Sophia Pace, age 4; and
Henrietta Pace, age 1 --- all born in Ala. Also listed
with this family: James Scruggs, age 29, b. in Ala.

Census Data from Shelby County
1860 Census

1046-6: Allen Elliott   age 45   b. Tenn.
         Caroline   "   44   b. S. C.
         Charles   "   17   b. Ala.
         Hugh   "   15   "

1026-30: Madison Elliott   33   b. Ala.
         Mary   "   22   "
         Elizabeth   "   5   "
         Eliza   "   3   "
         Nancy   "   2   "
         Amos   "   6/12   "

654-8:   Starlin Baker   69   b. S. C.
         Nancy   "   56   b. Tenn
         Leonard   "   19   b. Ala.
         Jefferson Elliott   19   "
         Miley   "   16   "
         Elizabeth Gasaway   80   b. S. C.

642-6:   Wm. H. Elliott   27   b. Ala.
         Nancy   "   30   b. S. C.
         Eliza Jane "   10   b. Ala.
         Alsa Ann   "   8   "
         John C.   "   6   "
         Mary L.   "   4   "
         Wm T.   "   2   "

643-7:   Willis Elliott   63   b. S. C.
         Martha   "   26   b. Ala.
         Charles   "   22   b. Ala.

641-5:   Bennett Elliott   29   b. Ala.
         Caroline   "   20   b. Ala.
         Elizabeth   "   1   b. Ala.

540-44: William Elliott   61   b. S. C.
         Mary   "   50   b. Tenn.
         James   "   20   b. Ala.
         Amos   "   17)   "
         Elizabeth   "   17)   "   (twins)
         Martha   "   15   "

```
431-35:   Green Elliott        age 29     b. Ala.
          Stacy S.    "           28        "
          Ellen P.    "           10        "
          Mary A. M.  "            8        "
          Willis M.   "            5        "
          Jefferson F."            4        "
          Sabrina L.  "          6/12       "
```

In a Carden Family:

```
          Amos M. Elliott      age 22     b. Ala.
          Mary        "           21        "
          James A.    "            2        "
          Charles     "            1        "

33-34     James M. Nabors      age 53     b. S. C.
          Caroline M. "           39     b. Tenn
          Ezekiel     "           16     b. Ala.
          Catherine   "           14     b. Ala.
          Francis     "           10     b. Ala.
          Paralee     "            8        "
          Martha      "            6        "
          Louisa      "            2        "
```

From 1850 Census of Shelby Co., Ala.:

```
294-97:   Noah Haggard         age 62     b. Tenn. Bapt. Clergy
          Sarah                   60        "
          Henry O. Haggard        28     b. Ala.
          Margaret Haggard        20        "
          Samuel J.   "           17        "
          James R.    "           40     b. Tenn.
                                         (Bapt. Preacher)
          Willis Wood             21     b. Ky.
          Lucy E.     "           20     b. Ala.
          Margaret Wood         9/12       "
```

From 1860 Census, Perry Co., Ala., pp. 59-60:

Plantersville Beat: A. Mahan, age 63, male, b. in
Tenn.; Mary Mahan, age 50, b. in Ga.; John Mahan, age 18,
b. Ala.; James Mahan, age 17, b. Ala.; Elizabeth Mahan,
age 15, b. Ala.; Martha Mahan, age 14, b. Ala.; and
Laura Mahan, age 12, (or 13), b. Ala.

From 1840 Census of Monroe Co., Ala:

James Harris: 1 male 5 to 10; 1 male 30 - 40;
                1 female under 5; 1 female 5 - 10;
                3 females 10 - 15; 1 female 30 - 40

T. R. Watts: 3 males 40-50   1 female under 5
                1 male 50-60   1   "   15-20
                                     1 female 30-40

Charles T. Harris: 1 male 5-10   1 female 5-10
                    1 male 30-40   1 female 30-40

John Watts: 1 male under 5   2 females under 5
                1   "   30-40   1 female 5-10
                                     1 female 30-40

/Compiler's note: These are all the Harris and Watts
families listed in the 1840 Census of Monroe Co., Ala./

From Will Book C, Greene Co., Ala.:

pp. 70-71: Will of Joseph Hopkins, dated 23rd Dec.
1843, and probated on April 1st, 1844. Mentions
property to be equally divided among A. H. Hopkins,
Littleberry Hopkins, John Hopkins, and three daughters: Hixy, Rutha, and Emily Hopkins. "The balance
of my children not named, as I have given them their
shares." Executor, son A. H. Hopkins. Witnessed by:
A. P. Berry, Thos. Carpenter, Allen Hobson, and
James Carpenter.

From Deed Book A, Greene Co., Ala:

p. 51. 6 March 1820. Elizabeth Hopkins sold to
Samuel Swilley of Greene Co., Ala., a Negro boy, aged 15,
for $600.00. Witn.: Lambeth Hopkins, Thos. Childers,
and Sellar (x) Hopkins, her mark.

p. 52. 13 April 1821. William Hopkins of Greene Co.,
Ala., sold to Samuel Swilley, a Negro boy aged 13, for
$520.00. Attest: Lambeth Hopkins, Thos. J. Davis,
Dennis Hopkins.

p. 267. 10 Feb. 1826. Joseph Hopkins of Wake Co.,
N. C., sold to Hardy Hopkins* a Negro boy named
James. Witn.: Peter Hopkins and Wm Hopkins.

* In one place this is spelled Hardy Harkness.

Gibson of Marengo County

From Deed Book B:

p. 48:   I, William Gibson of Marengo Co., Ala., for love
and affection to my father, Samuel Gibson, also of
Marengo Co., and in consideration of the harmony which I
wish may prevail among my sisters and our families
..... give him 4 Negro boys ..... and Samuel in return gives
William 2 Negro women.   15 May 1829.

p. 313. Samuel Gibson sold slaves to William Gibson on
20th Feb. 1830. Sam'l acknowledged his signature to this
document on 24 Jan. 1832.

p. 349. I, Benjamin McKinney, in consideration of a
regular transfer of the right and title of Francis Gibson and Franciss Gibson to their legacy or share of the
estate of Josiah Scott, dec'd, of Scriven Co., Ga., do
grant unto Emeline Gibson, my sister, and dau. of said
Francis and Francess Gibson, aged about 10 years, a certain female slave... 26 March 1837.
Witn.: Wm J. Alston.

p. 43:   We, James C. Williams and Francis Gibson, both of
Marengo County, in consideration of the goodwill and
affection we have for Benjamin McKinney, have granted him
a certain Negro girl....   25 April 1829
Test: Alex'r Trotter, Jo. B. Earle.

p. 41. Clarke Co., Ala. James C. Williams and Francis
Gibson, in consideration of affection for William McKinney,
give him a Negro gril, Charlotte, 8 years old.
Dated 25 April 1829. Witn: Alex'r Trotter, Jo. B. Earle.

p. 41   Clarke Co., Ala. James C. Williams and Francis
Gibson, both of Marengo Co., for good will and affection
to Turner Stark McKinney, a Negro girl, Mary Ann, aged
6 years. 25 April 1829. Witn: Jo. B. Earle and
Alex'r Trotter.

p. 42. Clarke Co., Ala. James C. Williams and Francis
Gibson of Marengo Co., Ala., for good will and affection,
to James McKinney, a Negro girl, Martha, 12 years old.
25 April, 1829. Witn.: Alex'r Trotter, Jo. B. Earle.

p. 42. James C. Williams and Francis Gibson, a gift to
Samuel McKinney, a Negro girl, Eliza, 14 years old.

Tract Book, Conecuh County

/Compiler's note: Court records of Conecuh Co. were
destroyed by fire about 1865. This copy of the Tract
Book must have been made from records at the State Capital.

The Tract Book lists names of persons who had warrants to
purchase land direct from the U. S. Govt. The book is not
in alphabetical order.

I list here names of some early patentees, with approxi-
mate dates and page no., occasionally giving also the
Township and Range Number. These are names of persons
I have orders for searching.

51.	Mallard Pipkin	1836	T5 R9E
	David "	1825	"
	Martin "	1825	"
55.	Stephen Pipkin	1823	"
64.	Joseph Pickens	1819	T6 R9E
65.	John Campbell, Assignee	1819	T6 R9E
73.	Wm C. Jones, Asse.	1819	"
	Joshua Perry (Peavy?)	1819	"
75.	Joseph East, Asse.	1819	T7 R9E
79.	Bennett Lampkin	1819	"
102.	Andrew Pickens, Asse.	1819	T5 R10E
	Mayberry Thomas	1831	"
106.	John A. Thomas (?)	1843	
109.	Thos. Watts, Asse.	1819	
	John Gillis	1831	
111.	Wm Coleman, Asse.	1819	
112.	James Thomson	1833	
	Samuel Lindsay	1825	
	Thos. Jones, Asse.	1819	
113.	Smith P. Johnson	1811	
	Harris Brantley	1852	
116.	Lott M. Brantley	1854	
118.	John G. Riley	1833	
121.	Josiah Watts	1836	Certificate No. 29786
	Dan'l Watts	1836	" " 29785
129.	Harris H. Brantley	1855	
	James A. Watt	1869	
131.	Hilliard Brantley	1850	
136.	Mary Lamkin (date missing)		Sec. 13 T8 R10E
147.	Thos. Speights	1836	T9 R10E
155.	Willis Thompson	1814	T4 R11E
	James Thompson	1842	"
	Wm D. Thompson	1840	"

169.	Daniel D. Mobley	1825	Cert. No. 499 Tᶜ R11E
	Henry Chapman	1825	" " 535 " "
	Joseph A. Thomas	1854	" "
163.	James H. Thomas	1867	
	Mary Thomas	1836	
165.	William Jones	1819	
169.	John Hammond, Asse.	1819	Cert. No. 23ᶜ7 Tᶜ R11
170.	John Gillis	1837	
178.	Isaac Edwards, Asse.	1819	Cert. No. 297
179.	Simon Thomas	1869	
180.	Mitchell Burford	1836	
181.	Mitchell Burford	1831	T6 R11E
	Sam'l S. Lamkin	1819	" Cert. No 341
	John Mathews	1819	" " " 338
182.	Mitchell Burford, Asse.	1819	T6 R11E
183.	Levi Mobley	1819	Cert. No. 122
185.	Wm W. Hammonds	1856	
188.	Richard L. Hammonds	1859	
199.	Elijah Fuller	1826 or 1836	
	Samuel Fuller	1825	
204.	Nathan Sirman, Sept. 12	1821	T8 R11E Cert. No. 411
206.	John H. Sirmon, Nov. 23	1836	" "
	Richard R. Hammonds	1850	" "
	Chas. Hammonds	1851	" "
	Wm W. Hammonds	1854	
212.	Matthew Averett	1819	
	Thos. Speight	1830	
215.	Elbert Jones	1823	
216.	Henry Fountain	1823	T4 R12E
219.	Eli Atkinson	1823	
220.	Tabitha Brantley	1855	
222.	Stephen Anderson	1823	" " Cert. No 136
226.	Joseph Waits	1824	
	James Thompson	1823	
	William Rabun	1823	" "
227.	Wm Hammond	1832	
248.	Levi L. Mobley	1831	
250.	Ransom Thomas	1886	
	Mason L. Mobley	1836	
256.	Stephen W. Pipkin	1838	
258.	Peter Quarles	1823	T4 R13E Cert. No. 316
261.	Joseph Thomas	1836	
262.	Samuel Quarles	1823	
	James L. Thomas	1885	
263.	John Brantley	1823	
267	Robert Smilie	1823	
269.	Wilson Fountain	1836	
278.	Alfred Thomas	1835	
	Nathaniel B. Thomas	1856	
	Joseph Thomas	1825	

279.	Tristram Thomas	1836
281.	Philip P. Thomas	1854
	Mary A. E. Thomas	1851
282.	Wm Thomas	1835
292.	Thos. H. Watts	1836

From Will Book B, Lowndes Co,, Ala., pp. 3-5:

Will of Job. P. Givhan of Parish of St. Georges, Dorchester, Colleton Dist., S. C.:

1. To wife, Jamima, my horse called Telemachus, and my riding chare...

2. Also 1300 A. land known as the Cypress Place, belonging to me and my borther, Jacob Givhan.

3. To my children: Mary G. Appleby; George, Phillip, Jacob, John, Eliza, Jane, and Susan Givhan

4. The ferry to be hired out...

Executors: My son-in-law, Richard Appleby, and my son, Phillip Givhan

Dated 8th May 1824.   Witn.: Patrick Canady, Elizabeth Myers, and Sarah Canady
Proved on oath of Patrick Canady on 18 Sept. 1824, before Malachi Ford, Ordinary of Colleton Dist.

Lowndes Co., Ala., Minutes of Orphans' Court, Book D, pp. 312-3. May 1842. Asa T. May applied for letters of administration on the estate of Henry M. Bostick, dec'd, with the will annexed. Wm F. Browning, surviving executor of said will in Montgomery Co., Ala., has for many years lived beyond the jurisdiction of this court. Heirs of Henry Bostick are:

Mary C. May, wife of Asa T. May
        formerly Mary C. Bostwick
Jane, wife of Elias Daniel,
        formerly Jane Bostwick
John H. Bostwick

Wm S. May testified that it is impossible to divide the personal property of said Henry H. Bostwick without a sale. Slaves named Sam and Phillis.

Estate of Andrew Pickens of Butler Co., Ala.

From Minutes of Probate Court, Vol. 1:

p. 28.   May 28, 1853. About October 1852, Ezekiel M.
Pickens was appointed admr. of the estate of
Andrew Pickens, dec'd.

pp. 440-41: Final settlement of this estate on Apr. 26,
1854. Six heirs named:

1. Ezekiel H. Pickens
2. Mary A., wife of Thos. J. Black
3. Jane H., wife of Joseph S. Black
4. Eliza E. Kirkpatrick
5. Isabella Pickens
6. The heirs of John C. Pickens, to wit:

Elizabeth, wife of Richard Thompson;
Isabella, wife of John Hammonds;
Statira, wife of Matthew Hammonds
Sarah, wife of John Perry, Jr.;
John A. Pickens

Compiler's note: Each of the heirs of John C. Pickens
received $136.96; each of other heirs, $684.82.

From Deed Book A, p. 401: Ouichita Parish, La.
14 Feb. 1852. Matthew Hammonds and Statira, his wife,
appoint Ezekiel H. Pickens of Butler Co., Ala., their
attorney.... Witn.: Thos. L. Simpson, Notary Public
in Ouichita Parish.

Watts items from Butler County:

Minutes of Probate Court, Vol. 2, p. 380. Jan. 26, 1857.
Monroe P. and Thos. J. Watts, vs. heirs of Henry West,
dec'd. Margaret E. West is admx. of Henry's estate. The
papers were destroyed in the fire of April 12, 1853.

Marriage Record for 1858-64:

p. 33. James Murphy to Miss Prudence Watts on 21 Oct. 1858,
by Wingate Boggan, J. P., at residence of Mrs. Mary M. Watts.
Security: Charles Timothy Watts.

p. 231: Thaddeus C. Watts to Miss Mary F. Carter.
Security, Harris E. Carter.

p. 178.   3 Sept. 1855.   Wm T. Bates to Miss Emily
Rencher, by Daniel Herlong, L. E.
Sec. on groom's bond: Wm Rencher

p. 198.   Brassell, Andrew J. to Miss Martha E. Dean
on 25 Oct. 1855 by Henry Terry, J. P.
Sec., Thos. Dean.

p. 320.   Andrew J. Caldwell to Miss Eliza J. Boggan
on 25 March 1857 by D. C. Fowler...
Security: P. B. Waters

p. 99.   Gafford, David W. to Miss Maria Routon, on
Aug. 1854, by Samuel J. Bolling, Judge of Probate.
Sec., Joseph S. Hartley.

p. 90.   Matthews, John D. to Sarah F. Routon on
June 13, 1854 by J. C. Ramage, J. P.
Security: John Routon.

p. 427.   Matthews, Abram T. to Miss Martha J. Tillery
on 15 April 1858, by James W. (or M.) Tillery, J. P.
Security, John Tillery.

p. 191.   Vinson T. Watts to Miss Fanata P. Watts on
3 July 1855 by D. C. Fowler --.

p. 240.   Sirmon, Nathan J. to Elizabeth H. Simmons
on 28 Feb. 1856 by Sam'l J. Bolling, Judge of Probate.   Security: J. S. Peavy.

Parker marriages in this volume:

p. 65.   Noah Parker, Jr. to Isabella Bennett
p. 158. Wilson A. Parker to Mary E. Cravy
p. 176. James A. Parker to Mary E. Pugh
p. 271. Henry J. Parker to Rebecca S. Foster
p. 300. Thos. A. Parker to Martha Davis
p. 365. LeGrand Parker to Mily M. Moore
p. 394. John T. Parker to M. C. Wiggans

Also in this volume: John F. Thomas to Harriett L.
Josey; John T. Thomas to L. A. Davidson; Augustus
Murphy to Miss Amanda F. Watts; Augustus Watts to
Sarah Murphy; James F. Powell to Miss Nancy Boggan;
Wm Campbell to Mrs. Eliza Riley; Wm Watson to Miss
Ann E. Fuller (Sec., Joseph Fuller); Wm Hammonds to
Mrs. Nancy Allen.

Estate of Frederick Day, Butler Co.

From Minutes of Probate Court, Book 2:

pp. 261-3: Oct. 6, 1856. Joseph Day and Archer Cheatham, admrs. Heirs named: The widow, Mrs. Nancy Day and:

1. Mary, wife of Thos. M. King)   all of age and
2. Thos. C. King (Day?)   )   residing in
3. Jos. Day, one of the admrs.)   Butler County
4. Julia Ann King, Dora Ann King, Frances R. King,
   Elizabeth King, Nancy C. King, Trina Day, Caroline
   Day, and Martha Ann Cheatham -- all minors and
   residing in Butler Co.
5. Martha Ann, wife of Dempsey Boyd; Susan, wife of
   John T. Foster; Susan, wife of ___ Ratliff ...
   all residing in Montgomery Co., Ala.
6. Julia Ann Smith, of full age, and Stephen F., Lydia
   and James Smith, minors, all residing in Texas or in
   Louisiana (The admrs. do not know which.)
7. Barbara Dickson, widow of James Dickson, living in
   Texas.
8. Elizabeth, widow of Caleb Talley, who lives in Miss.
9. Matilda, wife of Jarrett Carter, who lives in
   Dallas Co., Ala.

From Minutes of Probate Court, Butler Co., Ala.:
Vol. 3, p. 236. Dec. 8, 1857. Nathaniel W. Barrett,
admr. of est. of Thos. C. Day, dec'd. Heirs named:
Sarah, Linny (?) Susan, wife of said Barrett; and
Caroline J. Day, a minor, who resides in Butler Co.

The marriage of Zacheus Day Jr. to Miss Elizabeth Talley
is recorded on p. 217 in Marriage Record for 1858-64.

In same volume: Marriage of John F.Day to Miss Martha A.
Davenport, on p. 381.

Also from Marriage Record of Butler Co., for 1853-58:

p. 222. Bates, James M. to Miss Julia A. Turner
p. 349. Bates, Anderson C. to Jane Zeagler
p. 390. Campbell, Jas. H. M. to Miss Sarah C. C. Prewett
         by Anderson Seale, J. P.
p. 333. John F. Thomas to Moannah F. Wilson

Will of Noah Parker Sr., Butler Co., Ala.

From Will Book 2, pp. 12-21: Oct. 30, 1867. John T.
Parker, as extr. of will of Noah Parker sr., presented
said will for probate. Said Noah Parker Sr. died 3 Oct.
1867, in Butler Co., Ala. Frances Parker, the widow, resides in Butler Co. Will proved 16 Dec. 1867.

Heirs named:

1. Nancy, wife of Richard R. Odum
2. Elisha Parker
3. Noah Parker
4. William Hawthorn Parker
5. Samuel Parker
6. Jane, wife of John W. Leflin (or J. M. Leflin)

   all of whom reside in Butler Co.   and

7. John T. Parker, res. in Covington Co., Ala
8. Mary Conadee (or Kenedy) wife of L. D. Conadee,
   residing in Texas
9. Eliza, wife of Andrew Searcy, res. in Lowndes
   Co., Ala.
10. Elizabeth, wife of Morton Savill, res. in Fla.
11. Sarah A. M., wife of Wm Hinson, res. in Fla.
12. Franklin Parker, a minor, res. in Butler Co.

The will is witnessed by Abraham Beasley, Wm Cross, and
John M. Liles, of Red Level, Covington Co., Ala.

Butler Co., Ala., Min. of Probate Court, Book 1:

p. 22. May 10, 1853. On ___ day of ___ 185_,
James Norman was appointed admr. of estate of Daniel B.
McDonald, dec'd, and on 12 April 1853, at night, all the
records were burned. Francis Sheppard was security on the
bond of Norman. The property belonging to the estate
was sold on 11 Jan. 1853.

p. 409. May 14, 1855. E.H. Pickens was apptd. gdn. ad
litem to represent the minor heir, _____ McDonald.

pp. 440-41. July 23, 1855. Final settlement of estate of
Daniel B. McDonald. Two heirs named: The widow, Frances R.
McDonald, and E. Ophelia McDonald, a minor.

From 1850 Census of Barbour Co., Ala.:

```
McDonald, Daniel B.      Age 60      b. N. C.
          Mary              48         "
          John              26         "
          Sarah             23         "
          Daniel            16      b. Ala.
          Mary              19         "
          Caroline          14         "
          William           11         "
          Hugh               9         "
```

In next house:

```
McDonald, Malcolm          54      b. N. C.
          Martha           43         "
          Sarah            19         "
          Robert     17 or 14      b. Ala.
          Eliza            15         "
          Catherine        12         "
          Hugh              9         "
          Daniel            6         "
          Mary              2         "
```

Compiler's note: There are other McDonalds in 1850 Census of Barbour Co ; also Parkers.

Also from 1850 Census of Barbour Co.:

```
Harvill,*David             45      b. Ga.
        Mahala             43         "
        Augustus           14         "
```

```
Strickland, Matthew        43      b. N. C.
            Elizabeth      45         "
```
and William, age 24; Matthew, age 17; Mary, age 14;
    Elizabeth, age 12; Martha, age 10; Jesse, age 8;
    John, age 6; and Lewis, age 4 -- all b. N. C.

Next house: Strickland, Harmon   age 30   b. N. C.
                        Feriby   22   "
            and Wm, age 6; Daniel, age 4; Elizabeth, age 2;
            and Emeline, age 2 -- all b. N. C.

House No. 669, Family No. 685: Elias Wilkes, age 68,
machinist, b. in S. C.; Hannah, age 70, b. S. C.;
James W., age 20; and Jesse, age 22, both b. S. C.

From 1850 Census of Barbour County:

House No. 1143, Family No 1144: James Wilkes, age 60,
b. in Ga.: Susan, age 16, b. Ga.; Blacston, male, age 15,
b. Ga.; Catherine, age 10, b. Ala.; Lidia, age 13, b Ga.;
and LeJeffries, age 7 (or 4), b. Ala.

House No 1984, Family No. 1950: Wm W. Wilkes, age 34,
b S C.; Sarah, age 28, b in Ga ; William, age 4, b. Ala.;
and Laura, age 2, b Ala

From 1850 Census of Choctaw Co., Ala.:

406.	Wisdom Trim	Age 25	b	Ala	
	Larra A. "	25	"		
	Lausiana "	7	"	Female	
	Wm W "	5	"		
	Mosonia " (?)	2	"	Female	
	Ann "	1/12	"		
407.	Cubbert Trim	60	b. N. C.	Male	
	Elizabeth "	63	b. Va.		
	Sarah A. Studivint	17	b. Ala.		
	William "	34	"		
517.	Asa Whitlock	55	b. S. C.		
	Nancy "	45	"		
	Sarah J. "	13	b. Ala.		
	John "	10	"		
	Espy A. "	9	"	Female	

From 1850 Census of Clarke Co., Ala.:

42.	Uriah Gill	45	b. S. C.	
	Elizabeth Gill	44	"	
	Caroline "	15	b. Ala.	
	Mary "	12	"	
	Martha "	13	"	
	Thos. "	11	"	
	Lewamisella" (?)	5	"	Female

In the home of Susan Mott, Clarke Co.:

Uriah Gill, Jr., age 28, b. Ala.

509.	A. Daffin	30	"
	Betty Daffin	22	"

and Harriett, age 4; Allice, age 2; and
May, age 3/12 -- all b. in Ala.

510. Charlotte (Daffin ?) age 47, b. Va.

Also from 1850 Census of Clarke Co., Ala.:

```
513.  E. J. Doty          age 37      b. Ala.  male
      Ann       "             31         "
      Nancy     "             12         "
      Julius    "              1         "
      Nancy Daffin           60      b. S. C.
```

From 1850 Census of Choctaw Co., Ala.:

```
353.  Powell, William    age 70      b. N. C. planter
              Sarah          55      b. Ga.
              Honor          27      b. Ala.
      Ingram, James          23      b. Tenn.
              M. A.          25      b. Ala..
              F. M.           4      b. Miss., female
              James M.        1      b. Ala.
      Richardson, Franklin   16         "

354.  Powell, Richard        32      b. Ala.
              M. Ann         28         "
              M. E.           4         "      female
              John R.         3         "
              Sarah E.        1         "
      Smith, Isaac           18         "      laborer

447.  Powell, John           57      b. N. C. planter
              Mary           55         "
              David          28         "
              Esther         24         "
              Selia          17         "
```

From 1850 Census of Clarke Co., Ala.:

```
Powell, John               49      b. Ala.
        Sarah              21         "
        Josey              18         "      female
        Nancy              16         "

Powell, John               41         "
        Francis            36         "      female
        Theophilus         18         "
Hart, Harriett             64      b. N. C.
Johnson, James             19      b. Ala.
```

House No. 747, Family No. 747, Clarke Co., Ala.:

James Daffin, age 76, b. N. C., living alone

From 1850 Census of Clarke Co., Ala.:

536-6.   Gill, James   age 60   b. S. C.
              Catherine   55   b. S. C.
              Walter   26   b. Ala.
              John   24   "
              Martha   18   "
              James   17   "
              Washington   30   "

In house No. 556, living with the James Cranford family:

D. Daffin, age 23, printer, b. Ala.

In house No. 740, living with Ellen Walker family:

R. Gill, age 42, male, b. S. C.

House No. 749, family No. 749:

Daffin, Oran   37   b. Ala.
           Julia   30   "
           John   10   "
           Sarah   8   "
           Rebecca   5   "

In house No. 844, living with the family of Gardner
Cherry: Rebecca Daffin, age 28.

From 1860 Census, Perry Co., Ala., Hamburg Beat:

Turnbo, Thomas   57   b. In Ky.
            Sarah   57   b. in Ga.
            J. M.   24   b. in Ala.   male
            W. J.   22   b. in Ala.   male
            S. R.   17   "   female (or L.R.

From Will Book A, Perry Co., Ala.: Will of Jesse Heard,
dated 22 Aug. 1840 and recorded Nov. 7, 1840, mentions:
Wife, Elizabeth, and all my lawful heirs except son William,
who has had his share; all my sons, and 3 daughters. Witnessed by Wm M. Heard, Charles Heard, and Jno. B. Fuller.

Omitted above: From 1850 Census of Clarke Co., Ala.:

836-36: Daffin, George   age 28   b. Ala.
              Frances   24   "
              Edwin   3   "
              Benjamin   6/12   "

Index of Persons

Elliott L. F. 35
   Louisa 39
   Louisa C. 43
   Madison 86
   Maggie 41
   Margaret 32
   Martha 39 86
   Martha W. 43
   Mary 40 42 87 87
   Mary A. M. 87
   Mary L. 86
   Miles (?) 38
   Miley (?) 37
   Nancy 34 41 43 44 86
   Narcissa R. 43
   Narcissa K. 39
   Paralee 43
   Parthena 39 43 44
   Parthenia 35
   Sabrina 87
   Sarah Ann 43
   S. J. (or S. G.) 39
   Stacy S. 87
   Sylvanus J. 43
   Virginia 40
   W. A. 41
   Wiley 86
   Wiley J. 43
   Willie 41
   Willie 40
   Willis M. 87
   Wm 33 35 38
   Wm H. 86
   Wm T. 86
   W. T. 40
Elliotte Chas. B. 46
Ellison Robt. 20
Ellit Wm 32 41 42 43 86
   Willis 38 41 86
Espy David A. 4
Estill James 34 46
Etheridge Elizabeth 78
Ethridge Wiley 78
Everett Geo. 22
Ezel Miel 63

Farr Geo. 41
Fates S. E. 62
Farrington Jos. 13 15
Farrington Jos. 13 14

Figures John W. 79
   C. C. 81
Fikes Ferry Road 9
Finley Jas. M. 41
Finnegan John T. 70
Fletcher David 32 45
Fluker Geo. 66
   Nancy 66
   William 83
Foot James (2) 64
Ford Malachi 91
   Pinkey 1
Forwood S. 82
   Samuel 64
Foscue J. & Co. 78
Foster James 64
   John 95
   John W. 72
   Mary 72
   Rebecca S. 94
   Richardson 26
   Susan 94
   Wm H. 78
Fountain Henry 90
   Wilson 90
Fowler, Wm 83
   D. C. 94
Fowlkes Sam'l H. 11
   S. H. 10
Franklin Thos. B. 81
Freeman S. R. 58
Freeze Rima 46
Frenage Marc Anthony 4
Frierson Reese 7
Frost Benj. 34
   Hannah 45
   John 45
Fulford Clifford 83
Fuller John A. 22
   Alfred 25 53
   Miss Anna E. 94
   Blake J. 25
   B. J. 53
   Cenith B. 52
   Cynthia J. 25
   Cynthia P. 54
   Delany 25 53
   E. H. 54
   Elijah 91

Fuller Elijah W. 52
  E. W. 51
  Wm 53
  E. Wm 53
  Frances 51 53
  Geo. W. 53
  Green 51 52
  Green H. 53
  James A. 25
  James M. 25
  James R. 53 54
  Jesse 52 53 54
  Jesse M. 54
  Jesse S. 25
  John A. 52 54
  John B. 53 100
  John Jr. 54
  Joseph 94
  Josephine L. 53
  Laura 53
  Lexington 25
  L. S. B. J. 52
  M. A. F. 54
  Margaret 51
  Margaret C. 53
  Martha 53
  Martha H. 53
  Mary 51
  Mary C. 53
  Mary E. 54
  Mary P. 53
  Melissa 51 53
  Richard R. P. T. 53
  Robert 53
  Sam'l T. 51 53
  Sam'l P. B. 22 25
  Sam'l W. J. 25
  Sarah 51
  Sarah A. 54
  Sarah D. 53
  Sarah H. 53
  Seaborne 54
  Senith B. 53
  Susan 51 53
  Susan J. 54
  Susan T. 53
  Susannah 25
  Thos. 53
  Thos. A. 25

Fuller Wm L. 54
Fulton David 46
  Elijah L. 46
  Elizabeth 32
  Engline 46
  Hulda 47
  John 48
  Rhoda 48
  Sam'l 32 46

Gafford David W. 94
Galaway Alfred 13
Galloway G. 37
Garner Elvira 18
  John 14 48
  Sarah S. 48
  Wm 18
Gates Martha 75
Gayle J. M. 61
Gentry David 9
George James H. 63
Gholston T. T. 76
Gibbs Chas. R 43
Gibson Emeline 89
  Francis 89
  Franciss 89
  Samuel 89
  Wm 89
Gill Caroline 98
  Catherine 100
  Elizabeth 98
  James 100
  John 90 91 100
  Lewamisella 98
  Martha 98 100
  Mary 98
  R. 100
  Thos. 98
  Uriah 98
  Uriah Jr. 98
  Walter 100
  Washington 100
Givhan Eliza 91
  Geo. 91
  Jacob 91
  Jamima 91
  Jane 91

Givhan Job 91
   John 91
   Phillip 91
   Susan 91
Glaze Abner Jutson 59
   Elizabeth Gena 52
   John Calbert 52
   Jonathan 53
   Joseph Green 52
   Samuel Jesse 52
Godbold Abram
Goggans James 52
Goodbread Minerva 1
   Phillip 5
Goode Wm 64
Goodwin James 17
   Julius 16
Gouch Henry 34
Graham H. C. 70
Grayson H. C. 82
Gregory James 49
Green Guilford D. 64
Greene James 4
Griffin Bird 16
   H. P. 15
   James 16
Guyse A. C. (or G.) 24
   A. G. 54
   Frances E. J. 54
   Lysander B. 54
   Joel 54
   M. E. 54
   Sarah G. 54
   Wm J. H. 54
Guyse or Guise A. G. 51
   Margaret 51

Haggard Henry O. 87
   H. O. 49
   Jos. R. 87
   Lucy E. 49
   Margaret 87
   Noah 87
   Samuel 49
   Samuel J. 87
   Sarah 87
   Susan 49
   T. W. 49

Hale Ann 33
   Joseph 33
Hall J. 57
   John 58
Hamilton Wm R. 64 79
Hammond John 91
Hammonds Isabells 93
   John 93
   Matthew 93
   Richard L. 91
   Richard R. 91
   Statira 93
   Wm 94
   Wm W. 91
Hamner James 12
   Laura H. 11
   Laura M. 12
   Laura V. 12
Hancock Joseph 32
   Wm B. 78
Handley Wm F. 63
Hanes Elizabeth 60
   John 82
Haney Chas. W. 35
   Geo. 38
   John W. 35
   Mary 35 38
   Mary J. 35
   Polly 43
   Wm 35
Hanna _____ 7
   Emma C. 10 12
   Mary 10
   Mary O. 12
   Mary V. 9 10
   Nancy V. 9
   William S. 7 9 12
   Wm T. 10 12
Hannah Emily C. 6
   John C. 41
   Mary O. 6
   Wm S. 6
   W. T. 6
Hanson T. R. 62
Haralson Jon. 68
   Jonathan 69

Harbour Abner 22 23 24
    Barsheba 22 23 24
    Bazel 54
    Calloway 22 23 24
    Christopher 25
    Christopher C. 54
    David 22 23 24
    Elijah 22 23 24
    Elisha T. 24
    Elizabeth 22 23 24
    Ezekial 25 54
    E. F. 54
    E. T. 24
    Isaiah 22 23 24
    Jamima 22 23
    John 22 23 24
    John R. 25 54
    Lucretia 24 25 54
    Maria 24
    Martha 54
    Mary (Polly) 22 24
    Mary F. 54
    Mina 24
    Nancy 22 23 24
    Nancy Jane 25
    Polly 24
    Sarah 22 23 24
    Talman 22 23
    Thos. 22 24
    Wm 22 23 25
    Wm C. 24 54
Hardee Bessie 69
    Miss Eliza 69
    Mrs. Mary Lewis 69
    Mrs. Mamie 69
    Miss Sallie 69
    Sallie F. 69
    Lt.-Gen. Wm J. 68
    Mrs. W. J. 69
    Wm J. 69
    Wm Joseph 69 70
Hardin Thos. 27
Harkins Andrew 31 32
Harper John W. 84
Harris Mrs. Amanda 26
    Chas. F. 26
    Chas. T. 88
    James 28 88
    James B. 26
    Josephine Bell 29
    Judith 52 53
    Margaret 28
    Margaret Jane 29

Harris Martha Ann 26
    Micajah 79
    M. J. 29
    Sarah 51
    Susan 52
    William 51 52 53
    William Jr. 52
    William H. 53
Harrison Asbury 85
    Ewel S. 34
    Martha 85
    Middleton 56
Hart Harriett 99
Hartley Jos. S. 94
Hartwell Jesse 29
Harvey Emily 14
    G. B. 14
Harville Augustus 97
    David 97
    Mahala 97
Harwood J. A. 70
Hasty Robt. 82
Heard Chas. 100
    Delana 22
    Elizabeth 100
    Ephraim Q. 22
    Jesse 100
    Wm 100
    Wm M. 100
Hearon Maria 82
Hemeter Michael 23
Hemitor Michael 23 22
Henderson Daniel 78
Hendrix Althea V. 6 9 10
                11 12
    A. Q. B. 6
    A. V. 12
    Bradley 11 12
    Chas. 6
    David 6
    Donna 11 12
    James T. 6
    Laura V. 7
    Margaret 6
    Martin T. 6 11 12
    Murrell W. 6
    Murrell W. 6
    Roswell 6 11 12
    William 6 7 9 10 12
Hendrix, Oliver & Co. 9

Herlong Daniel 94
Hewitte Wm M. 79
Hightower Rebecca 21
Hildreth James 84
Hill Alexander 45
    Ephraim 45
    John 60
Hinson Sarah A. M. 96
    William 96
Hobson Allen 88
Hodge H. C. 57
Hoffman Elizabeth 17
Holman Sarah R. 30
Holsombeck Abraham 46
    Derrick 50
    Elenor 50
    Hiram 46
    John 50
    Margaret 50
Hopkins A. H. 88
    Dennis 88
    Elizabeth 88
    Emily 88
    Hardy 88
    Hixy 88
    John 88
    Joseph 88
    Lambeth 60 88
    Littleberry 88
    Peter K. 88
    Rutha 88
    Sellar 88
    William 88
Hopkins Lambeth Co. 60
Houston John C. 66
Howze J. A. 81
Hosea S. S. 44
Howard J. 19
    James 48
    John 44
    Margaret 48
Howze A. C. 54
    James A. 57
    John 11 12
Huckabee John G. 30
Huffman Chas. 13 18
    Chas. A. 14
    Elizabeth 13 14
Hunter James 27
    Ruthy 30
Hurt Isaac 56
Hyde Jesse 78

Ikerman M. M. 49
Ingram F. M. 99
    James 99
    James M. 99
    M. A. 99

Jackson A. G. 52
    F. B. 62
Jarvis Susannah 81
    Thos. 79
Jemison Joseph 55
Jennings Martin 43
Jervey James 30
Jessop Israel 19
    Mary 19
Johnson Isaac 45
    James 99
    Lewis 70
    Samuel H. 35
    Smith P. 90
    Wm 45
    Wm M. 32
Johnston John L. 71
Jones Elbert 91
    Genetta Woolley 21
    Hugh 21
    Joseph White 21
    Jordan 46
    Louisa J. 19
    Lydia 21
    Samuel J. 19
    Thos. 90
    Wm 91
    W. C. 90
Josey Harriett L. 94
Julian Lewis 76 81

Kenedy (See Canadee)
Kennan Robt L. Jr. 60
Keene (or Keese) R. W. 82
Keese (or Keene) R. W. 82
Kenan Robert L. Jr. 60
Kennan Robt. L. Jr. 60
    W. H. 60
    Wm H. 60
    Woodson 60
Kennedy Edward 76
    John L. 59 61
    Warren E. 59
Kidd D. N. 40
    Mrs. D. N. 40
    Leroy A. 70

Kidd W. H. 40
W. W. 46
King Dora Ann 95
Edwin I. 8
Elizabeth 95
Frances R. 95
Julia Ann 95
Nancy C. 95
Thos. C. 95
Thos. M. 95
Kirkland Hamblin 20
Kirkpatrick Elize E. 93
James 78

Lacy Austin 2
Elisha 2
LaGrone Sarah 58
Lambkin Bennett 90
Lamkin Mary S. 91
Sam'l S. 91
Lane Chas. L. 67
Large Mary M. 14
Wiley 14 15
Larkin James 67
Lawler Elijah G. 50
Joab 31 33 50
Levi 33
Lawson P. B. 7 12
Pinckney B. 11
W. B. 11
Leaper S. 38
Ledyard Austin 81
Austin R. 79
Lee Robt W. 55
R. W. 55
Sarah 36
Thos. 30 48
Leeper John S. 40
J. T. 42
Leflin Jane 96
John 96
Lenoir Chas. 70
Levert O. V. 57 59
Lewis Arthur M. 4
Liles John M. 96
Lindsey Benajah B. 49
Catherine 49
Elijah 49
Margaret 49
Mary 49

Lindsay Samuel 90
James M. 26
Joseph 26
Thos. 34
Little Gray 82
Lolly Andrew 50
Catherine 50
Christopher 50
Elenor 50
Elizabeth 50
Henry 50
Jeremiah 50
John 50
Joseph 50
Margaret 50
Mary A. 50
Miles 50
Nancy 50
Louise 50
Lovelady David 58
Elijah 58
Henry 48
James 48
John 34 48
Joseph 48
Lydia 48
Obed 22 23
Polly 48
Rachel 48
Rhoda 48
Sarah S. 48
Wm 42
Lucas Abraham 50
Bradley 50
George 50
James 50
Lucus Elizabeth 34
Lyles Catherine 14
John 14
Lyman E. S. 40
F. May 40

Maberry Bartholomew 45
Mackey John 64
Maddison John 58
Madison James M. 55
Peyton 56
Magaha Elizabeth 21
James G. 21

Mahan A. J. 24
   Anthony 13 14
   Aquelaus 13
   Catherine 13
   Edward 13 14 15
       17 18 45
   Elizabeth 13 14 87
   Emiline 17
   James 13 17 18 87
   Jesse 16 18
   Jesse W. 13 15 16
   John 15 16 32
      34 45 87
   Laura 87
   John S. 14 16 17
   Martha 16 17 87
   Mary 14 87
   Mary E. 15
   Mary M. 16
   Nancy 14 16 17
   Nancy R. 15
   Polly 17
   Rebecca 17
   Robt. 14
   Susannah 18
   Thos. J. 16 17
   Wm 14
   Wm G. 13 15
Mardis John W. 18
   Napoleon B. 42
Maroney Catherine 13 14 18
   Emily M. 45
   Hannah 45
   Isaac 44 45
   John 44
   John A. 45
   Mary 45
   Matilda 45
   Nancy E. 15
   Rhoda 33 45 46
   Thos. 17 45
   Thos. D. 15
   Thos. E. 13 14
Marshall John L. 26
Martin Andy 76
   Celia 65
   Eleanor 66
   John 65
   Norman 66
   Thos. 66

Mason Noel 34 43 50
Mathews John 91
Matthews Abram 27
May Asa T. 91
   Benj. 48
   Elizabeth 66
   Jonathan 1 2 3 4 66
   Mary C. 91
   Robt. C. 66
   Wm A. 66
Mayberry Bartholomew 45
Meggs John 56
Melson (Nelson ?)
   Hardy S. 38
Melton John W. 24
   Sarah 52
Meredith David 33 39
Meroney (See Maroney)
Merrell (Merrill)
   Amos 41 44 38
   Elizabeth 43 38
Milbern Williamson 84
Milhous Phillip 27
Miller Daniel 64
Mink James 18
Miree Lewis 17 18
Misendahl Michael 81
Mitchell G. W. 77
Mixon George 70
   James 66
Mobley Daniel D. 91
   Levi 91
   Mason L. 91
Molett W. P. 70
Monts Frederick 55
   J. F. 55
Moore Alisander J. 39
   Caroline S. 5
   Elizabeth J. 39
   Emily 45 46
   Josephine 39
   Miley M. 94
   Silas 56
Moreland Geo. W. 15
Morgan Asa T. 63
   Daniel 63
   Dr. 69
   Elizabeth 63
   Eppy (Effy?) 63
   Isaiah 69
   Isham 63

Stedham James 43
Sterrett A. A. 42 47
Stevens Benj. 13
Steward or Stewart
  Chas. J. 15
  Geo. W. 1
  Nancy 14
  John 66
Stokes Wm W. 56
Stone Abner 27
Strain Wm 41
Strickland Daniel 97
  Elizabeth 97
  Emeline 97
  Feriby 97
  Harmon 97
  Jesse 97
  John 97
  Martha 97
  Mary 97
  Matthew 97
  Wm 97
Stringfellow Wm 60
Strong Titus 47
Strudwich Sam'l 60
Sturdavint Sarah A. 98
  Wm 98
Suttle A. J. B. 24
  John W. 24

Tadlock A. G. 61
Talbird H. 58
Talley Caleb 95
  Elizabeth 95
Tarrant Leonard 31 45
  Mary Ann 30
Taylor Benj. 45
  Christopher H. 62
  J. R 41
  Ward 26
Teague Elizabeth 42
  John W. 41 43 44
  Mary 43
Temple Martha J. 14
Terry Henry 94
  John 29
Thirman M. M. 49
Thomas James M. 91
  James L. 91
  John 60

Thomas John A. 90
  John F. 94 95
  John T. 94
  Joseph 91
  Joseph A. 91
  Mary 91
  Mary A. E. 92
  Mayberry 90
  Phillip 92
  Simon 91
  Tristram 92
Thompson Elizabeth 93
  James 90
  Richard 93
  Wm D. 90
  Willis 90
  Thornton E. 81
  Eli S. 76
  E. S. 77
  James 78
  J. W. 76
  Levi 76
  Wm L. 76 78
Tiller Mary 26
Tillery Jas. W. 94
  John 94
  Martha J. 94
Tilman Harris 78
Todd Louisa M. 29
Toland H. A. 76
  Henry A. 76
Traylor Paschal B. 21
Trim Ann 98
  Cubbert 98
  Elizabeth 98
  Larra A. 98
  Laury 4 5
  Louisiana 98
  Martha 4
  Mosonia 98
  Turner 4
  Wisdom 4 98
  Wm W. 98
Trotter Alex'r 89
Troutman Jesse 84
Tubb John 10
Turnbo (Turnbow)
  J. M. 100
  Sarah 100

Turnbo Thos. 100
    W. J. 100
Turner A. A. 77
    H. H. 81
    Julia A. 95

Underwood J. 34
    James 10
    T. 34

Vanderbilt Jacob 33
Varnell James 22
Varnell or Varner or Varnum
    James 22

Wade Joshua A. 4
Walker Allen 100
    James 50
    Jas. Sanders 31
    N. M. 51 52
Wallace Samuel 34
Walters G. W. 25
    Wm W. 55
Walthal Richard B. 60
Ward David 17
Ware Bennett 45
Warner James 57
Warren John 23
    Polly 23
Washam Jeremiah 83
Waters P. B. 94
Watrous Daniel E. 34
Watson Benj. H. 51 52
    Francis 51
    Joab 52
    John B. 52
    Laura 6
    Lemuel 6
    Mary T. 52
    Sarah E. 52
    Seeney Susan 52
    Sophronia 6
    Sophronia D. 9 10 12
    Thos D. 6
    William 94
Watts Agnes 28
    Althea C. 30
    Amanda 94

Watts Augustus 94
    Celia 27 28
    Chas. 27 28
    Chas. Timothy 93
    Daniel 90
    Edward T. 30
    Elizabeth 27
    Elizabeth A. 30
    Ella T. 30
    Fanata P. 94
    Finetty 28
    Frances 27 28
    James 30
    James A. 90
    Jeremiah 27 28
    Jesse 30
    John 27 28 88
    John B. 28
    John H. 27
    Josiah 27 28 90
    Julia Ann 30
    Louisa M. 30
    Margaret 30
    Martha Ann 26
    Mary H. 26
    Mary Jane 26
    Mrs. Mary M. 93
    Monroe P. 93
    Murry 30
    Prudence 93
    R. S. 26
    Rumsey 30
    Sarah 30
    Sarah Jane 26
    Simeon Andrew 30
    Thaddeus C. 93
    Thos. 27 28 29 30
    Thos. H. 30
    Thos. J. 30
    Thos. Jr. 30
    Thos. Sr. 30
    Thos. R. 26 28
    T. R. 88
    Vinson T. 26 94
    Wm W. 30
Weaver P. J. 13
Webb Caroline 64
    H. 59